ANNOTATED
MYTHS&
LEGENDS

ANNOTATED
MYTHS &
LEGENDS

NEIL PHILIP

DORLING KINDERSLEY
London • New York • Sydney • Moscow
www.dk.com

A DORLING KINDERSLEY BOOK
www.dk.com

Art Editor Sasha Howard
Project Editors Antonia Cunningham
and Fergus Day
Senior Art Editor Heather McCarry
Senior Managing Editor Anna Kruger
Deputy Art Director Tina Vaughan
Production Controllers Meryl Silbert
and Manjit Sihra
Picture Researcher Jo Walton

For Ruth and Michael

First published in Great Britain in 1999
Dorling Kindersley Limited,
80 Strand, London WC2R 0RL

This edition published in 2001

Bellerophon
Detail from page 47

Colour reproduction by GRB Editrice s.r.l
Printed and bound in Spain
by Artes Gráficas Toledo, S.A.U.
D.L. TO: 1341 - 2001

CONTENTS

Osiris, Isis, and Nephthys
Detail from page 17

Venus
From page 32

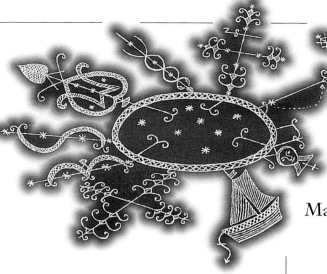

Voodoo Symbols
Detail from page 91

Tristan Kills Mordred
Detail from page 82

Lumaluma
Detail from page 104

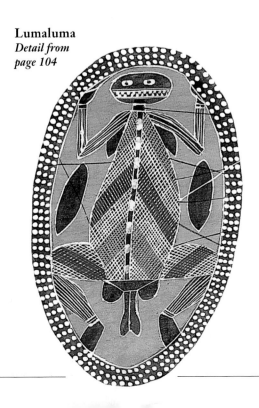

Japanese Dragon
Detail from page 120

INTRODUCTION

IT IS IN THE NATURE OF HUMANKIND TO TELL STORIES, and at the root of every culture are the stories we call myths – stories of the creation of the world and of humankind, of the deeds of gods and heroes, and of the end of time. Such stories explain and justify the world, and define our role within creation. Once a civilization has become established, the myths that formed it may dwindle into superstition or entertainment, but even so, they never lose their intrinsic power. For the world's mythologies enshrine all the poetry and passion of which the human mind is capable. From ancient Egypt to Greece and Rome, from West Africa to Siberia, from the Hindu concept of Brahman and the endless cycle of creation to the eternal Dreaming of the Australian Aboriginals, the same themes recur, as humankind engages with the great mysteries of life and death. The best definition of myth is Maya Deren's in her book on the Voodoo gods: "Myth," she writes, "is the facts of the mind made manifest in the fiction of matter."

WHAT IS MYTH?

The word myth derives from the Greek *mythos*, signifying "word" or "story". A myth has different meanings for the believer, the anthropologist, the folklorist, the psychologist, the literary critic. That is one of myth's functions – to celebrate ambiguity and contradiction. There is no more point expecting a myth to offer a single, clear, consistent message than there is in trying to turn one of Shakespeare's sonnets into plain prose. Like poetry, mythology offers a way of understanding the world through metaphor. Stories adapt and change according to the teller and the context; myths are not fixed and dogmatic but fluid and interpretive.

MYTH AND TIME

Many mythologies start before the dawn of time, with the coming into consciousness of a creator god, such as the Egyptian Re (see p.12). Re himself is described as the awareness of an all-encompassing divine being, Nebertcher, the lord without limit. Mythological time, unlike clock time, is cyclical rather than linear. It presupposes what the writer Mircea Eliade called "the myth of the eternal return". It is set going by a particular event – in Egypt, the call of the Benu bird as it alighted upon the first land. It will come to an end eventually, and the cycle of creation will begin again.

The mythology of the Aztec and Maya, and of Native American nations such as the Navajo, describes this world as being the fifth one. For the Navajo, the first four worlds were beneath this one, from which humanity climbed up in the myth of the emergence. For the Aztec, four suns had shone on previous creations before this, the world of the sun Nahui Ollin, which is blown across the sky by the breath of the god Quetzalcoatl.

The First People
This West African carving shows the world in the form of a calabash, with the first man and woman and the cosmic serpent. The Fon call this serpent Aido-Hwedo, and he carried the creator in his mouth when the world was made. Aido-Hwedo is said to have accompanied the first man and woman to earth.

The Maya believed that this current cycle of creation began on August 13, 3114 BC. Although they projected events forward until at least AD 4772, they did not think it would continue forever. Their sacred book, the *Chilam Balam*, tells us: "All moons, all years, all days, all winds, reach their completion and pass away. So does all blood reach its place of quiet, as it reaches its power and its throne. Measured was the time in which they could praise the splendour of the Trinity. Measured was the time in which they could know the sun's benevolence. Measured was the time in which the grid of the stars would look down upon them; and through it, keeping watch over their safety, the gods trapped within the stars would contemplate them."

Even the dualistic philosophy of Zoroastrianism, with its opposing gods of good and evil, Ahura Mazda and Ahriman, was set in motion when the god of eternal time, Zurvan, gave birth to the twin gods.

The Eternal Wheel of Time
This Aztec calendar stone, found beneath the central plaza of Mexico City, is a wheel of time commemorating the five world creations, of which the latest is the current world. The fifth sun, Nahui Ollin, was made by the gods at Teotihuacan (just north of modern Mexico City), which was also the birthplace of the gods themselves. The stone is not a fully-functioning calendar; the complex Aztec calendar was based on a 52-year cycle known as the calendar round, which reconciled the concurrent 260-day and 365-day years.

Our notion of time, the limited time of creation, is merely a trick of Ahura Mazda's to limit the power of Ahriman. At the end of time, all will be purified, and – as in Norse mythology – a fresh, new creation will arise.

THE FLOOD

Just as many mythologies look forward to the destruction of this world in a catastrophe, such as the Norse cataclysm called Ragnarok, so many record a time, within this creation, when the gods grew angry with humankind, and attempted to destroy them with a flood. The biblical story of the deluge is one of many such accounts, and owes much to the Sumerian/Babylonian account in the Epic of Gilgamesh, in which the Noah figure is named Utnapishtim (see p.19).

The ancient Greeks told how Zeus tried to destroy mankind with a flood, but Prometheus (see p.24) warned Deucalion and Pyrrha. Manu was saved from the Hindu deluge Vishnu in the form his fish *avatar*, Matsya (see p.110). Flood myths can be found in Peru and in China, among the Australian Aboriginals and in many Native American cultures, including the Mandan myth of Lone Man (see p.94) Even in the 19th century, folklorists could still collect in Serbia a cycle of Slavonic myths about the great flood from which the sole survivor Kranyatz was preserved by the trickster god of wine, Kurent.

THE CREATOR

One thing that all mythologies agree on is that the world was created by the deliberate act of a divine being, and that men and women were created especially to live in it.

In the Mandan creation myth, First Creator and Lone Man send a mud hen down to fetch sand from the bottom of the primeval flood, in order to make the land. The Ainu of Japan tell how the creator Kamui sent a water wagtail down from heaven to accomplish the same task (see p.120). According to the Yoruba people in West Africa, the world was made when Obatala, the son of the great sky god Olorun, threw earth from a snail shell, and got a pigeon and a hen to scatter it.

The supreme gods of Africa tend, like Olorun, to withdraw from their creation leaving the main work to their successors. In the original myth preserved by the priests of the Fon sky-cult, it is the androgynous deity

Noah and the Flood
Noah's ark rides the flood after the biblical deluge, in a wood-engraving from the Nuremberg Bible of 1483. God decided to destroy humanity because of its wickedness, but warned the pious Noah of the coming flood, and told him to build the ark and take on board two of every living creature. After the ark had grounded on Mount Ararat, God sent the rainbow as a symbol of his covenant never again to destroy the creatures he had made. Noah lived to be 950 years old.

Vishnu the Preserver
Vishnu and his wife Lakshmi (or Shri) are shown riding on their mount, the celestial bird Garuda. Vishnu, the "wide-strider", measured out the cosmos in three strides. He is regarded as the protector of the world, and because of his compassion for humankind, descends to earth in various avatar forms, such as Prince Rama, to fight evil. Whenever Vishnu is incarnated, so is Lakshmi, to be his bride. Here, Garuda is taking the loving couple to their own heaven, Vaikuntha.

the world, to take on his many *avatar* forms in order to help humanity in times of crisis. His final *avatar*, Kalkin, the white horse, will appear at the end of this era, to usher in a new age.

THE GREAT MOTHER

Creator gods tend to be male, but much of the work of creation may be delegated to a goddess. For example, among the Keres of the American Southwest, Utsiti, the creator god, who made the world from a clot of his own blood, sent his daughter Iatiku with her sister to make the earth fruitful. Iatiku sends her son to lead the people up into this world, and then Iatiku and her sister sing a creation song, all the while casting seeds and images of their song out of a basket given them by Spider Woman (see p.93).

We still talk of "mother earth". Native Americans consider this as a fact. Smohalla, the Wanapam founder of the Dreamer religion in the mid-19th century, said: "You ask me to plow the ground! Shall I take a knife and tear my mother's bosom? Then when I die she will not take me to her bosom to rest. You ask me to dig for stone! Shall I dig under her skin for her bones? Then when I die I cannot enter her body to be born again. You ask me to cut grass and make hay and sell it, and be rich like white men! But how dare I cut off my mother's hair?"

An Anglo-Saxon charm beseeches the favour of "Erce, Erce, Erce, Mother of Earth" with similar fervour. Yet, despite the obvious connection between agricultural and human fertility, the earth is not always

Nana-Buluku who creates the world, and then gives it into the keeping of his children Mawu and Lisa (see pp.88–89); but Nana-Buluku is now almost forgotten, and the work of creation credited to Mawu.

The Ashanti tell how the supreme god Onyankopon (or 'Nyame) used to live near men, but moved to the top of the sky because he was constantly annoyed by an old woman who used to knock him with her pestle as she pounded yams in her mortar. When the old woman realized what had happened, she told all her children to gather mortars and pile them on top of the other. At last they had a pile that nearly reached to Onyankopon. They only needed one more mortar. So the old woman told them to take the mortar from the bottom, and put it on the top. When they did so, the whole pile collapsed,

killing them all. So the lesser gods, the *abosom*, act as intermediaries between the sky god and humanity.

Often, as with the Yoruba god of fate, Eshu (see pp.86–87), such intermediaries may be tricksters who introduce an element of chance, play, and humour into humanity's relationship with the gods. Obatala, the creator, is hymned by the Yoruba as the father of laughter, who rests in the sky "like a swarm of bees". The Mandans believe that First Creator actually turned into the trickster god Coyote. Such tricksters, whose mischief may lead them into wickedness, are found throughout mythology, from the Greek Dionysus to the Norse Loki to the Japanese Susano (see pp.58, 69, and 123).

But another theme is the Creator's care for the beings he has made. It is this care that leads Vishnu, the Hindu preserver of of Gilgamesh, in which she first desires Gilgamesh and then, when he rejects her, exacts a terrible revenge (see p.18).

The Egyptian Isis became absorbed into Roman myth, and it is she who speaks, with the unmistakable voice of the great goddess, to Lucius, the hero of Apuleius' novel *The Golden Ass*, when he is initiated into her cult: "I am Nature, the universal Mother, mistress of all the elements, primordial child of time, sovereign of all things spiritual, queen of the dead, queen also of the immortals, the single manifestation of all gods and goddesses that are."

HOLDING THE WORLD TOGETHER

In the Mysteries of Eleusis in ancient Greece, the great goddess formed the central focus of Greek religion (see p.29). These rituals, open only to the initiated, related to the myth of the corn goddess Demeter, and her daughter Persephone, the ineffable maiden. Those who witnessed the rites were assured of a new birth in death. The Mysteries were thought by the Greeks to "hold the entire human race together".

Such a belief illustrates the crucial importance of myth in holding the world together, just as the cosmic serpent coils securely around the earth in the Fon creation story. Australian Aborginal stories about the Dreamtime, such as the Gunwinggu story of Lumaluma (see pp.102–3), are not just entertainments or nursery tales – they are sacred charters for existence. To understand them fully one must enter eternal time. Similarly the myths underlying Navajo rituals such as Mountainway (see pp.92–93), and its sandpaintings of the Holy People, define and express what it means to be Navajo. At the end of such a ritual, "The world before me is restored in beauty." When Jasper Blowsnake revealed the sacred Winnebago Medicine Rite to anthropologist Paul Radin (published under the title *The*

Nut, the Egyptian All-Mother
The Egyptian sky goddess Nut arches over the earth in this ancient tomb painting. She is about to swallow the evening sun, which is shown again on her upper arm as it starts its night journey. Nut became regarded as the mother of all, for even the sun god Re entered her mouth each night to travel through her body and be reborn next morning. A figure of Nut inside Egyptian coffin lids promised the same nurture and rebirth for the souls of the dead.

Neolithic Mother Goddess
The Venus of Willendorf, a stone figurine of a fertility goddess found at Willendorf in Austria, dates from the neolithic period. The breasts and belly are deliberately exaggerated in this representation of the great mother goddess.

female. The Egyptians, for example, worshipped Geb as god of the earth, and his sister-bride Nut as the goddess of the sky.

Nowhere has worship of the eternal female been so strong as in India, where various goddesses are worshipped under the enveloping spell of Mahadevi, the great goddess. Devi is the consort of the god Shiva (see pp.112–13), and is worshipped as benign Parvati or Uma or as ferocious and vengeful Durga or Kali. Sankara wrote of her in the 9th century, "Your hands hold delight and pain. The shadow of death and the elixir of immortal life are yours."

The combination of "delight and pain" is not confined to India. The great goddess of ancient Mesopotamia, variously called Ishtar and Inanna, also combined the roles of goddess of love and goddess of war. These dual aspects are explored in the Epic

Triptolemus, Culture Hero
Triptolemus, who taught mankind how to use the plough, stands between the two goddesses of the Eleusinian Mysteries, Demeter, and Persephone. Demeter is handing him a golden ear of grain (now lost). This marble relief of the second half of the fifth century BC was found at Eleusis, probably in the temple of Triptolemus.

Road of Life and Death), he was unveiling a mystery as great and as secret as that of Eleusis. "Never tell anyone about this Rite," ran the ritual. "Keep it absolutely secret. If you disclose it the world will come to an end. We will all die." The absolute secrecy required of initiates into the Mysteries of Eleusis was so strictly kept that we are left to guess from fragments of evidence both what the rituals were and what they meant.

CULTURE HEROES
One of those fragments is the moment in the Demeter myth when, having taken a position in a royal household while searching for her daughter, the goddess places the royal prince, her charge, into a divine fire to burn away his mortal parts and give him eternal life, but is interrupted before she can complete the ritual. The same incident occurs in Egyptian mythology, when the goddess Isis becomes nursemaid to a prince while searching for her husband, Osiris (see p.16). In the Egyptian story the prince dies, but in the Greek, the boy,

Triptolemus, became a benefactor of humankind – a culture hero – when Demeter gave him corn, a plough, and the knowledge of agriculture to teach to humankind. Triptolemus had his own cult and temple at Eleusis.

The role of the gods in giving the gift of knowledge to humankind is found in every mythology. Greek Prometheus, Aboriginal Ancestors, Mandan Lone Man, Aztec Quetzalcoatl, Polynesian Maui – all are revered for teaching us how to live in the world.

Alongside such figures stand the heroes who teach us by their example – their bravery, virtues, persistence and, sometimes, their flaws. The exploits of the Greek heroes such as Heracles and Theseus, who are half-human, half-divine (see pp.50–51, 54–55) offer a pattern after which the wholly human can model themselves.

The Indian story of Rama (see pp. 114–15), still inspires the devotion of all Hindus, and his story has even been adopted as the national epic of Buddhist Thailand. The Celtic hero King Arthur (see pp.80–81, 84–85) is the centre of similar legends, in which Celtic myth and the aspirations of medieval Christendom meet.

The Hero Heracles
This Greek vase shows Heracles killing the Stymphalian Birds, the sixth of his 12 labours (see pp.50-51) in which he killed or captured several ogres and monsters. Before performing the last of his labours Heracles had to be initiated into the Eleusinian Mysteries. On his death, he ascended to Olympus to live with the gods.

Taoist myths of the Eight Immortals (see pp.118–19) show how human beings can aspire to the divine. In their search for perfection, the Immortals earn not long life on earth, in linear time, but everlasting life in heaven, in eternal time.

DEATH AND THE UNDERWORLD
For most of humanity, the moment when linear time stops is at death. All mythologies hold out the hope that was so dear to the initiates of Eleusis, that there may be a new life beyond this one. The Egyptians hoped to be reborn to live a new life in the Field of Reeds, which was a perfected version of the Egypt they knew. They were sustained

in this belief by the daily rebirth of Re, the sun. The Vikings believed that warriors who died in battle would feast in the golden-roofed hall of Valhalla among the gods, before fighting for Odin, the lord of hosts, in the final battle of Ragnarok.

The Roman poet Virgil tells us how the hero Aeneas found his father Anchises in the fields of Elysium in the underworld (see p.67). But when he tried to embrace him, he was as insubstantial as air. When he then saw souls flocking to drink the water of oblivion to forget their former lives, and be born again, he asked Anchises what was happening. Anchises explained that in the beginning the world was pure spirit, but we become bound to life by love and fear. Only a few are able to rest quiet in the afterlife, waiting for the circle of time to be completed, when they will become pure spirit once more. Most people hunger for the world again.

The Guarayú Indians of Bolivia tell of the soul's quest after death, when it is faced with the choice of two paths to reach Tamoi, the Grandfather, who lives in the west. One is wide and easy, the other narrow and dangerous. The soul must choose the hard path and overcome many trials before reaching its destination and being welcomed and refreshed. Once washed in Grandfather's restoring bath, the soul will be young once more, and able to laugh, hunt, live, and love once again in the land of the west.

Myths tell not only of what happens after death, but of how death arrived in the world – according to the Zulus, it was all a mistake. The Great One sent the Chameleon, Unwabu, to tell people they would live forever, but he lingered, and was passed by Intulo the Lizard, with the message that all people must die. There are also stories of heroes who tried to conquer death – Maui, Gilgamesh, the Mayan hero twins (see pp.100–1).

In his search for the secret of everlasting life, the Sumerian hero Gilgamesh crosses the ocean of death in search of Utnapishtim, the sole survivor of the great flood. But Utnapishtim tells him: "There is no permanence. Do we build a house to stand for ever, do we seal a contract to hold for all time? Do brothers divide an inheritance to keep for ever, does the flood-time of rivers endure? It is only the nymph of the dragon-fly who sheds her larva and sees the sun in his glory. From the days of old there is no permanence."

Utnapishtim's lesson is repeated in a haunting little Aztec poem, addressed perhaps to the lord of life Quetzalcoatl, who descended to the underworld to restore humanity to life (see pp.98–99):

> **"**Can it be true that one lives on earth?
> Not forever on earth; only a little while here.
> Be it jade, it shatters.
> Be it gold, it breaks.
> Be it a quetzal feather, it tears apart.
> Not forever on earth; only a little while here.**"**

In a world where the only certainty is uncertainty, the great myths offer us wisdom and comfort to prepare us for our own journey to the Grandfather, into the hands of the unknown god.

Neil Philip

Hermod Descends to the Underworld
This 18th-century manuscript illustration shows Hermod, the son of Odin, descending to the underworld on Odin's eight-legged steed Sleipnir to try to rescue his brother Balder, who had been slain through the treachery of the god Loki. Hel agreed to let Balder go if all the world wept for him; but Loki refused. As a result, the gods hunted Loki down and tied him up in torment – but at Ragnarok, Loki will break loose, and lead the hordes of the dead to war in a ship made from dead men's nails.

THE CREATION

IN THE BEGINNING, Egyptian myth tells us, there was nothing but the dark endless ocean of Nun. All the elements of life were in the ocean, inert and senseless. Then the lord without limit came into being, and called himself Re. He was alone. With his breath he created Shu, the air, and with his spittle he created Tefnut, moisture, and sent them out across the water. He caused the waters of Nun to recede so that he had an island on which to stand. Then he took thought in his heart of how things should be, and called forth from Nun all the plants, birds, and animals. He spoke their names, and they came into being. Shu and Tefnut had two children: Geb, the earth, and Nut, the sky. Nut lay on top of Geb and the sky mated with the earth. But Shu was jealous and wrenched the sky away, holding her aloft, and pinning the earth down with his feet. The children of Nut and Geb were the stars.

Ankh

Djed pillar

Symbols of Life and Stability
This figure is Ha, the god of the western desert, who protected Egypt from enemies in the west, especially the Libyans. Raising his arms in blessing, he carries the ankh, symbol of the life-giving elements of air and water, from which hangs a sacred djed pillar, signifying stability.

THE EGYPTIAN GODS

All the gods of ancient Egypt are, like the Hindu gods, aspects of the great divine essence, named in one account of the creation as Nebertcher, "Lord to the uttermost limit". Re, the sun god, represents the creative consciousness of this all-powerful god, and the rest of the gods, brought into being by Re, represent other aspects. Egyptian gods were also interrelated or merged: Amun, "the hidden", the chief god worshipped at Karnak, was a god of the air, but as Amun-Re he was a sun god and as Amun-Min, a fertility god. Known by various names, most of the gods could also be depicted in animal as well as human form.

SHU, THE AIR
Shu, father of the goddess Nut, can be identified by his ostrich plume. He is usually shown holding Nut and Geb, the sky and the earth, apart.

GOD OF THE WESTERN DESERT
Ha, the god of the western desert, wears a bull's tail from his waist. This was part of the Egyptian royal regalia, signifying power and fertility.

NUT, THE MOTHER OF ALL
Nut arches her body to make the dome of the sky. Each night she swallowed the sun, giving birth to it again each morning. Because of her role as the mother of the life-giving sun, Nut was regarded as the universal mother. The dead were entrusted to her and her image was marked on the underside of coffin lids.

SYMBOL OF REBIRTH
Shu's staff is in the form of a snake. Because snakes have the ability to slough off their skins, they became a symbol of rebirth with life-giving powers.

ANKH
The ankh was the symbol of life and whoever possessed it had the power to give or take life from lesser persons. Only gods, kings, and queens had the authority to hold an ankh.

GEB'S GOOSE
Geb is sometimes represented as a goose, and one of his names is "the Great Cackler" – a reference to the cackle he gave when he produced the great egg from which the Benu bird emerged at the dawn of time (see p.13).

GODDESS OF ORDER
Maat, the goddess of order and justice, who is often described as the "daughter of Re", accompanies the god, who sits opposite her.

GEB, THE EARTH
The earth god Geb is shown sprawling recumbent beneath his sister-spouse the sky. The Egyptians were unusual in comparison with other cultures, because they thought of the earth as male.

THE EGYPTIAN YEAR was made up of 12 lunar months of 30 days, plus another five days to make up the number to 365. However, the Egyptians did not add the extra quarter day to make a true solar year. Therefore, their calendar drifted slowly out of sync with the astronomical calendar, so that it might officially be summer in the wintertime, or vice versa. The two calendars came back into line every 1,460 years, a mystical cycle for the Egyptian priesthood.

THE BENU BIRD

At the beginning of time, the waters of Nun lay in darkness, until Re thought himself into being. At the first dawn, the Benu bird flew across the waters, its great wings flapping soundlessly, its long legs trailing. The Benu bird reached a rocky pyramid, just breaking through the surface of the water. It opened its beak, and let out a harsh cry. The sound rang out across the endless waters, shattering the eternal silence. As the light of the first dawn broke over the darkness, the world was filled with the knowledge of what was, and what was not, to be. The Benu bird was depicted as a gigantic heron; the Greeks later called it the phoenix, recognizing that the bird was really an aspect of the sun god, Re. At the great temple of Amun at Karnak, a duck was released across the waters of the sacred lake each morning, in imitation of the Benu bird.

This tomb painting shows the worship of the Benu bird.

MOTHER OF THE STARS
Nut's union with her brother Geb and the birth of her children, the stars (often shown as decoration on her clothing), infuriated her father Shu, who cursed her so that she would never again give birth in any month of the year. But Nut gambled with Thoth, the moon god and reckoner of time, and won from him five extra days outside the 12 lunar months of 30 days each. In these days she gave birth to her children Osiris, Blind Horus, Seth, Isis, and Nephthys.

WEDJAT EYE
The left eye of the sky god Horus (see p.16) was identified with the moon. It was destroyed in his fight with his uncle Seth, but made whole again; the symbol of the Wedjat eye stands for wholeness and renewal.

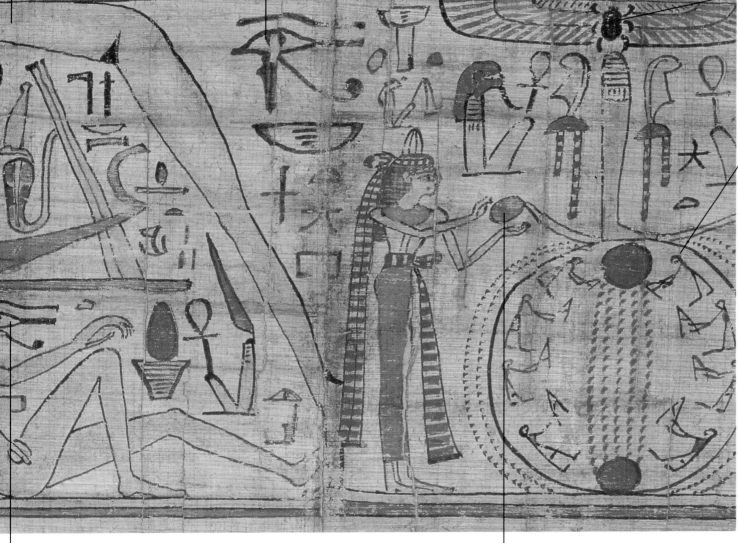

SCARAB BEETLE
The winged scarab beetle of Re is shown joined with the mummified body of Osiris, which rises from the fertile earth. This motif symbolizes the resurrection of Osiris and the daily rebirth of Re.

TENDING THE EARTH
Men plough the earth and sow seed. As Re makes his daily journey across the sky (centre), the warmth of the sun will make the crops grow – another symbol of Osiris' resurrection from the dead.

Feather of justice

Uraeus

Sun disc

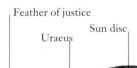

THE EGYPTIAN WORLD PICTURE
This image shows the Egyptian gods in relation the world. In the centre, the sky (Nut) arches over the body of earth (Geb), his bent knees indicating the uneven nature of the land, while the sun (Re) courses between them. On the left stands Shu (air), next to Ha, god of the western desert. On the right, the goddess Nephthys waters the earth.

Creator of the Universe
Re, creator of the universe, the gods, and the first people, wears the sun on his brow. He will rule the world until the end of time, when all creation shall pass away, and once more the world shall be covered by the infinite flood of Nun.

EYE OF THE SUN GOD
The sun was said to be the eye of Re, which he sent to seek Shu and Tefnut. When it returned, another eye had taken its place. The first eye wept, and its tears became the first human beings. So Re placed it on his brow as the uraeus, or cobra, to rule the world and spit fire at his enemies.

WATERS OF FRUITFULNESS
The goddess Nephthys, sister of Isis, pours the waters of fruitfulness over the earth, where men hoe the land. The mummified body of Osiris (see p.16) is reborn where the water makes contact with the earth.

Re's boat

RE, THE SUN GOD

RE, THE SUN GOD, took three main forms: Khepri, the scarab beetle, who was the rising sun; Re, the sun's disc, who was the midday sun; and Atum, an old man leaning on a stick, who was the setting sun. Each evening, as the sun reached the westernmost peak of Mount Manu, the sky goddess, Nut (see p.13), swallowed it, whereupon the sun god journeyed perilously through a netherworld in his night barque. Here, he was assailed by demons led by the monstrous snake Apophis, his enemy who, according to one myth, came into being at the very same moment as Re himself. In the darkest hour before dawn, Apophis made his most desperate attack. Each night, Re, in the form of a cat, would cut off the snake's head before being born once again in the east at dawn from Nut, the universal mother. He would then rise and travel across the sky until the following twilight, when Apophis would be lying in wait once more. If Apophis were ever to vanquish Re, the sun would not rise. This daily cycle of death and rebirth came to symbolize the life cycle of humankind, who hoped after death to find a new birth. From the Middle Kingdom, the visible sun god Re was complemented by an invisible divinity, Amun, "the hidden one", who as Amun-Re was worshipped as the king of the gods.

RE'S SECRET NAME

Re called the world into being with words. But one word – his own secret name – he kept to himself. Isis, daughter of Geb and Nut, the earth and the sky, and wife of Osiris, decided to learn the names of all things, so that she would be as great as Re himself. At last, the only word she did not know was Re's own secret name. To trick Re into telling her, Isis gathered the spittle that had dripped from his mouth as he sailed across the sky day after day (for he was now old and dribbled) and shaped it into a snake, which she left lying in his path. Inevitably, Re was bitten and, letting out a terrible cry, he trembled, and a fog blurred his vision. Taking advantage of his pain, Isis offered to counteract the poison if he would tell her his name. At last, he passed his name from his heart to hers, giving her power even over himself. Using Re's name, she commanded the poison to flow away, leaving him fit and strong. The text of this story also had a practical purpose as a spell against poison. Reciting the text over the images of four gods, including Isis and Horus, and making the patient eat a paper inscribed with the spell was guaranteed to be "successful a million times".

Scarab Beetle

The scarabeus, or dung-beetle, is the symbol of Re in his role as Khepri, the rising sun. Rolling along a ball of dung, the scarab beetle is a symbol of the sun itself. It was also a symbol of self-generation and rebirth, because of the way the young appear from the ball of dung.

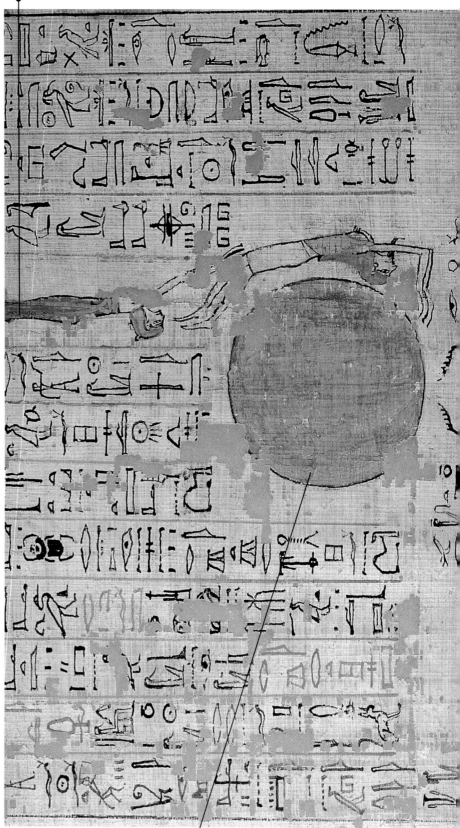

• INTO THE UNDERWORLD

Here, the sky goddess Nut raises Osiris, the son of Geb and Nut and ruler of the underworld, to receive the sun disc before it goes on its terrifying night journey. In the deepest night, Osiris and Re become one, and are described both as "Re who rests in Osiris" and "Osiris who rests in Re".

THE EGYPTIANS believed that a dead person, armed with the right spells, could counter the terrors of the underworld, Duat, and live a new life in the Field of Reeds. All the elements that made up the living person had to be preserved and resurrected – not just the physical body and the two parts of the soul, the ka (life force) and the ba (personality, or genius), but also the individual's name and shadow. These five elements made the complete being.

PAPYRUS OF ANHAY
c.1250 BC

This papyrus is part of a "Book of the Dead" written for Anhay, a priestess of Amun-Re, king of the gods. Nun, the god of the primeval waters (see p.12), holds up the barque of sun, upon which the scarab beetle, another symbol of the sun, is shown pushing the sun disc, as a scarab rolls a dung ball.

DISC OF THE SUN
As Re, the sun god was represented by the disc of the sun itself.

THE EGYPTIAN BOOK of the Dead (or Book of Coming Forth by Day) is a collection of spells, many deriving from the earlier Pyramid and Coffin texts, designed to ensure power for the deceased in the afterlife. Copies were made for most wealthy individuals and buried with them. A typical, and essential, spell is for "not dying again in the realm of the dead".

BARQUE OF THE SUN
Re is shown in his solar barque, in which he travels through the sky.

Oh you who are great in your barque, bring me to your barque, so that I may take charge of your navigating in the duty which is allotted to one who is among the Unwearying Stars.
THE BOOK OF THE DEAD

BASTET

When human beings began to plot against the ageing Re, he transformed the goddess Hathor (the sacred cow of fertility) into a raging lioness, Sekhmet. Her bloodlust brought plague and death into existence. This goddess, who could only be appeased by being made drunk, gradually became revered under a more gentle guise as the cat goddess Bastet. The domestic cat was regarded as sacred to her, and many were mummified in religious rituals. Young girls were often nicknamed "kitten". But cats were also trained for the hunt, and are depicted in Egyptian art retrieving birds felled by their masters' throwing sticks. The Greeks identified Bastet with Artemis, goddess of the hunt (see pp.36–37), and Herodotus describes her annual festival as an orgy.

The Egyptian cat goddess Bastet

URAEUS
The enraged cobra is the symbol of the sun god (and of the pharoahs, who wore it on their foreheads); it is often depicted attached to the sun disc.

HORUS
The falcon-headed Horus, son of Isis and Osiris, was one of the greatest Egyptian gods. He was essentially a sky god; his left eye was the moon and his right eye was the sun. In his role as the sun god he merged with Re as Re-Harakhty.

NUN, FERTILITY OF THE NILE
The god Nun, who represents the primeval waters or flood, holds up the barque of the sun. To some extent the mythology of ancient Egypt simply reflects the land of Egypt itself. Egypt was described by the Greek historian Herodotus as "the gift of the Nile", and without the annual flooding of the Nile, which made a strip either side of the river fertile, Egypt could not have survived. The importance of the sun god's journey from east to west, and the primeval flood represented by the god Nun, is clear.

ACCORDING TO one myth, the world was created by the archer goddess Neith from the primeval waters of Nun.

She created the gods by saying their names, and then (in cow form) gave birth to the all-powerful Re. Re was born in an egg, and when he emerged from the egg he was dazzled by the light, and cried: mankind was formed from his tears.

Company of Gods
Re is accompanied on his journey by seven (four not shown here) other gods with Horus at the helm. The other gods cannot be identified beyond doubt. The company usually includes three of the earliest-created gods, Sia (perception), Hu (utterance) and Hike (magic) as well as such important gods as Shu, Geb, Osiris, Horus, and Thoth. Sometimes there are also goddesses in the barque, especially Hathor.

Horus

OSIRIS, ISIS, AND HORUS

OSIRIS, THE RULER OF THE UNDERWORLD, was originally a king in the upper world where he taught the Egyptians (and later, the rest of the world) how to live, worship, and grow corn (when they had previously been cannibals). He earned the name Wennefer, "eternally good". He was murdered by his jealous brother Seth who tricked him into a wooden chest, which he sealed up, and sent down the Nile. Osiris' wife Isis rescued the corpse, but when Seth found it, he cut it up and scattered the pieces all over Egypt. Sorrowfully, Isis and her sister Nephthys collected every piece and, with the help of Anubis, the guide of souls to the underworld, and Thoth, the gods' scribe, they pieced Osiris back together, as the first mummy. Isis transformed herself into a kite and, hovering over the body, she fanned life into it with her wings; it was at this moment that she conceived a son, Horus, who would avenge his father. The revived Osiris went down to the dark and desolate underworld, to be the lord and judge of the dead.

Horus

Horus is shown here as a falcon-winged wedjat eye. His origins lie in the early Egyptian conception of the sky as the wings of a falcon. The eyes and speckled belly of the falcon were the sun, moon, and starry night sky.

ISIS AND THE SCORPIONS

Pregnant, Isis fled from Seth to the Nile delta accompanied by seven scorpions. One night, she begged shelter of a rich lady named Usert, but she refused her. Furious, the scorpions pooled all their venom and bit Usert's son. Pitying the dying child, Isis cured him. She then went to Khemmis and gave birth to Horus. Desperately poor, Isis often had to leave the baby alone while she found food. One day, she returned to find Horus lying rigid, bitten by a scorpion. But Isis could not save him, having used her power to cure Usert's son. Her anguish halted Re as he crossed the sky and the world went dark. Re sent Thoth to cure Horus for until he recovered, there would be no light, the wells would dry up, and the crops would wither.

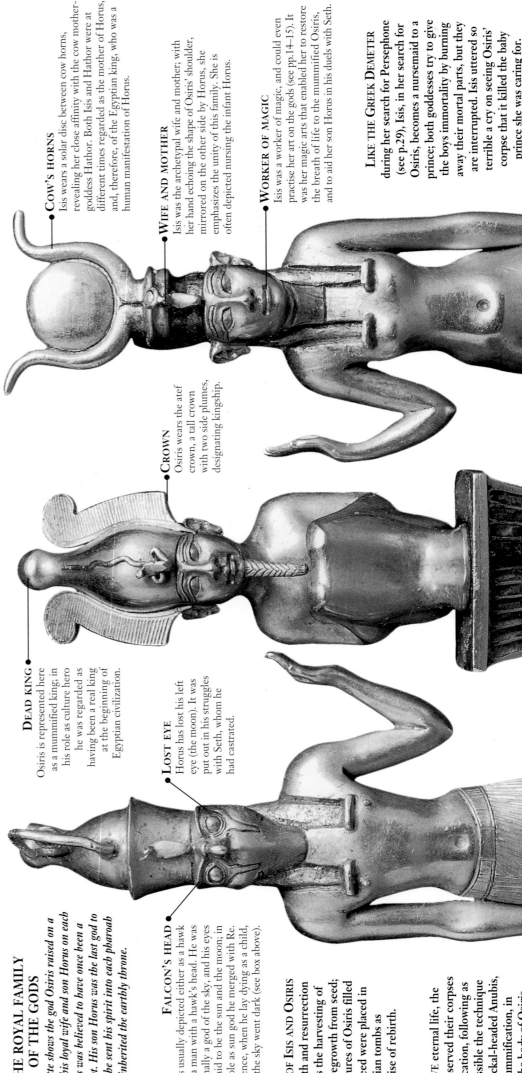

COW'S HORNS
Isis wears a solar disc between cow horns, revealing her close affinity with the cow mother-goddess Hathor. Both Isis and Hathor were at different times regarded as the mother of Horus, and, therefore, of the Egyptian king, who was a human manifestation of Horus.

WIFE AND MOTHER
Isis was the archetypal wife and mother; with her hand echoing the shape of Osiris' shoulder, mirrored on the other side by Horus, she emphasizes the unity of this family. She is often depicted nursing the infant Horus.

WORKER OF MAGIC
Isis was a worker of magic, and could even practise her art on the gods (see pp.14–15). It was her magic arts that enabled her to restore the breath of life to the mummified Osiris, and to aid her son Horus in his duels with Seth.

CROWN
Osiris wears the atef crown, a tall crown with two side plumes, designating kingship.

DEAD KING
Osiris is represented here as a mummified king; in his role as culture hero he was regarded as having been a real king at the beginning of Egyptian civilization.

LOST EYE
Horus has lost his left eye (the moon). It was put out in his struggles with Seth, whom he had castrated.

FALCON'S HEAD
Horus is usually depicted either as a hawk or as a man with a hawk's head. He was originally a god of the sky, and his eyes were said to be the sun and the moon; in his role as sun god he merged with Re. Hence, when he lay dying as a child, the sky went dark (see box above).

LIKE THE GREEK DEMETER during her search for Persephone (see p.29), Isis, in her search for Osiris, becomes a nursemaid to a prince; both goddesses try to give the boys immortality by burning away their mortal parts, but they are interrupted. Isis uttered so terrible a cry on seeing Osiris' corpse that it killed the baby prince she was caring for.

THE ROYAL FAMILY OF THE GODS

This statuette shows the god Osiris raised on a plinth, with his loyal wife and son Horus on each side. Osiris was believed to have once been a king of Egypt. His son Horus was the last god to be king but be sent his spirit into each pharaoh who inherited the earthly throne.

THE STORY OF ISIS AND OSIRIS tells of a death and resurrection that mirrors the harvesting of corn and its regrowth from seed; miniature figures of Osiris filled with corn seed were placed in Egyptian tombs as a promise of rebirth.

TO ACHIEVE eternal life, the Egyptians preserved their corpses by mummification, following as closely as possible the technique used by the jackal-headed Anubis, god of mummification, in preparing the body of Osiris.

HORUS FIRST performed the key mummification rite of opening the mouth on his father Osiris. With other rites, it ensured that all the bodily functions could be restored after death through the spells contained in the *Book of the Dead*.

Hail to you, Osiris Wennefer, the vindicated, the son of Nut! You are the first-born of Geb, the Great One who came forth from Nut . . . shout with joy, Osiris, for I have come to you; I am Horus, I have saved you alive today.

THE BOOK OF THE DEAD

AFTER OSIRIS DESCENDED to the underworld, he could no longer rule his earthly kingdom, so he bequeathed it to his son Horus. But his evil brother Seth, the god of chaos and confusion, laid claim to the throne. Only after 80 years did the god Re judge Horus the winner, award him the kingdom, and banish Seth to the desert.

Plaque with Cartouche
Royal sarcophagi, or coffins, were rectangular inside like the cartouche that encircled the royal name. Just as the cartouche protected the royal name, so the coffin protected the royal body.

Isis and Nephthys

Osiris

Horus as a wedjat eye

The four sons of Horus

Horus

Hunefer

Thoth

Feather

Ammit

Anubis weighs Hunefer's heart

Anubis

Heart

Re-Harakhty

The gods who sit in judgement of Hunefer include Utterance, Perception, and the Southern, Northern, and Western Ways.

Hunefer is lead by Anubis through the hall of two truths

Hunefer

SOULS IN THE BALANCE

After death, each person went before Osiris in the Hall of Two Truths. Here, a man named Hunefer is led by the jackal-headed god Anubis. Anubis checks the scales that weigh Hunefer's heart against the feather of Maat, which symbolizes truth. Ammit – a crocodile-headed monster with the forequarters of a lion and hindquarters of a hippopotamus – waits to gobble up the heart if Hunefer is judged guilty. Egyptians protected themselves against this outcome by including in their tombs a so-called Negative Confession – a list of sins they have not committed. To the right, ibis-headed Thoth, god of writing and knowledge, sets down the result. Further right, Horus takes Hunefer before Osiris; Isis and Nephthys stand behind the throne. Above, Hunefer adores a company of gods, led by Re-Harakhty, who stand as witnesses to the judgment of Osiris.

THE EPIC OF GILGAMESH

Gilgamesh was lord of Uruk in Mesopotamia. Two-thirds divine, he was so arrogant in his glory that the gods created the warrior Enkidu to be a comrade equal to him in strength. They fought each other furiously on their first encounter, then became very close companions and went together to the great forest to kill Humbaba, "the great evil". On his return, the goddess Ishtar, seeing his beauty, asked Gilgamesh to marry her, but he refused. Furious, she demanded that her father Anu create a Bull of Heaven to ravage the land. But Enkidu and Gilgamesh struck it dead. At that, the gods decided that one of the heroes must pay and Enkidu fell ill and died. Weeping, Gilgamesh set out to find Utnapishtim, the ancestor of mankind, to ask him why we must all die. He travelled beyond the ends of the earth to find him and on his way back found a plant that returned youth to the old. But as he stopped to drink at a pool one day, a snake ate the plant, which is why snakes shed their skins and become young again, but men still age and die.

Gilgamesh
This colossal statue dates from the eighth century BC and shows Gilgamesh in royal regalia, carrying a lion and a serpent-headed staff. These are both references to episodes in the story of his journey beyond the Ocean to find out why humans must die.

TWO EPISODES IN THE LIFE OF GILGAMESH

This is an impression from a seal that dates from between 2340 and 2180 BC. On the left, it appears to show Gilgamesh and Enkidu killing the monster Humbaba; on the right, Gilgamesh is being ferried across the Ocean in search of Utnapishtim, the mortal survivor of the great flood, whom he hopes will tell him the meaning of life.

HUMBABA •
This lion-like figure may represent Humbaba, a forest giant with a "countenance . . . like a lion", fiery breath, and terrible jaws. When he roared, it was like a storm, and his eyes blazed with the power of death. At the suggestion of the sun god Shamesh, Gilgamesh and Enkidu travelled into the faraway forest where they found and killed him. By doing so they incurred the anger of the gods, especially Enlil, the chief god, lord of earth and air.

AFTER KILLING HUMBABA and the Bull of Heaven, the god Anu said that either Enkidu or Gilgamesh must die as a punishment. The gods Ea and Enlil agreed so, despite the pleas of Shamash the sun god (to whom the heroes had sacrificed the bull's heart), Enkidu was marked for death. He fell ill, forewarned of death by a dream in which he was seized by a black bird and taken down to the House of Dust – the palace of Erishkegal, the Queen of Darkness.

ENKIDU •
This bull-headed figure is Enkidu, the only creature to equal Gilgamesh in strength. He was created from mud and spit, had a rough and hairy body, and grew up in the forest with the animals knowing nothing of mankind.

GILGAMESH TRIUMPHANT •
Gilgamesh defeated Humbaba, who begged for mercy with tears in his eyes and promised to be his servant. Gilgamesh almost agreed, but Enkidu said he was not to be trusted and persuaded Gilgamesh to kill him.

THE GODS WHO CREATED GILGAMESH gave him a perfect body. Shamash, the sun god, gave him beauty, and Adad, the storm god, gave him courage. Until the gods created Enkidu to curb his arrogance and be his companion, no one could surpass his strength.

"*Gilgamesh . . . struck Humbaba with a thrust of the sword to the neck, and Enkidu his comrade struck the second blow*"
THE EPIC OF GILGAMESH

> *"I will proclaim to the world the deeds of Gilgamesh . . . the man to whom all things were known . . . He was wise . . . knew secret things, he brought us a tale of the days before the flood. He went on a long journey, was weary, worn-out with labour, returning he rested, he engraved on a stone the whole story."*
>
> PROLOGUE TO THE EPIC OF GILGAMESH

AFTER THE DEATH OF ENKIDU, Gilgamesh set out to solve the mystery of death. He marched to the top of the twin peaks of Mashu, guardians of the rising and setting sun, and demanded entry to the underworld from the dreadful scorpion guardians at the gate, who were half-man and half-dragon. Inside he journeyed for 12 leagues in utter darkness, before coming to the garden of the gods where he met the goddess Siduri who advised him to seek out the ferryman Urshanabi (see below).

ISHTAR, GODDESS OF LOVE

The goddess Ishtar (or Inanna) was the mistress of heaven, a powerful goddess of both love and war. Her first consort was her brother Tammuz (see p.33). When Tammuz died, Ishtar descended to the underworld to wrest the power of life and death from her sister, the dread Erishkegal. Leaving her servant Papsukal with orders to rescue her if she did not return, Ishtar descended into the dark land. She started full of bold defiance, shouting at the gatekeeper to open it up before she smashed it down. But at each of seven doors she was stripped of items of her clothing, and with it her power, until she came naked and defenceless before Erishkegal, who killed her and hung her body on a nail. With her death, the whole world began to wither. But faithful Papsukal went to the gods, and asked them to create a being to venture into the land of death and revive Ishtar with the food and water of life. So Ishtar was brought back to life, but she had to pay a price. For six months of each year, Tammuz must live in the land of the dead. While he is there, Ishtar laments his loss; when he rises in the spring, all rejoice.

Sumerian statue of the goddess Ishtar

> *"Which of your lovers did you ever love forever? . . . There was Tammuz . . . for him you decreed wailing, year after year. You loved the many-coloured roller but you struck and broke his wing . . . You have loved the shepherd of the flock . . . You struck and turned him into a wolf . . ."*
>
> GILGAMESH REFUSES ISHTAR

WHEN GILGAMESH reached the far shore, he met Utnapishtim and told him of his despair at Enkidu's death. "Because of my brother I am afraid of death. Because of my brother, I wander through the wilderness." Utnapishtim told him that death was like sleep; it comes to all, and is not to be feared. He then told him the story of the flood.

THE FLOOD

Utnapishtim, the only man to survive the great flood sent by the gods, had lived in the city of Shurrupak, where he served the god Ea. The city and the gods grew old, and the goddess Ishtar caused such strife among men that the gods could not sleep for the noise. So Enlil, god of earth, wind, and air, said, "Let us loose the waters on the world, and drown them all." The gods agreed, but Ea warned Utnapishtim of the impending disaster in a dream and told him to build a boat, and take on board two of every creature. For seven nights the tempest raged, until the entire world was covered in water. At last, the boat ran aground on the top of Mount Nisir. To check the water level, Utnapishtim set free a dove, then a swallow, then a raven. When the raven did not return, Utnapishtim knew it had found a resting place and the waters were subsiding. In thanks, he lit a fire to make a sacrifice to the gods. Enlil was furious when he smelled the smoke, but wise Ea interceded, and Enlil made Utnapishtim and his wife immortal; they are the ancestors of all humanity.

• **GILGAMESH CROSSES THE WATERS OF DEATH**
Gilgamesh acts as a human mast in the ferryboat of Urshanabi, the ferryman of the gods. Distraught at Enkidu's death, he was advised by Siduri, the goddess of wine and wisdom, to seek out the ferryman and cross the bitter waters of death in his search for Utnapishtim.

• **FERRYMAN OF THE GODS**
Urshanabi takes Gilgamesh across the Ocean. "For three days they ran on as it were a journey of a month and fifteen days and at last Urshabani brought the boat to the waters of death." He punts while Gilgamesh acts as a mast because, in a fury, Gilgamesh had broken the sacred stones that made the boat safe in these perilous waters.

AHURA MAZDA AND AHRIMAN

Ahura Mazda Sun Emblem
This glazed brick relief from the sixth or fifth century BC was found at Susa in Iran. It shows the winged sun emblem of Ahura Mazda placed above two winged sphinxes, who appear to be standing guard.

IN THE DUALISTIC MYTHOLOGY of Zoroastrianism, twin brothers Ahura Mazda, who lived in the light, and Ahriman, who lurked in the dark, are in opposition. Between them there was nothing but air. The twins were born from the god Zurvan, "Time", the ultimate being who existed in the primal void. Ahura Mazda, the wise and all-knowing, created the sun, moon, and stars. He brought into being the Good Mind that works within man and all creation. Ahriman (also known as Angra Mainya meaning "the destructive spirit") created demons and attacked Ahura Mazda. But Ahura Mazda sent him back into the darkness, saying "Neither our thoughts, teachings, plans, beliefs, words, nor souls agree". Then Ahura Mazda created Gayomart, the first man and the first fire priest. But Ahriman renewed his attack and broke through the sky in blazing fire, bringing with him starvation, disease, pain, lust, and death. So Ahura Mazda set a limit to time, trapping Ahriman inside creation. Ahriman then tried to leave creation, but he could not. So he has remained, doing evil until the end of time.

WHEN AHRIMAN CAUSED A DROUGHT and poisoned the first man, Gayomart ("Dying life"), Ahura Mazda sent rain, which brought forth, from the seed of Gayomart, the mother and father of humanity, Mashya and Mashyoi.

AHURA MAZDA
Ahura Mazda (also known as Ohrmazd) was the culmination of Zurvan's desire. He is an all-knowing creator, whose plans for a perfect world are frustrated by Ahriman.

Youth
This figure is a representation of youth. All men are born good, although Ahura Mazda allows them to choose between good and evil. It is said that the earth is happiest where one of the faithful is standing. At the end of time (see box opposite), those who die as children will be re-born at the age of 15.

BARSOM TWIGS
Barsom twigs are sacred and a symbol of priesthood. Zurvan gave them to Ahura Mazda, in recognition that he was his true son. Their use was spread by the god Sraosha ("Obedience"), who is present at every religious ceremony. He is embodied in men's prayers and hymns, which he takes to heaven in a chariot drawn by four white horses with golden hooves.

MATURITY
These figures represent mature human beings. When the world is recreated at the end of time, all adults will be brought back to life at the age of 40.

ZURVAN
Worship of the unified god Zurvan became a heresy of Zoroastrianism, which regards Ahura Mazda and Ahriman as having existed in duality from the beginning of time.

WHEN IT WAS TIME for the twins to be born, Zurvan promised that his first-born should rule the world. Ahura Mazda, who was gifted with foresight, told his brother this, and evil-hearted Ahriman forced his way out first, and lied to his parent, saying, "I am your son, Ahura Mazda". But Zurvan was not deceived, and answered, "My son is light and fragrant, but you are dark and stinking". And Zurvan wept.

MITHRA

Mithra was a Persian god who became widely venerated in the West, especially in the Roman Empire, as Mithras. He was said to be the son of Ahura Mazda – one of the seven divinities created by Ahura Mazda to oppose the demons created by Ahriman. He was a god of order; but in the need to maintain order, became a god of war and warriors. He was seen as a more approachable god – one who in a sense mediated between the pure goodness of Ahura Mazda and the pure evil of Ahriman. His shrines depict him slaying a bull, a ritual act thought to ensure new life in the renewed creation; worshippers bathed in the blood from sacrificed bulls. The mystery cult of Mithras as practiced in the Roman Empire was solely for men; it was an ascetic cult that emphasized truth and right living, holding out in return the promise of life after death.

This Roman statue shows the god Mithras slaying the bull.

• **AHRIMAN**
Ahriman – the personification of Zurvan's doubt – spoilt the world by creating sin and evil. He defiled everything he touched, and rejoiced as he did so. "My victory is perfect," he crowed. "I have fouled the world with filth and darkness, and made it my stronghold. I have dried up the earth, so that the plants will die, and poisoned Gayomart, so he will die."

• **OLD AGE**
These elderly people are approaching the day when they must cross the Cinvat Bridge, the Bridge of Judgement, to reach either the joy of heaven or the horrors of hell, according to their acts and consciences. The bridge is wide for the faithful, but narrow as a needle for the sinner.

THE END OF ALL THINGS

As the end of time draws near, the saviour, Saoshyant, will arise. He will prepare the world to be made new, and help Ahura Mazda to destroy Ahriman. In the time of Saoshyant, people will grow pure. They will stop eating meat, then milk, then plants, then water, until at last they need nothing. Then there will be no more sin, and Az, the demon of lust created by Ahriman, will starve. She will turn on her creator, and try to swallow him up. Ahriman will beg Ahura Mazda to save him, and Ahura Mazda will cast him from creation, through the very hole he made when he broke in. Then time will be at an end, and the world will begin again. Saoshyant will raise the dead, and Ahura Mazda will marry body to soul. First to rise will be Gayomart, the first fire priest, then the mother and father of humanity, Mashya and Mashyoi, then the rest of humanity. All the metal in the mountains of the world will melt, and each man and woman will pass through the stream of molten metal and emerge purified. To the good, the stream will feel like a bath of warm milk; to the evil, it will be agony, as their sins are burned away. The new world will be immortal and everlasting, and free of taint.

• **SACRIFICE OF A THOUSAND YEARS**
The god Zurvan, a unified, androgynous, undifferentiated god, longed for a son. He offered a sacrifice of 1,000 years to create one. But as the 1,000 years drew to an end, he began to doubt his power to produce a son.

THE BIRTH OF AHURA MAZDA AND AHRIMAN
This silver plaque from Luristan, from the eighth century BC, shows the twins, Ahura Mazda and Ahriman, emerging from the body of Zurvan, the supreme god and personification of time. On either side stand figures representing the three stages of man – youth, maturity, and old age.

GODS OF OLYMPUS

THE GODS OF THE ANCIENT GREEKS lived at the top of Mount Olympus, the highest peak in Greece. Later their home was conceived of as a heaven in the skies. From Olympus, the gods loved, quarrelled, watched the world, and helped and hindered mortals according to their whims. Presided over by Zeus (Roman Jupiter), ruler of heaven and earth, there were many gods and immortals of whom 12 are usually regarded as the most important: Aphrodite (Venus), Apollo (Apollo), Ares (Mars), Artemis (Diana), Athena (Minerva), Demeter (Ceres), Dionysus (Bacchus), Hephaestus (Vulcan), Hera (Juno), Hermes (Mercury), Hestia (Vesta), and Poseidon (Neptune). Hades (Pluto), Zeus' brother, ruled the underworld. These Olympian gods succeeded earlier generations of gods. Gaia (Mother Earth) was the first goddess, and bore the race of Titans by her son Uranus. The Titans, led by Cronos (Saturn), seized power from Uranus; and in turn were defeated by their own children, led by Cronos' son Zeus. After the defeat of the Titans, Zeus and his brothers Poseidon and Hades drew lots for the governance of the sky, the sea, and the underworld.

> ❝Zeus is the first, Zeus is the last, the god with the dazzling lightning. Zeus is the head, Zeus is the middle, of Zeus all things have their end. Zeus is the foundation of the earth and of the starry sky. Zeus is male, Zeus is an immortal woman. Zeus is the breath of all things.❞
>
> AN ORPHIC HYMN TO ZEUS

PERSEPHONE
Persephone was the daughter of Demeter and Zeus. She was seized by Hades to be his bride in the underworld (see pp.28–29).

HESTIA
Hestia, Zeus' sister, was goddess of the hearth and a sworn virgin. She was more important to the Romans than the Greeks and was venerated as Vesta, and served by the Vestal virgins.

ATHENA
Athena, Zeus' daughter by the nymph Metis, was goddess of war and wisdom. Her approach was very different from that of the brutal war-god Ares. She was born from Zeus' head and is usually shown wearing armour.

POSEIDON
Poseidon was the god of the sea. He is shown here astride a fish, carrying his three-pronged trident. Poseidon is particularly noted for his persecution of the hero Odysseus (see pp.64–65).

CRONOS AND RHEA
This couple may depict Zeus' parents, Cronos and Rhea, who were banished to Tartarus in the underworld. Cronos, whose name means "time", castrated his father Uranus with a sickle.

HADES
Hades (see pp.28–29), Zeus' brother, was the god of the underworld. He was married to Persephone (see above).

Zeus brandishes thunderbolts, his chief weapons, made for him by the cyclopes

Zeus
Zeus, originally a sky god, was the supreme ruler of heaven and earth. He was married to Hera but had many other sexual liaisons.

ARES
Ares, the god of war (see p.27) was the only son of Zeus and Hera. His militant agression was often pitched against the strategy of Athena (see above). Aphrodite was his lover.

EROS
Eros, the god of love, represented as a child or a youth, is usually said to be Aphrodite's son. He is shown here as winged cherub, carrying his arrows of desire.

APHRODITE
Aphrodite (see pp.26–27), the goddess of sexual love, was born from the foam after Cronos cast his father's genitals into the sea. She had power over everyone except Hestia, Athena, and Artemis.

PAN

The goat-god Pan (see pp.42–43), the son of Hermes, was the god of pastures and wild places. He was very lustful and is typically shown, as here, carrying off a nymph.

APOLLO

Apollo (see pp.38–39) and his sister Artemis were Zeus' children by the Titaness Leto. He was god of prophecy, divination, and the arts, especially music, and also a sun-god, although he was not the sun itself – this was represented by the god Helios.

FOUR WINDS

The winds, Zephyrus (see pp.35–5), Eurus, Notus, and Boreas (see p.43) and the stars were the children of the Titan Astraeus, and Eos, the dawn.

CRONOS, THE CHILD-EATER

Saturn
by Francisco de Goya (1746–1828)

Cronos (Saturn) was the youngest of the Titans, the children of Gaia and Uranus (the earth and the sky). Uranus hated his children and hid them in Mother Earth, causing her great pain. In revenge, she made Cronos a sickle and encouraged him to kill his father. When he had done so, he then married his sister Rhea, but fearful that his own children might rise against him, he swallowed them as soon as they were born: first Hestia, then Demeter, Hera, Hades, and Poseidon. However, when her sixth child, Zeus, was due, Rhea gave birth to him at the dead of night, and entrusted him to the care of her mother Gaia. She gave Cronos a stone to swallow in the baby's stead. When Zeus was grown, he asked to be made Cronos' cup-bearer. He mixed his father a powerful emetic, causing him to vomit up both the stone and the five older children. Zeus then led his brothers and sisters to war against the Titans whom they defeated and confined to Tartarus in the underworld. Thereafter, Zeus reigned supreme among the gods.

HEPHAESTUS

Hephaestus, the lame blacksmith god (see pp.26–27), was the son of Hera – produced without a mate, although some sources say that Zeus was his father. He was married to Aphrodite.

HERMES

Hermes was the messenger of the gods and Zeus' son by Maia, daughter of the Titan Atlas. He is wearing his winged hat and carrying his herald's staff, the *caduceus*.

DIONYSUS

Dionysus (see pp.58–59), god of ecstasy and wine, was the child of Zeus by a mortal, Semele. He is shown with goat's legs and horns.

HERACLES

Heracles (see pp.50–51) was a son of Zeus by a mortal. Hera hated him. He earned immortality by performing 12 impossible tasks. When he went to Olympus he married Zeus' daughter Hebe.

DEMETER

Demeter, Zeus' sister, was the Greek earth-goddess. Her brother Zeus fathered her daughter, Persephone. Her search for Persephone formed the basis of the Mysteries of Eleusis (see p.29).

THE CREATION

The Greeks had several creation myths. In one, Euronyme, the goddess of all things, divided the sea from the sky, and then gave birth to a world egg, from which hatched the planets, earth, and all creatures. In another, Eros was born from the cosmic egg and, as the first god, set the universe in motion. Before that, all was chaos. Gaia, Mother Earth, inspired by Eros, then brought forth Uranus, the sky, and mated with him, to produce the first immortals, the forefathers of the Olympian gods.

"Hear us blessed Goddess, beloved wife sister of Zeus, Goddess of the moon and stars, shine joy and peace upon us"
ORPHIC HYMN TO HERA

GANYMEDE

Ganymede was a young prince of Troy; Zeus was so overwhelmed by his beauty that he descended in eagle form and snatched the beautiful youth to be his cup-bearer on Olympus.

ARTEMIS

Artemis (see pp.36–37) was Apollo's twin sister and the goddess of hunting and archery. All wild animals were in her care.

THE GODS OF OLYMPUS
by Giulio Romano (c.1499–1546)
This 16th-century ceiling painting shows the gods and some of the immortals of Mount Olympus. It would have been painted to suggest the power and glory of the patron.

Hera, Queen of the Gods

Hera was Zeus' wife and sister. In one account it was she, not her mother Rhea, who saved Zeus from being swallowed by their father Cronos (see above). She was the goddess of marriage, and many of the stories about her centre on her jealousy of Zeus' many affairs.

PROMETHEUS

PROMETHEUS, A TITAN, was the creator of humankind, whom he made out of clay and water. Although he and his brother Epimetheus sided with the Olympian god Zeus (Roman Jupiter) during the war of the Titans (see box), Prometheus' relationship with Zeus was uneasy because Zeus thought him wily and, being mortal, more loyal to humankind than to the gods. In an argument over which parts of an animal should be sacrificed to the gods, Prometheus tricked Zeus into choosing the bones and the fat rather than the meat. In retaliation, Zeus removed the gift of fire from the world, causing great suffering to humankind. In response, Prometheus stole fire from the sun, which he gave back to the world. Furious, Zeus chained Prometheus to a rock, where his liver was eaten each day by an eagle, and grew back each night.

CLASH OF THE TITANS

The 12 Titans, children of Uranus, the sky, and Gaia, the earth, were the first gods. They were deposed after a 10-year struggle by Zeus, son of Cronos (see p.23), and sent to Tartarus in the underworld, locked behind bronze doors guarded by three 100-armed giants. Zeus and his siblings then became the gods of Mount Olympus. Prometheus and Epimetheus sided with Zeus in this war; his older brothers, Menoetius and Atlas, supported the Titans – Zeus killed Menoetius and sent him to Tartarus; Atlas he condemned to support the heavens on his shoulders for eternity.

Watched from Above
Zeus, shown here in his chariot, did not trust Prometheus and kept a watchful eye on his activities, suspecting that the Titan's loyalties lay with mortals rather than immortals.

TURNED INTO A MONKEY
When Prometheus was chained to the rock by Zeus, Epimetheus, his not-so-clever brother, was turned into a monkey and banished to the island of Pithecusa.

HUMANKIND
The first human race lasted until Zeus decided to send a great flood to destroy it. The only survivors were Deucalion (Prometheus' son) and his wife Pyrrha (daughter of Epimetheus and Pandora). Zeus then offered them any gift they desired, so they asked for more people. Each stone they threw over their shoulders became a new man or woman.

THE MYTH OF PROMETHEUS
by Piero di Cosimo
(1461/62–1521)
This painting depicts several stories from the myth of Prometheus; the creation of man (assisted by Epimetheus); the theft of fire from heaven, helped by Athena (Minerva); and there are references to the later story of Pandora's box.

EPIMETHEUS
The name Epimetheus means "afterthought" or "hindsight"; Prometheus means "forethought" or "foresight". As the names suggest, Epimetheus, shown here making human beings out of clay to Prometheus' model, was rather foolish and entirely without his brother's guile and cunning.

JAR OF SORROWS
When the world first came into being, it was a happy place, all the sorrows and ills having been shut tightly into a jar (or box) never to be opened. But the enmity between Zeus and Prometheus jeopardized paradise. When Zeus created Pandora (see p.25), she opened the jar and paradise was destroyed.

PANDORA'S BOX

Pandora, the first mortal woman, was created by several gods, on Zeus' orders, to wreak havoc after Prometheus stole fire from heaven. Hephaestus (Vulcan) shaped her; Aphrodite (Venus) gave her beauty; Helios taught her to sing; Hermes (Mercury) to flatter and deceive; and Athena (Minerva) clothed her. Although Prometheus told Epimetheus to refuse any gifts from Zeus, he accepted Pandora and married her. As intended, she brought chaos, opening a forbidden jar and releasing all the ills of the world that had been shut away. Only blind Hope remained – Pandora coaxed it out to comfort humankind.

Pandora by Dante Gabriel Rossetti (1828-82)

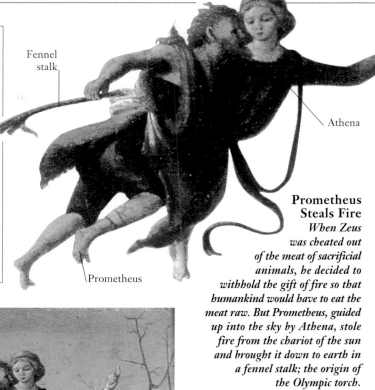

Fennel stalk

Athena

Prometheus

Prometheus Steals Fire

When Zeus was cheated out of the meat of sacrificial animals, he decided to withhold the gift of fire so that humankind would have to eat the meat raw. But Prometheus, guided up into the sky by Athena, stole fire from the chariot of the sun and brought it down to earth in a fennel stalk; the origin of the Olympic torch.

CHAINED TO A ROCK by Zeus, Prometheus was doomed to 30,000 years of agony. He escaped the full term, however, by warning Zeus of the oracle that foretold that any son borne to the sea nymph Thetis, with whom Zeus was in love, would be greater than his father. (Later, she married a mortal and gave birth to Achilles, see p.63.) Freed by Heracles (see pp.50–51), with Zeus' consent, Prometheus joined the immortals on Mount Olympus by swapping his own mortality with the immortality of the centaur Cheiron (see p.39), who, accidentally wounded by Heracles, was doomed to an eternity of suffering and wished to die.

● **CHARIOT OF THE SUN**
Helios (later identified with Apollo) drove the sun across the sky in his chariot each day; once he allowed his son Phaethon to take his place, but the youth was unable to control the horses of the sun. The earth would have been destroyed by fire had not Zeus struck Phaethon down with a thunderbolt.

● **SICKNESS AND MISERY**
Prometheus passed on only good gifts to mankind; the ills of the world he shut up in a jar. Until these were released by Pandora, the first woman, men lived carefree lives with no sorrow, hard work or disease.

ACCORDING TO ONE Greek tradition there have been five ages of man: the Golden Age during the time of the Titan Cronos, when humankind lived in ease and harmony; a Silver Age; two Bronze Ages (the second in the time of the heroes); and then the present Iron Age.

● **THE FIRST MAN**
Prometheus shaped the first man in the image of the gods, by mixing earth and water into clay; Athena, the goddess of wisdom, breathed life into him. Whereas the other animals hung their heads to look at the ground, Prometheus stood man upright, his head held high with his gaze to the stars.

● **PROMETHEUS**
Prometheus gave humankind the gift of thought, and the secrets of many skills, including how to navigate and how to tell the time.

● **GODDESS OF WISDOM**
Athena passed on her knowledge and wisdom to Prometheus, who shared it with humankind. According to one myth, Prometheus had assisted at Athena's birth from Zeus' head, although other sources name the god Hephaestus (Vulcan).

APHRODITE AND ARES

APHRODITE (ROMAN VENUS), THE GODDESS OF LOVE, was married to the smith god Hephaestus (Vulcan) to whom she was never faithful. One day, Helios, the sun god, came to Hephaestus and told him that he had seen Aphrodite with her lover Ares (Mars), the god of war, in Hephaestus' own palace. Deeply jealous, Hephaestus went to his workshop and – in a white heat of fury – fashioned a net of metal so fine and light that it was almost invisible, yet so strong that it could not be broken. This he fastened to the bedposts and rafters in the bedroom. When Aphrodite and Ares next went to bed, the net was released and bound them so tightly that they were unable to escape. Hephaestus then invited all the gods to come and laugh at the trapped lovers. Poseidon (Neptune), Hermes (Mercury), and Helios came. Hephaestus demanded that Zeus (Jupiter) should repay him all the gifts he had made in order to win Aphrodite's hand, but in the end settled for a fine to be paid by Ares. Amid much laughter, Poseidon offered to stand surety for the debt, and so the lovers were freed.

ALL-SEEING SUN
Helios, the sun, saw Aphrodite and Ares together in the palace of Hephaestus, and immediately informed the cuckolded god.

IMP OF DESIRE
Some sources say that Eros (Cupid) was Aphrodite's son by either Ares, Hermes, or even by her father Zeus. Others say that he was the first god, and hatched from the world egg at the beginning of time.

CUNNING NET
When Hephaestus learned of Aphrodite's betrayal, he made a net of fine metal to catch the lovers. Hephaestus was the blacksmith god and was worshipped in Athens as the patron of craftsmen.

THE BIRTH OF APHRODITE

Some sources say that Aphrodite was a daughter of Zeus, but in the poet Hesiod's account, she was born from the seafoam (*aphros*) that gathered around the genitals of Uranus after they had been cut off and flung away by his son Cronos (Saturn – see p.23). The drops of blood that fell became the Furies, Giants, and the ash-tree nymphs called the Meliae. Aphrodite came to shore at Paphos in Cyprus. As she stepped onto land, grass grew under her feet. Also called Anadyomene – "She who emerges" – she was accompanied by Eros (desire) from the beginning.

Wet hair

Aphrodite

Scallop shell

Foam

This Greek sculpture shows Aphrodite emerging from the sea, wringing the water from her hair as she comes to the island of Paphos on a giant scallop shell.

APHRODITE, HEPHAESTUS, AND ARES
by Tintoretto, originally Jacopo Robusti (1518–94)
This painting shows Hephaestus fixing a net to the bed to trap Ares and Aphrodite together. Oddly enough, Aphrodite does not realise that he is setting a trap and he does not notice Ares under the bed.

GOLDEN GODDESS
Aphrodite is called "golden" by the poet Hesiod. She is also called "laughter-loving", although here the joke is on her.

JEALOUS HUSBAND

Hephaestus was enthralled by Aphrodite, and deeply jealous of her infidelities. Hephaestus himself is earlier represented as the husband of Aglaia, the youngest of the Graces, and also as having been smitten with passion for Athena. His attempted rape of Athena was unsuccessful, but where his seed fell on the ground it gave birth to Ericthonius, the king of Athens who invented the chariot.

APHRODITE, GODDESS FROM THE EAST

The worship of Aphrodite emanated from the island of Cyprus, which was culturally influenced from the Near East. She is related to the goddess Ishtar (see p.19); her love for Adonis (see pp.32–33) echoes that of Ishtar and Tammuz and the existence of temple prostitutes in her temple in Corinth reflects the custom in the temples of Ishtar. Herodotus points out that the Babylonian custom of every woman prostituting herself once in the temple of the goddess was also to be found in Cyprus.

CRIPPLED BLACKSMITH

Hephaestus was the son of Hera (Juno). Some say that Zeus was his father, but other writers say that he was conceived without intercourse. A volcanic deity, he is the smith and metal-worker of the gods. When he was born lame, Hera threw him from Olympus in disgust.

Aphrodite, Goddess of Love

Aphrodite was only interested in making love. On the one occasion when Aphrodite worked at a loom, Athena, goddess of arts and crafts, protested most vigorously at this invasion of her own domain. Aphrodite humbly apologized, and has never done a day's work since.

BED OF LOVE

Aphrodite had many lovers including Dionysus (Bacchus), who fathered her son the phallic god Priapus, and Hermes who fathered the twin-sexed Hermaphroditus. Mortal lovers included Adonis (see pp.32–33) and Anchises, who was the father of her son, the hero Aeneas (see pp.66–67).

THE STORY OF APHRODITE'S affair with Ares, and the revenge of her husband Hephaestus, is sung by the blind bard Demodocus at the Phaeacian Games in *The Odyssey*, to the delight of Odysseus (see pp.64–65).

ARES, THE WARRIOR

Ares cowers under the bed until Hephaestus leaves the room. Ares, although he was the god of war, was not the god of victory and on several occasions suffered humiliation in battle, as he does in this story of love.

Ares, God of War

Ares loved to stir up trouble, often in league with Eris, the goddess of strife (see p.63). He was a bully and a braggart and, apart from Aphrodite, no one, not even his parents Zeus and Hera, cared for him. Hades, however, appreciated the steady stream of young men who entered the underworld thanks to Ares' warmongering.

GODDESS OF SENSUAL PLEASURE

While Hera (Juno) blessed the marriage bed, Aphrodite, her daughter by Zeus, was the goddess of love and passion. She offered aid to human lovers, but cruel and vengeful punishment to those who scorned her.

BARKING DOG

The dog tries to alert Hephaestus to the presence of Ares under the bed but he remains oblivious. Ares and Aphrodite, although they were caught on this occasion, managed to have several children together: Deimos (fear), Phobos (panic), Harmonia (concord), and, according to some sources, Eros (desire).

THE RAPE OF PERSEPHONE

PERSEPHONE (ROMAN PROSERPINE), the daughter of Zeus (Jupiter) and Demeter (Ceres), was carried off by Hades (Pluto) to be his queen in the underworld. Devastated, Demeter, the earth goddess, refused to fulfil her duties until she was returned to her. But Persephone had eaten a pomegranate seed while she was away, which bound her to Hades. Zeus agreed to a compromise: Persephone would spend four (some sources say six) months on earth with her mother and the rest of the year in the underworld. This story explains the annual death and rebirth inherent in nature's cycle – when Persephone is away, Demeter is too sad to fulfil her duties, but when she returns, Demeter works with renewed vigour. The myths of Persephone are complex because in their inner meanings they go to the heart of ancient Greek religion. In one version of her story, Zeus himself falls in love with her, and seduces her by taking the form of a snake and enveloping her in his coils – the resulting child is Dionysus (Bacchus). In the more common version, she is abducted by Hades – but a Hades who reveals many features of Dionysus in his archaic role as lord of the underworld (see p.59).

PURE MAIDEN
Persephone, first known as Core, "the maiden", was pure and beautiful. Persephone means "bringer of destruction" – as Hades' queen, no one could die unless she cut a hair from their heads.

THE ISLAND OF SICILY
The story is set in Sicily, where the maiden Core is wandering innocently through the meadows picking flowers - usually said to be poppies, which were sacred to Demeter, although violets and lilies are also mentioned.

HADES IN LOVE
Hades carries Persephone away. According to Ovid's Roman version of the story, Aphrodite (Venus) instructed Eros (Cupid) to pierce the underworld god with an arrow of desire for his niece, in order to demonstrate her power over the other gods.

CERBERUS
Hades galloped over the fields, guarded by Cerberus, the three-headed watchdog of the underworld, breathing venomous fire.

Hades and Persephone
Hades was sometimes called Pluto, which derives from the Greek word for "riches". The recipent of buried treasure, he was, therefore, considered the god of agricultural wealth. As such, he exerted influence over crops and cultivation – hence his marriage to the earth goddess' daughter. (In earlier times Persephone and Demeter may have been a single divinity.)

Persephone

WEEPING WATER NYMPH
When Hades seized Persephone, the nymph Cyane rose from the lake and rebuked him – but he ignored her. Desolate, Cyane wept so much that her blood turned to water, and she dissolved. When Persephone's grieving mother Demeter came looking for her, all the mute Cyane could do was bear up Persephone's lost girdle on the surface of the water.

ROYAL TRIDENT
Hades struck the ground with his trident to open up a way to the underworld, where he took Persephone to be his queen.

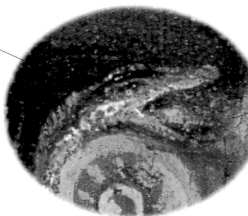

PERSEPHONE WAS stolen away from the island of Sicily. The earth giant Typhoeus was imprisoned beneath the island and his struggles were creating earthquakes. Hades was concerned in case the earth gaped open and let in daylight, which would frighten the dead.

Snake
Snakes have many meanings in Greek myth depending on the context. A symbol of fertility in earlier religions, the snake had similar connotations as an attribute of Persephone's mother, Demeter, the earth/corn goddess. The artist may also be referring here to the story of Zeus taking the form of a snake and enveloping Persephone in his coils.

THE STORY OF DEMETER

The daughter of Cronos (Saturn) and Rhea (Ops), Demeter was sometimes portrayed with a horse's head. One of the Olympians, she left Olympus in despair when Persephone disappeared. One day, she came to Eleusis, near Athens, where she stayed with the king and queen in the guise of an old nurse. Grateful for their kindness, she bathed their son in fire each night to make him immortal. But one night she was interrupted and the spell was broken. She then revealed herself in her divine form and ordered that a temple should be built to her (see below). She also gave the child, Triptolemus, cornseed, a plough, and the knowledge of agriculture, so that he could teach the skill to humankind.

Demeter is shown on this Greek black-figure amphora together with her daughter Persephone and the god Apollo in his chariot.

THE RAPE OF PERSEPHONE
by Christoph Schwartz (or Shwarz) (1545–92)
The painting shows the early part of the story of Persephone, when her uncle, Hades, whisks her into his infernal chariot and carries her off to be his queen in the underworld. He ignores the pleas of the water nymph Cyane, who sees what is happening and tries to stop him.

• BLACK HORSES
Hades' black horses drew his fiery chariot towards the chasm of the underworld. They were among his most prized possessions, along with his helmet of invisibility, which he once lent to Perseus (see pp.46–47).

THE MYSTERIES OF ELEUSIS

The Mysteries of Eleusis were the most profound and secret rituals of Greek religion, and it was believed that they "held the whole human race together". Therefore, it was vital to observe them each year. Initiates were seen as superior beings because of the vision they had received of life beyond death. The secrecy the initiates maintained was so strict that it is not known exactly what they experienced, but they seem to have had a three-fold revelation: the assurance that Persephone had given birth in fire to a divine child, the Aeon; a beatific vision of the maiden herself; and the display of an ear of corn, with its promise of new life. The Mysteries were observed for 2,000 years; they came to an end when Alaric, king of the Goths, sacked Eleusis in AD 396.

ORPHEUS AND EURYDICE

Oʀᴘʜᴇᴜꜱ ᴡᴀꜱ ᴍᴀʀʀɪᴇᴅ ᴛᴏ ᴛʜᴇ ɴʏᴍᴘʜ Eurydice, whom he loved dearly. One day she was walking by the banks of a river when she met the shepherd Aristaeus. Amazed at her beauty, Aristaeus immediately fell in love and pursued her through the countryside. Eurydice fled, but as she ran, she stepped on a snake – the bite proved fatal. Desolate at her loss, Orpheus determined to journey into the underworld (from which no living mortal had ever returned), to beg for his wife to be returned to him. Persephone (Roman Proserpine), queen of the underworld, was so moved by his sorrow, that she agreed to his request on condition that he did not look at Eurydice on the way back to the daylight. But as they neared the end of their journey, Orpheus could not help glancing back to make sure his beloved was still with him – as he looked she faded before his eyes, lost to him forever. Orpheus never recovered and lived in misery until his death.

ORPHEUS IN THE
UNDERWORLD
RECLAIMING EURYDICE,
OR THE MUSIC
**by Jean Restout II
(1692–1768)**
*This painting shows Orpheus
begging Hades (Pluto) and his
wife Persephone, rulers of the
underworld, to return his wife
Eurydice to him because he cannot
live without her. He is singing and
playing his lyre in an attempt
to soften their hearts.*

THE MUSES

The nine Muses were the daughters of Zeus and the Titaness Mnemosyne (memory). They were regarded as the goddesses of art, poetry, and music – hence artists, writers, and musicians still speak of being "inspired by the muse". Calliope, the muse of epic poetry, was the mother of Orpheus; when he was torn apart by the Maenads (see p.31), the other Muses helped her gather his limbs and bury them at the foot of Mount Olympus. The Muses themselves lived on Mount Helicon. The other eight Muses were: Clio (history), Euterpe (flute-playing), Terpsichore (dance), Erato (lyric poetry), Melpomene (tragedy), Thalia (comedy), Polymnia (mime), and Urania (astronomy).

Oʀᴘʜᴇᴜꜱ ꜱᴀɴɢ ɪɴ ᴘʀᴀɪꜱᴇ of the god Dionysus (Bacchus, see pp.58–59) and founded Orphism, a cult whose mysteries centred on the god Dionysus Zagreus, who was torn apart by the Titans. Human sacrifice may have played a role in Orphism, and Orpheus himself is said to have been torn apart by the Maenads, who were punished by Dionysus.

THE FATES

The Three Fates were the daughters of the night: Clotho ("the spinner"), Lachesis ("the drawer of lots"), and Atropos ("the inevitable"). Even Zeus was not more powerful than the fates, who measured out each man's destiny like a length of thread – one spun it, one measured it, and the third cut it.

Lord of the Dead

Hades was made ruler of the dead when he and his brothers Zeus and Poseidon drew lots for the lordship of the sky, the sea, and the underworld. The earth was left as common territory, though Hades rarely ventured there except when absolutely necessary – as he did when he seized Persephone to be his bride (see pp.28–29).

The usually merciless
Hades signals to his
wife Persephone that
he has relented.

QUEEN OF THE UNDERWORLD

Persephone, the dread queen of the underworld, was the mother of the god of the Orphic mysteries, Dionysus Zagreus, who was fathered by Zeus in the form of a serpent. This may be the reason why she took pity on Orpheus, the poet who had sung Dionysus' praises.

THE UNDERWORLD

The underworld, also called Hades after its ruler, was the land of the dead. Hermes took the souls of the dead to the River Styx where they paid Charon, the ferryman, to row them across. Cerberus the three-headed watchdog prevented escape. Hades had several entrances to the upper world and could also be reached by sea, as Odysseus did (see pp.64-65). The majority of ghosts – conceived of literally as shadows of their former selves – stayed on the featureless Plain of Asphodel. A lucky few went to Elysium, the islands of the blessed. An unlucky few were condemned to everlasting torment in Tartarus – among these were the Titans (see p.23); King Tantalus, who killed his son, abused the gods' friendship and was condemned to stand chin-deep in water that he could never drink (thus forever "tantalized"); and Sisyphus, deceitful and disobedient, who was forced to roll a heavy rock uphill for eternity – every time it neared the top, the rock rolled back down.

Cerberus by William Blake (1757–1827)

ARISTAEUS, the shepherd who chased Eurydice, was a son of Apollo, and taught mankind the art of beekeeping. For his part in Eurydice's death, the gods destroyed his bees. His mother, the nymph Cyrene, advised him to ask the advice of the sea god Proteus. Proteus told him to make offerings to the shade of Eurydice; when he did so, the bees recovered and swarmed up.

ORPHEUS SINGING
The singing of Orpheus even eased the torments of the damned. According to Ovid, the ghosts ceased from their rounds of fruitless labour and constant torment, and listened to his plea in tears. Even the Furies cried. Hades and Persephone were so moved that they could not refuse him.

ORPHEUS WAS TORN APART by Maenads, the wild women in the retinue of Dionysus (see pp.58–59), because he would not join in their revels. Only his head survived – this floated down the river Hebrus singing, and was washed ashore on the island of Lesbos, where it began to prophesy, until it was silenced by Apollo.

Orpheus
Orpheus was revered as a great poet and musician – the son of the muse Calliope and the son or pupil of Apollo. Orpheus charmed all the nymphs with his music, but was indifferent to them until he met the lovely Eurydice, whom he married. He invited the marriage god Hymen to the wedding, but Hymen was in low spirits; his torch sputtered and smoked and would not stay alight.

GUIDE OF SOULS
The god Hermes (Mercury) has a role in the underworld as the *psychopompos*, or guide of souls. Here, he leads Eurydice down to her new home. Unusually, he is shown with wings, rather than winged sandals.

HESITANT WALK
Eurydice, newly arrived in the land of the dead, still walked slowly with a limp from her injured foot. When she was returning to the upper world, this caused her to lag behind Orpheus, making him doubt that she was still with him and glance back.

APHRODITE AND ADONIS

ADONIS WAS A BEAUTIFUL YOUTH with whom the goddesses Aphrodite (Roman Venus) and Persephone (Proserpine, see pp.28–29) fell in love. He died as a result of their quarrels, killed at the request of Persephone (who wanted to keep Adonis in the underworld with her forever) by Ares (Mars), Aphrodite's jealous lover, who was disguised as a boar. Adonis was the son of Cinyras, king of Paphos in Cyprus, and his daughter Smyrna (Myrrha). Aphrodite had made Smyrna fall in love and sleep with her father while he was drunk, in revenge for Cinyras boasting that his daughter was more beautiful than she was herself. When Smyrna fell pregnant, her father tried to kill her but Aphrodite, now feeling sorry for Smyrna, turned her into a myrrh tree. The tree subsequently split in two and the beautiful infant Adonis tumbled out. Aphrodite placed the baby in a chest and gave him to Persephone for safekeeping. Persephone was immediately besotted.

• BORN FROM A TREE
Some sources say that after his mother had been turned into a myrrh tree, the baby Adonis continued to develop inside the tree. When it was time for him to be born, Ilithyia, the goddess of childbirth, released him. Others say that – in a pre-echo of his death – a wild boar charged the tree and split it in two.

APHRODITE AND ADONIS
by Hendrick Goltzius
(1558–1616/17)
This painting shows the goddess Aphrodite and the youth Adonis in a summer embrace, just before he goes off on a hunting trip. Aphrodite entreats him not to go because she is frightened for his safety.

CARELESS CUPID •
According to the Roman poet Ovid, Aphrodite fell in love with Adonis because her son Eros (Cupid), the god of love, accidentally grazed her with one of his arrows while he was kissing her one day, thus inflaming her with passion for the beautiful youth.

THE STRUGGLE between Aphrodite and Persephone for Adonis led Zeus to ask the muse Calliope (see p.30) to make a decision about the situation. She decided that Adonis should spend a third of his time with Aphrodite in the upper world, a third with Persephone in the underworld, and the rest he could do with as he pleased. To Persephone's anger, Aphrodite, with the aid of her magic girdle, persuaded him to spend his free time with her as well.

White Roses
The rose, a flower sacred to Aphrodite, was originally white. According to one story, as she ran to help the dying Adonis, Aphrodite trod on a thorn and the blood that fell onto the white rose petals stained them red.

• HUNTING DOGS
Adonis loved hunting and only laughed at Aphrodite who, prophetically, was terrified that he would be harmed on one of his hunting trips.

• WARNINGS OF A GODDESS
Aphrodite clings to Adonis, trying to persuade him not to go hunting. She constantly warned him against exposing himself to the dangers of hunting wild beasts – fearing especially the wild boars that could so easily take his life.

TAMMUZ, THE EASTERN ADONIS

Adonis is the Phoenician word for "lord" and the story of Adonis' death and resurrection reflects aspects of the Near-eastern god Tammuz (see p.19). Tammuz was the spouse of the goddess Ishtar, who descended to the underworld to rescue him from death. He is essentially a fertility god, associated with the miracle of the harvest. His death and rebirth were celebrated each spring and autumn and the spectacle of women weeping for Tammuz is mentioned in the Bible (Ezekiel viii:14). Like Adonis, he was killed by a boar and while he is in the underworld all vegetation withers. The Sumerian "Innanna's Journey to Hell" is an early version of Ishtar and Tammuz, under the names Innanna and Dumuzi, and records an early song for the lost god: "Who is your sister? I am she. Who is your mother? I am she. Day dawns the same for you and me. This is the same day we shall see."

Chariot of a Goddess
Aphrodite's golden chariot is drawn by two swans. Aphrodite was often accompanied by birds, especially doves and sparrows.

DETERMINED TO HUNT
Adonis comforts Aphrodite, but is determined to take his leave while the sun is shining and his dogs are keen to take up the chase.

THE DYING DAYS OF SUMMER
It is harvest time and the summer is coming towards an end, indicating that it will soon be time for Adonis to visit Persephone in the underworld. Symbolically, it also prefigures Adonis's death.

> *I shall sing of Aphrodite, born on Cyprus Who brings sweet gifts to mortals and whose lovely face ever shines with a radiant smile.*
> HOMERIC HYMN TO APHRODITE

RED MATERIAL
The red material suggests the drops of blood that fell to the ground as Adonis lay dying, charged by a wild boar. Where these drops fell, there sprang up blood-red anemone flowers. Aphrodite wept as she clasped him in her arms.

WHEN ADONIS DIED, he should have remained in the underworld, never to see the upper world and Aphrodite again. But she begged Zeus not to allow Persephone to take him from her completely and he agreed to let Adonis join her above ground for the four months of the summer each year.

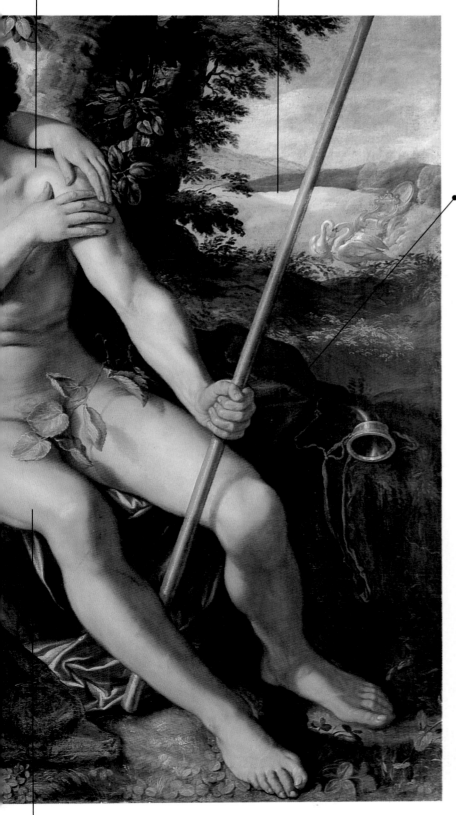

ECHO AND NARCISSUS

Echo was a nymph who, because she offended one of the gods, was doomed not to speak, except to repeat the last syllable of whatever had been said to her. Some say that Hera (Juno) laid this curse on her, exasperated by her constant chatter; others that it was Pan (see p.42), annoyed by her cloying love. It was her misfortune to fall in love with Narcissus, the beautiful son of the river Cephissus and the nymph Liriope. But as she was only able to echo him, Narcissus ignored her, and she faded to a shadow. Retribution, however, awaited Narcissus. Selfish and dismissive of all his admirers, he fell in love with his own reflection in a pool on Mount Helicon. Sick for love, he lay by the water's edge gazing at his own reflection until he died, and the gods turned him into the narcissus flower.

Echo and Narcissus
by Nicholas Poussin (1594–1665)
Echo, fading to a shadow from her unrequited love for Narcissus, gazes on him as he lies dead by a pool in a forest glade, while Eros, the god of love, looks on.

FEARLESS YOUTH
Adonis was a fearless youth and his bravado in ignoring Aphrodite's warnings led to his downfall. Persephone, angered that Aphrodite should have twice as much of Adonis' time as she did, complained to Aphrodite's lover Ares (see pp.26–27). Furiously jealous, Ares changed into a wild boar and, evading Adonis' spear, mortally wounded him.

CUPID AND PSYCHE • 34

CUPID AND PSYCHE

THE STORY OF CUPID AND PSYCHE is a Roman one in which Venus (Greek Aphrodite), the goddess of love, became infuriated by Psyche's beauty and told Cupid (Eros) to make her fall in love with the vilest of men. Unexpectedly, Cupid fell in love with her himself and married her. But Psyche became lonely because her new husband only visited at night, and told her that she must never look at him or their unborn child would not be immortal. To combat the loneliness, her sisters came to stay but, jealous of her lovely home, they convinced her that her unseen husband must be a monster. Terrified, Psyche took a lamp and looked at him while he slept – he awoke and fled. Full of remorse, Psyche searched for him everywhere, eventually coming to the palace of Venus, where she was set several impossible tasks. The last led to her falling into a deathlike sleep – Cupid revived her and took her to Olympus, where Jupiter (Zeus) made her immortal.

Love Falls in Love
Cupid, sent by his mother Venus to visit vengeance on Psyche by making her fall in love with a vagabond, was himself captivated by her beauty, and enlisted the god Apollo to help him win her.

TEMPLE OF APOLLO
Concerned for Psyche, her father consulted the oracle of Apollo at Miletus. He was told that Psyche must dress for her wedding, climb a mountain, and there await a non-human suitor.

CUPID AND PSYCHE – A FAIRY TALE

The story of Cupid and Psyche shows myth shading into fairy tale. It is included as a story-within-the-story in a Latin novel, the *Metamorphoses* of Apuleius, usually known as *The Golden Ass*. Although Apuleius presents the story as an allegory of the Soul (Psyche) in search of Love (Cupid), and sets the story in the world of the Roman gods, it is recognizably a version of a fairy tale widely distributed in the Indo-European tradition, known to folklorists as "The Search for the Lost Husband" or "The Animal Bridegroom". Variants include "Beauty and the Beast" and "The Black Bull of Norroway"; over 60 versions have been recorded from Italian oral tradition.

THE BIRTH OF PSYCHE
The story of Cupid and Psyche has many fairy-tale characteristics. In true fairy-tale style, Psyche's parents are never named except as "a king and queen". Psyche's two older sisters, shown here holding the newborn Psyche, were eclipsed by the beauty of their new sister.

WORSHIPPING SUITORS
Every day, people from far and wide came to admire the beautiful princess. They said she was Venus in human form, and began to neglect the worship of the goddess – much to Venus' anger.

THE STORY OF CUPID AND PSYCHE by Jacopo del Sellaio (1441/42–93)
This wooden panel from a wedding chest, shows the love story of Cupid and Psyche. Designed to concentrate on the love angle, several important episodes within the story are left out and less important references, such as the conception and birth of Psyche, are included. Presumably this is because, as it was painted on a wedding chest, a reference to having children was considered appropriate.

PSYCHE'S SEARCH FOR CUPID

Psyche searched everywhere for Cupid and eventually braved Venus' palace. Here, she became a slave and was given various tasks: the first, to separate a roomful of mixed grain, she achieved with the help of a colony of sympathetic ants; the last, borrowing a box of beauty from the goddess of the underworld (see pp.28–29), was accomplished with the help of a speaking tower. Aware of the danger, Psyche acted upon the tower's advice and took two sops of bread soaked in honey to appease the watch dog Cerberus, and two coins in her mouth to pay Charon, the ferryman, to take her across the River Styx and back. But against its advice, she opened the box, and fell into a deathly sleep. Finally she was revived by Cupid, granted immortality, and gave birth to their daughter Voluptas (pleasure).

Psyche and Charon *by John Roddam Spencer-Stanhope (1829–1908)*

GRIEVING PARENTS
Psyche's parents – shown here with her two sisters and their elderly husbands – were shocked at Apollo's prophecy. But Psyche – realising that the worship of her beauty must have offended Venus – begged them not to grieve.

ALONE ON A MOUNTAIN TOP
Psyche stood on the mountain top to await her spirit suitor. Zephyrus, the west wind, lifted her off her feet and wafted her to Cupid's beautiful palace.

DIRE WARNING
Cupid, who made himself invisible to Psyche, told her not to try to see him, because if she did so, their unborn child would not be born immortal.

PALACE OF LUXURY
Cupid's palace had jewelled floors and gold and silver walls. But despite the luxury, Psyche was lonely, for Cupid's servants, like Cupid himself, remained invisible to her.

WINGED FLIGHT
Cupid, angry that Psyche had disobeyed him, flew away. Psyche tried to hold on to his leg, and was carried some distance into the air, but soon had to let go.

DOOMED CONSPIRATORS
Psyche's sisters' plan to ruin her happiness proved their downfall. In revenge, Psyche (who had been prevented from committing suicide by Pan) told them that Cupid now wished to marry one of them instead. Each, in turn, climbed the mountain to meet him – but when they jumped off, Zephyrus did not catch them and they plunged to their deaths.

LAID ON THE TURF
The wind laid Psyche down on the soft turf, where Cupid's invisible servants found her. Obedient to the will of the gods, Psyche had declared herself ready for her new husband, even if he was born to destroy the world.

JEALOUS SISTERS
Psyche's sisters were summoned to keep her company. But they were jealous of her happiness, claiming that her husband was really a serpent, who would devour both her and her unborn child.

A GOD DISCOVERED
When Psyche shone her lamp on Cupid's face, meaning to slay him if he were indeed a monster, she was so shocked by his beauty that she spilled hot oil on his shoulder. But first she wounded herself on one of his arrows, so falling in love with Love.

Sleeping Beauty
Psyche's sleep here is a reminder of the deathly sleep that came upon her when she opened the box of beauty from the underworld (see above). In true fairy-tale style, she could only be woken by her true love, Cupid.

ARTEMIS AND ACTAEON

Crescent Moon
Artemis wears a crescent-moon diadem in her hair, showing her also to be a moon goddess.

ARTEMIS (Roman Diana) was goddess of the hunt and the moon. Like her brother Apollo (see pp.38–39), she was a child of Zeus and the Titan Leto. She was also the goddess of childbirth and, by extension, of all young creatures because her mother gave birth to her without pain. The story of Actaeon seeing her bathe and her revenge in turning him into a stag to be set upon by his own dogs, is best told in Ovid's *Metamorphoses*. This is a Roman source, although the story is Greek in origin. Artemis' reaction may be accounted for by the importance of her eternal virginity, which she begged Zeus to grant her at the age of three. However, some sources claim she was taking revenge on Actaeon for having claimed to be a better hunter than she was.

ARTEMIS SURPRISED BY ACTAEON
by Titian, originally Tiziano Vecelli(o) (c.1488/90–1576)
This picture shows the moment when Actaeon, while hunting in the forest, accidentally comes upon Artemis and her nymphs bathing. The virgin goddess is horrified, tries to cover herself, and will avenge herself by turning Actaeon into a stag to be hunted down and killed by his own hounds.

CALLISTO, TRICKED BY ZEUS

Callisto, Artemis' favourite nymph, caught the eye of Zeus, who seduced her disguised as Artemis. Artemis was furious when she learned of this and banished Callisto, even though she had tried to resist Zeus' advances. Shortly afterwards, when Callisto gave birth to a son, Arco, Zeus' jealous wife, Hera (Juno), turned her into a bear and Callisto fled. Arco was rescued and 15 years later pursued and caught his mother during a hunt. To prevent him from killing her, Zeus whisked them both up into the sky where they became the constellations of the Great Bear and Arctophylax, or "guardian of the bear".

Zeus seduces Callisto disguised as Artemis
by Jean-Simon Barthélemy (1743–1811)
Zeus kneels before Callisto disguised, wearing the crescent moon of Artemis.

● **DOGS OF DEATH**
Actaeon's faithful hounds did not recognize their master once the furious Artemis had transformed him into a stag. True to their nature, they chased and killed him.

● **ACTAEON**
Actaeon's father Aristaeus was the son of Apollo; his mother Autonoë was the daughter of Cadmus, founder of Thebes (see p.49), and brother of Europa (see p.45).

SACRED GROTTO

Artemis is seen bathing in her secret cave at the heart of the valley of Gargaphie near Thebes. She carved the arches from the living rock, and made the pool from a spring of pure water.

ANIMAL SKINS

Animal skins hang out to dry from the boughs of a tree, reminding us of Artemis' role as the goddess of hunting.

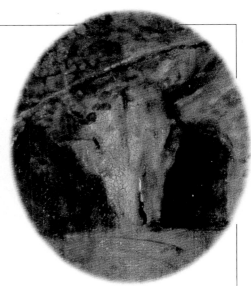

Stag's Head
The stag's skull placed on a column is a forewarning of Actaeon's metamorphosis and death.

ARTEMIS, GODDESS OF HUNTING, used her skills to protect her mother Leto in the sacred grove at Delphi, striking down the giant Tityus who was trying to rape her.

UNARMED GODDESS

Unprotected, her bow and arrow in the care of her nymphs, Artemis could do nothing but dash spring water in Actaeon's face. At the first touch of water, he sprouted antlers and gradually turned into a stag, a form in which he would be unable to tell anyone that he had seen her naked.

"The blazing eye of a young girl does not escape me, if she has tasted of a man: for such I have an experienced eye"
ACTAEON, IN *TOXOTIDES* OF AESCHYLUS

DAUGHTER OF THE RIVER

Artemis is attended by the nymph Crocale whose father was Ismenus, god of the river Ismenus in Boeotia, near Thebes, and a son of Apollo and the Nereid, Melia. As Crocale binds her hair, Artemis suddenly starts back in horror at the sight of Actaeon.

GODDESS OF THE CROSSROADS

Hecate was the Greek goddess of the night, ghosts, and magic, and a haunter of crossroads. Her statue with three faces – lion, dog, and mare – used to be placed where three roads met, one face looking down each road. Hecate is said to be the daughter of Asteria, Leto's sister. She is sometimes identified with her cousin, Artemis, and like her she is closely associated with the moon. In her triple aspect she is said to represent Selene (Luna) in heaven, Artemis on earth, and Persephone (Proserpine) in the underworld (see pp.28–29).

WATER NYMPHS OF ARTEMIS

Artemis was always attended by water nymphs, both Naiads – spring, river, and lake nymphs – and Nereids, or sea nymphs. In classical mythology, every principal spring and river was inhabited by one or more Naiads.

ARTEMIS' MAIDS OF HONOUR

The six nymphs depicted here are Crocale, Nephele, Hyale, Rhanis, Psecas, Phiale – just a handful of Artemis' huge retinue that included 60 ocean nymphs, who acted as maids of honour, and 20 river nymphs who looked after her clothes and her dogs.

APOLLO AND DAPHNE

Eros, God of Love
The god of sexual desire, Eros, was often portrayed as a spiteful child, who delighted in causing mischief with his arrows of desire.

APOLLO, THE GOD OF ARCHERY, music, prophecy, and light, was very powerful but not always successful in love. His first love was the nymph Daphne, who refused him. Apollo's fiery passion and Daphne's cold resistance were both the fault of Eros (Roman Cupid), who, angry at jokes Apollo had made, shot him with a golden arrow to make him fall in love, and Daphne with a leaden one so that she would reject him. Apollo pursued Daphne with loving entreaties, all of which she spurned, as far as the banks of the River Peneus. Here, just as he reached out for her, she called upon her father, the river god, for help and was immediately transformed into a laurel tree. Apollo was left bereft.

Unlike his father Zeus (Jupiter), Apollo did take "no" for an answer, although he sometimes exacted terrible revenge. For example, when the Sibyl Deiphobe refused him – despite being offered as many years of life as she could hold grains of sand – he was so angry that he gave her a thousand years more life but without eternal youth. She lived out her dessicated days in a jar at Cumae, refused her only wish – to die.

Apollo
Apollo, his halo showing his role as the god of light, had special care for flocks and herds. This relates to his stint as a herdsman for King Admetus – work given to him by his father Zeus as punishment for killing the cyclops (see box below).

TRANSFORMATION
Daphne was transformed into a laurel tree when she called upon her father, Peneus, to help her. Here, the first laurel leaves are springing from her fingers.

LAUREL WREATH
Heartbroken, Apollo swore that if he had lost Daphne, he would at least honour her memory by wearing a wreath of laurel leaves from then on. The laurel and the palm were both sacred to Apollo.

LONG HAIR
Apollo let his hair grow long. In tribute to him, Roman men did not cut their hair short until they were 17 or 18.

APOLLO AND DAPHNE
by Giovanni Battista Tiepolo (1696–1770)
This painting shows the god Apollo reaching out to clasp in his arms the reluctant nymph Daphne. She has called to her father, the river god Peneus, who answers her plea and is turning her into a laurel tree. Eros hides behind Daphne.

DAPHNE
Daphne rejected Apollo when she was a nymph; as a tree she still trembled and shrank from his kisses and caresses.

AMONG APOLLO'S loves was Hyacinthus, mortal, good-natured, and handsome son of the muse Clio. But Zephyrus, the west wind, also wished to be Hyacinthus' friend and in a fit of jealousy caused his death by blowing Apollo's discus off course while the two were having a sporting match. The blue hyacinth flower appeared where the young man's blood fell.

SPITEFUL CHILD
Eros, the cause of Apollo's unhappy love affair, hides from the god behind Daphne. He is sometimes punished for his deeds, particularly by Artemis (Diana) and Athena (Minerva) who both represent chastity. Daphne was one of Artemis' retinue of nymphs (see pp.36–37).

RIVER GOD
Daphne's father listens to her desperate pleas and saves her. The oar and the overturned water urn are traditional symbols of a river god.

*"Apollo even the swan sings of you.
As it lands upon the banks of the river Peneus.
The sweet-singing bard sings of you
First and last with his high-tuned lyre.
Hail lord! Hear my song."*
HOMERIC HYMN
TO APOLLO

CHEIRON

Cheiron was the greatest of the centaurs, who were half-man, half-horse. He was the son of Cronos (Roman Saturn, see p.23) and the nymph Philyra, to whom Cronos had appeared as a horse. The other centaurs were descended from Centaurus, a grandson of Ares (Mars), who mated with the mares on Mount Pelion. Unlike the gentle and intelligent Cheiron, the centaurs were uncivilized and brutish. Apollo taught Cheiron archery, medicine, and music; he, in turn, tutored Apollo's son Asclepius, as well as the hero Jason and his own great-grandson Achilles (see pp.52–53 and p.63). Cheiron was an immortal, but ceded his immortality to Prometheus (see pp.24–25) to escape an eternity of pain after Heracles accidentally wounded him (see p.51). Zeus granted him the lesser immortality of the skies, where he is the constellation Centaurus.

DAPHNE, the water nymph pursued by Apollo, was also loved by a mortal, Leucippus. Leucippus followed her disguised as a maiden, but the jealous Apollo advised the nymphs to bathe naked. When Leucippus removed his clothes his deception was discovered, and the nymphs tore him to pieces.

ARROWS
It was Apollo's role as the archer god that led him to be identified with the sun, whose rays fall like arrows to earth, and earned him the name Phoebus, "the bright".

THE LAUREL was sacred to Apollo as a result of his love for Daphne. At his shrine at Delphi, his high priestess, Pythia, chewed a laurel leaf before uttering an oracle. The answers given in her divinely-inspired ecstasy were often obscure and ambiguous. The philosopher Heraclitus wrote, "The lord whose oracle is in Delphi neither declares nor conceals, but gives a sign".

ASCLEPIUS

Asclepius was the son of Apollo and the nymph Coronis. But Coronis took a human lover, Ischys, and, in a fit of anger, Apollo killed her. He soon repented and told Hermes (Mercury) to rescue his unborn child from her womb. Apollo then entrusted the child, Asclepius, to Cheiron (see box), who educated him, and he grew up to be the god of health and medicine. Athena (Minerva), also helped him by giving him two phials of blood from the Medusa – blood from her left side raised the dead; blood from the right caused death. When Asclepius raised Hippolytus, Theseus' dead son (see p.57), Hades (Pluto), the god of the underworld complained to Zeus, who felled Asclepius with a thunderbolt. Apollo retaliated and killed the cyclopes (see p.64) who had made the thunderbolt. Zeus later restored Asclepius to life.

This Greek votive relief dating from the 5th century BC shows a family sacrificing a bull to Asclepius and his daughter Hygeia.

KING MIDAS

MIDAS, KING OF PHRYGIA, was unlucky in his dealings with the gods. Doomed (at his own request) in his early years as king, to turn everything that he touched into gold, he learnt his lesson and wanted only to live a simple country life. But in doing so, he upset the god Apollo, who took revenge. Out walking one day in the countryside he came across a musical competition in progress between the gods Apollo and Pan, with Tmolus, the spirit of the mountain, acting as judge. Apollo played the lyre, and Pan played the pipes (see pp.42–43). Apollo was so skilful that Tmolus awarded him the prize, demanding that Pan admit his pipes were inferior. Midas disagreed with Tmolus' judgement, preferring Pan's playing. Apollo was so offended by this that he changed Midas' ears into those of an ass. Midas was so ashamed that he hid them under a turban, but finally his secret became public and he killed himself.

Foolish King
Midas, freed by Dionysus from the double-edged gift that turned everything he touched to gold, then despised riches. He left his kingdom to live simply in the country and worship Pan, the god of wild and lonely places.

Ass's ears

ATHENA
The goddess Athena (Minerva) stands next to Aphrodite, the goddess of love. Athena's presence may be a confusion on the artist's part with the story of Marsyas (see opposite), or simply a reference to that other famous musical competition between Apollo and a rival.

A WHISPERED SECRET
When Apollo turned his ears into those of an ass, Midas hid his shame under a turban. Only his barber knew the truth. At last the burden of secrecy was too much to bear, and the barber went to a lonely spot, dug a hole in the ground, and whispered the king's secret into the ground. Next year, reeds grew there, and when they were stirred by the wind they whispered, "King Midas has ass's ears." When Midas knew his secret was out, he killed himself.

A Vain Boast
The god Pan, playing his pipes to a group of impressionable nymphs on Mount Tmolus, boasted that his music was better than that of the god of music, Apollo. Apollo challenged him to a contest, with the mountain god as judge.

Goat's horns

LAUREL WREATH
Apollo is crowned with a wreath of wild laurel from Parnassus. It signifies his mastery of the creative arts, and recalls his fated love for the nymph Daphne, who was turned into a laurel tree (see pp.38-39).

GOD OF MUSIC
Apollo, the god of music, played the lyre – the stringed instrument invented for him by Hermes (Mercury), Pan's father. It was played by either strumming or plucking with a plectrum.

GOAT-GOD
Here, Pan plays a flute, rather than the pan pipes. This is another indication, coupled with the presence of Athena, that the artist confused elements of the story of Marsyas with that of Pan.

KING MIDAS, the son of Gordius, a peasant who had been made king of Phrygia by the will of the gods, grew up convinced of the importance of money. As a result, when Dionysus (Bacchus) offered to grant him a wish for having helped his drunken satyr companion, Silenus, Midas asked that everything he touched should turn to gold. All went well, until he felt hungry – "Bring me food!" he cried. Alas, it turned to gold! "Bring me wine!" – the same thing happened. Horrified, Midas begged Dionysus to help him. The god told him to wash himself in the River Pactolus – which explains why the river and its banks are still flecked with gold dust.

THE FLAYING OF MARSYAS

Athena made herself a double flute but, because playing it distorted her beauty, she cursed it and threw it away. It was found by a satyr named Marsyas who taught himself to play the discarded instrument and, unwittingly, took on Athena's curse. He became such a fine player that he challenged Apollo to a musical contest, with the Muses as judges. The loser was to submit to any punishment the victor decided. Both musicians played so beautifully that the judges could not decide between them – until Apollo challenged Marsyas to play upside down, which was possible on Apollo's lyre but not on the flute. Apollo hung the impudent challenger on a pine tree and flayed him alive; so much blood flowed from the tortured satyr that it created the river Marsyas. Some say the river was formed from the tears of his fellow satyrs and nymphs, in grief at his torment.

This Greek ivory statue, c.200 bc, shows the satyr Marsyas tied to a tree before Apollo exacts his vicious revenge.

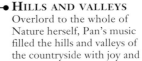

HILLS AND VALLEYS
Overlord to the whole of Nature herself, Pan's music filled the hills and valleys of the countryside with joy and an expectation of good things.

MOUNTAIN GOD
Tmolus, called to judge the relative merits of the music of Pan and Apollo, was the incarnated spirit of the mountain. Portrayed as an old man, he separates himself from his mountain form by shaking his locks free of trees, and creating a wreath of oak leaves on his brow.

THE JUDGEMENT OF MIDAS
by Gillis van Coninxloo (1544–1607)
This painting shows the end of Apollo and Pan's musical competition when Apollo has already cursed Midas with ass's ears. There are also references to other stories, including Pan's invention of the pan pipes, and the secret of Midas' ears becoming widespread.

ASS'S EARS
Midas was the only one to disagree with Tmolus' judgment; he preferred Pan's simple flutings. Apollo, enraged that anyone so stupid should be allowed to have human ears, transformed Midas' ears into those of an ass – long, grey, and hairy.

THE MUSES
The women watching and listening to the competition are the Muses, deities of poetic inspiration, who often accompany Apollo.

THE CREATION OF PAN'S PIPES
The story of Pan's invention of the pan pipes from river reeds following his pursuit of the nymph Syrinx is alluded to here. These two satyrs, also half-man, half-goat, sit by a clump of reeds on the banks of a river.

PAN AND SYRINX

PAN (ROMAN FAUNUS) LIVED ON EARTH IN ARCADIA, rather than on Mount Olympus with other gods (see pp.22–23). Although essentially a good-natured god, he was extremely lustful and was renowned for pursuing nymphs, such as Syrinx, whom he chased from Mount Lycaeum to the banks of the River Ladon, before she escaped by turning into a clump of reeds. From these reeds, he fashioned the first "pan pipes". The god of flocks and shepherds, Pan's name derives from the early Greek "Paon", which means "herdsman". His parentage is obscure; most sources say his father was Hermes (Mercury), although others name Zeus (Jupiter). His mother Dryope, a granddaughter of Apollo, is sometimes called Penelope, which has led to stories of Pan being the son of Odysseus' wife Penelope, either by Hermes or Zeus in the form of a goat or ram; or even that Pan, a name meaning "all", was born after Penelope slept with all her suitors, while her husband was away (see p.65). Pan was also able to inspire the sudden, groundless fear known as "panic". For example, in 490 BC, he is said to have caused the Persians to flee in terror from the Athenians, in return for the Athenians worshipping him and performing ceremonial rites. These later became the Roman Lupercalia, a festival dedicated to the fertility god Faunus.

ALTHOUGH PAN boasted that he had seduced all of Dionysus' Maenads, as well as the moon goddess Selene (Luna), he was often rejected. His least dignified pursuit was of Heracles' lover, Omphale, queen of Lydia. Climbing into her bed, Pan tried to embrace her, only to discover the couple had exchanged clothes in their loveplay and he was embracing Heracles. Heracles kicked Pan out of bed and across the floor.

HALF-GOAT ●
Pan's goat-form inspired the conventional depiction of the Christian devil; some writers see the "devil-worship" of the European witch-cult as a continuation of the rites of Pan.

HERMES, MESSENGER OF THE GODS

Hermes was Pan's father. A son of Zeus by Maia, the eldest of the Pleiades, he helped Zeus to woo the princess Io by lulling the 100-eyed guard dog Argus to sleep with the story of Pan's pursuit of Syrinx. The messenger of the gods, flying with the aid of his winged sandals, Hermes also acted as a guide of souls to the underworld, and invented the lyre, which he gave to his brother Apollo in recompense for stealing his cattle (see p.40). Hermes was also the god of travellers and a fertility god, represented by stone statues with erect phalluses called herms. Herms were placed on roadsides, in public places, and in the home. One fateful night in Athens in 415 BC hundreds of phalluses were broken off; modern scholars suggest this was a women's protest against Athenian militarism.

Caduceus, a messenger's emblem in Ancient Greece to ensure safe passage

Winged sandals for swift travel

Hermes
Hermes, shown here on a Greek red-figure cup dating from the late 5th century BC, is depicted as an athletic young man.

PAN AND SYRINX by François Boucher (1703–70)
This painting shows Pan, who has fallen in love with the beautiful nymph Syrinx, pursuing her to the banks of the River Ladon. As he reaches to embrace her, she calls on the river goddess to help her to escape.

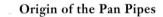

THE DEATH OF PAN

During the reign of the Emperor Tiberius (AD 14–37), a man called Thamus, sailing past the Greek island of Paxi, was hailed by a godlike voice calling, "Thamus, the great god Pan is dead!". This cry was repeated whenever the sailors saw land, and a terrible weeping arose from the countryside around. Some accounts place this event at the moment of Christ's birth, a fitting time as many of Pan's attributes have been assigned to the devil of Christian tradition. Some writers suggest the cry was a mis-hearing of "The all-great Tammuz is dead", a ceremonial lament for the death-and-rebirth of the oriental god Tammuz (see p.33).

CHAPLET OF FIR
Pan wears a chaplet of fir on his head, a reference to Pitys, a lover who was transformed into a fir tree.

BURNING TORCH
Eros (Cupid) inflamed Pan with love for Syrinx, symbolized by the burning torch.

Origin of the Pan Pipes
To escape Pan's advances, Syrinx was turned into a clump of reeds and the wind whistled through them and made sweet music. Pan, thwarted of his desires, cut the reeds into several unequal lengths, fastened them together with wax, and made the first syrinx, or pan pipes.

CHASTE NYMPH
Syrinx was a nymph of the virgin goddess Artemis (Diana, see pp.36–37), who demanded chastity from her attendants. Pursued by Pan, she was run to ground on the banks of the River Ladon, where, unable to escape and terrified of Artemis' fury, she called upon the river goddess to help her.

> *In the evening, he shouts as he returns from the hunt, And plays sweet music on his pipes of reed.*
> HOMERIC HYMN TO PAN

RIVER GODDESS
The river goddess heard Syrinx's cries and came to her rescue. Clasping her in her arms, she transformed her into a clump of reeds, thus disappointing Pan in his amorous pursuit.

The River Ladon
The River Ladon is shown here as a nymph with a water jar. In some versions of the story, the River Ladon, who transforms Syrinx, is her father. Transformation has many roles in Greek myth: while Syrinx uses it to escape, the nymph Pitys, another of Pan's lovers, is turned into a fir tree by Gaia, the earth, out of pity, because Pitys' angry and disappointed suitor, Boreas, the north wind, has crushed her against a rock, murderously jealous that she prefers Pan.

BEAUTIFUL NYMPH
Syrinx was so beautiful that she was often mistaken for her mistress, the goddess Artemis. The only way to tell them apart was that Syrinx carried a bow made of horn and Artemis one of gold.

WATER JUG
Water jugs or urns are often used to symbolize a river god or goddess.

ZEUS AND DANAË

DANAË WAS THE BEAUTIFUL DAUGHTER OF ACRISIUS, king of Argos, who was supposed to rule in rotation with his twin brother Proetus. But Acrisius refused to yield the throne, and Proetus, in anger, tried to seduce his daughter. Terrified by a prophecy that if Danaë ever bore a son the child would kill him, Acrisius shut her up in a bronze tower away from mortal men. Unfortunately, he could not guard against the gods and Zeus (Roman Jupiter), fulfilling the pattern of many of his conquests, came to her in disguise (here, as a shower of gold) and fathered the great hero Perseus (see pp.46–47). When Acrisius found out about the baby, he cast Danaë and her son out to sea. They drifted for several days before they came to the island of Seriphos, where they were taken in by Dictys, brother of Polydectes, the king of the island. Over the years, the old king tried to force Danaë to marry him. Seeking to protect his mother, Perseus succeeded in killing the terrifying Gorgon Medusa, using its lethal head to turn Polydectes into stone and save Danaë. Years later, the prophecy was fulfilled when Perseus accidentally killed Acrisius with a discus in a sporting competition.

THE SONS OF ZEUS AND EUROPA

Zeus and Europa (see below) had three sons: Minos (see p.56), Rhadamanthys, and Sarpedon. Minos, who had been made heir to the Cretan throne by his stepfather Asterion, quarrelled with his brothers and drove them from the island. As Zeus' sons, they both became kings elsewhere. Rhadamanthys also tutored Heracles (see pp.50–51) and is said to have married Heracles' mother Alcmene after her husband died. Both Rhadamanthys – who was a wise lawmaker – and Minos – who received new laws for the Greeks from his father Zeus every nine years – became judges in the underworld when they died.

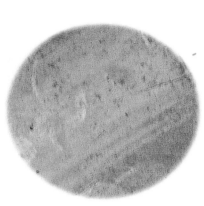

Shower of Gold
Zeus visited Danaë in a shower of gold. Some artists depict this as the burning rays of the sun, others as coins. Some, as here, combine both images. Later rationalizations of this myth explained the gold simply as a bribe to Danaë's guards.

ZEUS AND DANAË by Joachim Utewael (1566–1638)
This Renaissance painting shows Zeus appearing to Danaë as a shower of gold through the roof of her bronze prison. The child from this union was the hero Perseus.

● ZEUS IN LOVE
Looking down on the young and beautiful Danaë incarcerated in her bronze tower, Zeus fell in love and was determined to visit her.

❝ *... Danaë, when in the carven chest the wind blowing and the sea stirring shattered her with fear: Her cheeks were wet as she put her loving arm round Perseus, saying, 'Oh, child! What trouble is mine . . .* ❞
SIMONIDES

● EAGLE OF POWER
The eagle, Zeus' attendant bird, is symbolic of power and victory. In matters of love and war, Zeus never accepted defeat.

● CLOUDS GATHERING
God of the sky and ruler of weather, Zeus is often called "the cloud-gatherer". He is often shown with his weapon, the thunderbolt.

● BARRED WINDOWS
Although Acrisius is said to have loved his daughter Danaë, he selfishly shut her away behind closed doors, in order to save his own life.

● JEALOUS WIFE
Outside the window, silently observing her husband's betrayal, Hera, takes on the form of her totem bird, the peacock.

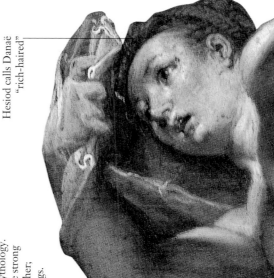

Hesiod calls Danaë "rich-haired"

GOD OF LOVE

Although he did not play an actual part in the story of Zeus' seduction of Danaë, Eros (Cupid), the god of sexual love, is depicted here. His presence indicates that love can overcome all obstacles, even barred doors and armed guards.

BOW AND ARROW

Eros always carries a bow and arrow. The poet Ovid said that there were two kinds of arrow – golden ones to inspire love and leaden ones to take love away.

ZEUS' COMPLICATED love life is the source of many stories. His overmastering sexual energy was, in fact, his primary characteristic – proof, perhaps, of his restless creative drive. Although married to Hera (Juno), he had many children by other women, immortals and mortals alike, who became gods or heroes. Zeus did not waste time on the niceties of courtship, and many of his seductions were, in fact, rapes, as is the case with both Danaë and Europa.

SURPRISED SERVANT

Danaë's handmaiden drops her spinning as Zeus appears through the roof as a shower of gold.

CONDEMNED TO DEATH

Accused of complicity in deceiving him, Danaë's handmaiden was put to death when Acrisius discovered the birth of his grandson Perseus.

I shall sing of Zeus, the best and greatest of the gods, Far-seeing, mighty, the fulfiller of designs.
HOMERIC HYMN TO ZEUS

SPINNING YARN

In Greek myth, spinning was often a symbol of the Three Fates, who spun the thread of life, measured it, and cut it off to the allotted length. The reference here indicates how hopeless it was for Acrisius to try to escape his fate, as decreed by the Oracle. As foretold, his grandson Perseus did accidentally kill him with a discus several years later.

GRIFFIN

The griffin, part-eagle, part-lion, is one of many fantastic monsters and beasts in Greek mythology. The griffin on Danaë's bed represents the strong guard under which her father had placed her; outside the doors was a pack of savage dogs.

Danaë, Princess of Argos

Danaë was the daughter of Acrisius of Argos by Eurydice, the daughter of Lacedemon (not to be confused with Eurydice, wife of Orpheus). Acrisius' twin brother Proetus, king of Tyryns, had quarrelled with his brother even in the womb, so it was no surprise that he should covet his brother's daughter, nor that Acrisius should try to prevent him.

EUROPA AND ZEUS

Europa was the daughter of the Phoenician king, Agenor. One day, Zeus saw her playing with her maidens by the sea and, overcome by lust, took the form of a handsome bull and mingled with the king's herd on the beach. Europa stroked him, hung garlands of flowers on his horns, and he seemed so gentle that she eventually climbed on his back. Zeus immediately charged out to sea, carrying her to Crete where he made love to her under a plane tree, which, according to tradition, has been green ever since. Europa gave birth to three sons: Minos (see p.56), Rhadamanthys, and Sarpedon. She subsequently married Asterion, the king of Crete, who adopted Minos as his heir.

The Rape of Europa
by Valentin Alexandrowitsch Serow (1865-1911)

PERSEUS AND ANDROMEDA

PERSEUS WAS THE SON of Zeus (Roman Jupiter) and Danaë (see pp.44–45), who was sent in search of the Gorgon Medusa's head by Polydectes, Danaë's unwanted suitor. The three Gorgons were sometimes beautiful, but always terrifying, serpent-haired creatures who turned people to stone with a single glance. Helped by Athena (Minerva) and Hermes (Mercury), Perseus managed to cut off Medusa's head, and put it in a bag. Flying home, aided by Hermes' winged sandals, he came upon Andromeda, a beautiful Ethiopian princess, chained to a rock and left as a living sacrifice for a sea monster, to assuage the anger of the sea god Poseidon (Neptune). Perseus fell in love, killed the monster, and married Andromeda. On his return, Polydectes, who presumed him dead, laughed scornfully when Perseus told him he had brought Medusa's head – smiling grimly, Perseus withdrew it from its bag and immediately Polydectes was turned to stone.

Perseus
Perseus was one of the great Greek heroes and, in his youth, accomplished daring deeds. Of royal blood, he did not wish to succeed to the throne of Argos after the death of his grandfather (see p.45), so ruled Tyryns and Mycenae instead. Here, he founded the family of the Perseids, from which Heracles was descended (see pp.50–51).

LOVE AT FIRST SIGHT
The infant Eros (Cupid), with his flaming torch, indicates that Perseus is in love with Andromeda.

BRONZE SHIELD
Perseus carries a bronze shield, which was lent to him by Athena. She warned him not to look at Medusa directly, but to look at the reflection in the bronze shield, to avoid being turned into stone. Athena later set Medusa's head on the shield and carried it as part of her armour.

MAGICAL GIFTS
Perseus received help in his quest from the Stygian nymphs. They lent him three magical items left in their care: Hermes' winged sandals, Hades' helmet of invisibility, and a bag in which to put the Gorgon's head.

SWORD OF HERMES
Fired by heroism and love, Perseus prepares to swing his sword and destroy the evil sea monster. The curved, unbreakable sword was also a gift from Hermes. Perseus first used it to strike off Medusa's head while she slept. He fled the scene undetected by the other Gorgons, thanks to the magic helmet that made him invisible.

PERSEUS RESCUING ANDROMEDA
by Charles-Antoine Coypel (1694–1752)
This painting shows Perseus about to rescue Andromeda from the sea monster. The sea is raging, and the angry sea nymphs look on in dismay. Andromeda's distraught parents and the crowds on the city walls pray to the heavens and beseech Perseus to succeed.

WHEN PERSEUS first set off to find the Gorgon Medusa, he was told by Athena to seek out the three Graiae, the Gorgons' sisters. The Graiae, hideous old hags with just a single eye and tooth between them, would tell Perseus how to find the Stygian nymphs who would help him to overcome Medusa. When the Graiae refused to help him, Perseus snatched their single eye as they passed it between themselves. Held to ransom, they told him what he needed to know. He then threw the eye into a lake so that they could not warn the Gorgons of his plans.

VENGEFUL NYMPHS
The sea nymphs, or Nereids, were offended by Andromeda's mother and called on Poseidon to avenge them. He sent a tidal wave and a terrible monster to maraud the coast of Ethiopia.

FLESH-EATING SEA MONSTER
The sea monster ravaged the coast, devouring men, women, and children. An oracle had told the king that it could only be assuaged by the sacrifice of his daughter.

BELLEROPHON SLAYS THE CHIMAERA

Bellerophon, like Perseus, was a heroic, royal figure who enjoyed the patronage of Athena. A guest at the court of King Proetus of Argus (see p.44), the queen falsely accused him of trying to rape her. Loath to kill a guest directly, Proetus sent him to his father-in-law King Iobates with a letter asking that the bearer be put to death. Iobates, expecting him to be killed, asked Bellerophon to slay the Chimaera, a fire-breathing monster with the front legs of a lion, the body of a she-goat, and the tail of a snake, which was devastating his kingdom. Bellerophon tamed the winged horse Pegasus with a golden bridle given to him by Athena, and, swooping down, riddled the beast with arrows and thrust a lump of lead between its jaws – the Chimaera's breath melted the lead and it choked to death. When he survived other trials, Iobates gave up trying to kill Bellerophon and made him his heir instead. When he heard the accusation that had been made against him, Bellerophon returned to Argos and killed the queen, pushing her off Pegasus' back into the sea. He eventually died a blind, lame beggar, having offended Zeus by trying to ride Pegasus up to heaven.

Bellerophon Slays the Chimaera by Giovanni-Battista Tiepolo (1696–1770)

ALTHOUGH CEPHEUS and Cassiopeia pledged Andromeda to Perseus, she was already betrothed in marriage to her uncle Phineas. Nonetheless, her wedding to Perseus went ahead, only to be interrupted by the arrival of an irate Phineas with a large armed guard. In danger of being overwhelmed by such numbers, Perseus used the Gorgon's head to turn Phineas and 200 of his men to stone.

DIVINE FATHER
Lightning in the sky shows the presence of Zeus, who fathered Perseus in a shower of gold.

DISTRAUGHT FATHER
When King Cepheus asked the oracle of horned Ammon (that is, the Egyptian god Amun, here assimilated into classical myth) how to turn aside Poseidon's anger, he was told that the only way was to sacrifice Andromeda to the monster. So, to save his people, he chained her to a rock for the monster to devour.

Monster Adversary
The sea monster, unaware that Perseus could fly, attacked his shadow on the water, enabling Perseus to swoop down and kill it using Hermes' sickle-shaped sword. Poseidon was furious: not only had Perseus rescued Andromeda but he had killed Medusa, one of Poseidon's former lovers. When she died, his two unborn children rose up from her spilled blood – the winged horse Pegasus and the warrior Chrysaor.

CHAINED MAIDEN
Andromeda was chained to a rock on the Phoenician coast as the final sacrifice to the monster. She was the daughter of Cepheus, king of Joppa, and his wife Cassiopeia.

BOASTFUL MOTHER
Cassiopeia had boasted that she and her daughter were more beautiful than the sea nymphs, thus bringing down Poseidon's vengeance upon the coast.

THE TRAGEDY OF OEDIPUS

Oedipus, the son of King Laius and his wife Jocasta of Thebes, was abandoned as a baby after it was prophesied that he would kill his father and marry his mother. Left to die, he was found and taken to King Polybus of Corinth who was childless. Oedipus grew up unaware of his origins, and, until he visited the Oracle at Delphi, unaware of the prophecy. When he was told, he was horrified and decided not to go home, thereby setting in motion the train of events that he most wished to avoid. Leaving Delphi, Oedipus met and killed King Laius who was on his way to ask the Oracle how to rid Thebes of the Sphinx, a monster who killed his subjects when they could not answer her riddles. Unaware of Laius' identity, Oedipus went to Thebes, rid the town of the Sphinx, became king himself and married Jocasta. When a plague broke out some time later, the Oracle blamed it on King Laius' murderer, and Oedipus gradually realized that he was the killer. The revelation of his birth soon followed. Aghast, Jocasta hanged herself and Oedipus put out his own eyes.

The Sphinx

This monster with a woman's head, an eagle's wings, a serpent's tail, and the body of a lion, was the daughter of Echidna (who was part-woman, part-serpent). Echidna's brood included many of the monsters of Greek mythology, including the Chimaera (see p.47), the Hydra, Cerberus (see p.31), the Nemean Lion, and the Crommyon Sow (see pp.54–55).

RIDDLE OF THE SPHINX

The Sphinx was sent by Hera (Roman Juno) to plague Thebes because, before he became king, Laius had abducted a youth, Chryssipus, to be his lover – a liaison that was a crime against marriage. The Sphinx used to ambush her victims outside the city, and ask her famous riddle, "What being walks sometimes on two feet, sometimes on three, and sometimes on four, and is weakest when it has the most?" When they failed to answer correctly, she devoured them.

OEDIPUS WAS ABANDONED as a baby because Laius was told by Apollo's Oracle at Delphi that he must remain childless or risk calamity to Thebes. Laius either disobeyed the Oracle's advice or was so upset that he got drunk and slept with his wife Jocasta anyway.

OEDIPUS AND THE SPHINX by Jean-Auguste-Dominique Ingres (1780–1867)
This painting shows Oedipus considering the answer that he should give to the Sphinx's riddle. He is surrounded by the bones of the unfortunates who have given the wrong answer. Below a man flees, in the expectation of yet another death.

> **❝** All unknowing you are the scourge of your own flesh and blood, the dead below the earth and the living here above, and the double lash of your mother and your father's curse will whip you from this land **❞**
>
> OEDIPUS REX
> BY SOPHOCLES C. AD 430

OEDIPUS

Oedipus ponders long and hard before he answers the Sphinx: "Man, who crawls on all fours as a baby, stands on two feet in maturity, and leans on a stick in old age". Cheated of her prey, the Sphinx casts herself from the rock to her death.

AT THE END OF HIS LIFE, Oedipus is depicted by Sophocles as a blind beggar, wandering from place to place, pursued by the Furies (see p.26). He died at Colonus, welcomed to the underworld in the end by Hades (Pluto) himself, and granted a beatific inner vision of Persephone (Proserpine) akin to that experienced by the initiates at Eleusis (see p.29).

OEDIPUS AND JOCASTA had four children – two sons, Eteocles and Polynices, and two daughters, Antigone and Ismene.

FLEEING MAN
This figure may be the only man in King Laius' entourage who escaped when Laius and Oedipus fought each other on the road – the same man who was instructed by Laius to abandon Oedipus as a child. He returned to Thebes and told the city that a band of robbers had set upon the king and murdered him.

THE CITY OF THEBES
The city of Thebes was the capital of Boeotia (not be confused with the Egyptian city on the site of present-day Luxor, called Thebes by the Greeks). It was founded by Cadmus, the brother of Europa (see p.45), on the instruction of the Oracle at Delphi. First Cadmus had to kill a dragon that guarded the spot and had killed all his men. To populate the city, he sowed the dragons' teeth and warriors sprang up. Oedipus' mother, Jocasta, was the daughter of one of the Sown Men, Menoeceus.

SPEARS
Oedipus is carrying the spears that he would have used when he met with the chariot of his natural father King Laius in the narrow mountain pass. Ordered to let the travellers pass, Oedipus became angry when one of his horses was deliberately killed, and a fight ensued in which Laius died – thus fulfilling the first part of the prophecy.

OEDIPUS' FEET
The name Oedipus means "swollen foot". When he was left to die as a baby, Oedipus' feet were pierced with a spike – perhaps to prevent his ghost from walking.

WHEN PLAGUE struck Thebes, the seer Teiresias said the gods demanded that one of the Sown Men (see opposite) should sacrifice himself for the city's good. Jocasta's father immediately leaped from the city walls. But Teiresias said another man had been intended : one "passing for an alien . . . [but] Theban born, to his cost . . . father-killer and father-supplanter".

Dead Men's Bones

When people could not answer her riddle, the Sphinx killed them, littering the countryside with their bones. Early sources describe the Sphinx as flying to the city wall, chanting her riddle, and snatching young men in her ravening jaws when the citizens failed to answer her. For this reason the anxious citizens of Thebes gathered every day to solve the riddle.

ANTIGONE, OEDIPUS' DAUGHTER

A ntigone, Oedipus' daughter, went into exile with her father, returning on his death to find her two brothers, Eteocles and Polynices, fighting for the throne. They killed each other and Creon, their uncle, who had supported Eteocles, buried him with honour, leaving Polynices to rot on the battlefield. On pain of death, Antigone performed a token burial. Furious, Creon shut her up in a cave to die, refusing the pleas of Haemon, his son and Antigone's betrothed, to forgive her. On the advice of the seer Teiresias, he finally relented. But on opening the cave, he found that Antigone had hanged herself. Cursing his father, Haemon killed himself.

Antigone and her Sister Ismene on the Battlefield by Marie Spartelli Stillman (1844–1927)

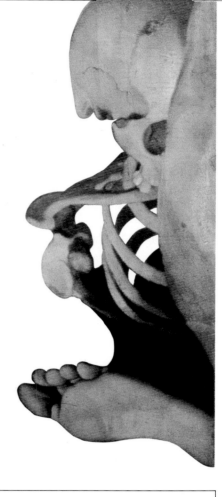

THE LABOURS OF HERACLES

HERACLES WAS A SEMI-DIVINE HERO, the child of Zeus (Roman Jupiter) by Alcmene, a mortal. Although Zeus meant him to be a great king, Hera (Juno) made sure that this honour passed instead to Heracles' cousin Eurystheus. Heracles grew into a great hero, fiery-eyed, skilled with the bow and javelin, and possessed of superhuman strength, which he used to wield a huge club cut from an olive tree. However, Hera, still jealous of Zeus' infidelities, afflicted the adult Heracles with madness and he killed his wife and children. Devastated, he visited the Oracle at Delphi, where he was told that he could be cleansed of this blood-guilt and gain immortality if, for 12 years, he served King Eurystheus. Eurystheus, an inferior man, set him ten seemingly impossible tasks, later extended to 12 as the petty-minded king quibbled over the means used to achieve two of them. The most difficult tasks were the last: the capture of the watchdog of the underworld, Cerberus, and the acquisition of the apples of the Hesperides (shown here), which were guarded by a fearful serpent. Heracles completed his tasks successfully, encountering many adventures along the way. When he died several years and exploits later from putting on a poisoned shirt, he rose to Olympus, causing Atlas to stagger under the sudden extra weight.

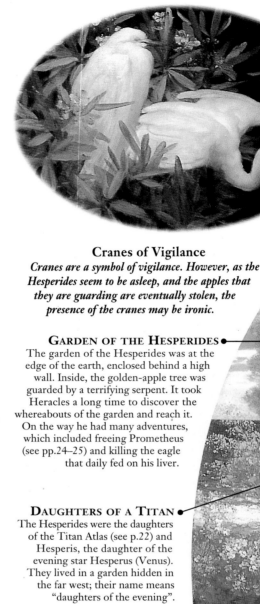

Cranes of Vigilance
Cranes are a symbol of vigilance. However, as the Hesperides seem to be asleep, and the apples that they are guarding are eventually stolen, the presence of the cranes may be ironic.

GARDEN OF THE HESPERIDES
The garden of the Hesperides was at the edge of the earth, enclosed behind a high wall. Inside, the golden-apple tree was guarded by a terrifying serpent. It took Heracles a long time to discover the whereabouts of the garden and reach it. On the way he had many adventures, which included freeing Prometheus (see pp.24–25) and killing the eagle that daily fed on his liver.

DAUGHTERS OF A TITAN
The Hesperides were the daughters of the Titan Atlas (see p.22) and Hesperis, the daughter of the evening star Hesperus (Venus). They lived in a garden hidden in the far west; their name means "daughters of the evening".

LYRE
Singing was the chief recreation of the Hesperides. Here, one of them dreamily strums on an upside-down lyre. (It was by playing the lyre upside-down that Apollo vanquished his challenger Marsyas in a musical contest [see p.41].)

THE CHILDHOOD OF HERACLES

Heracles was conceived when Zeus came to Alcmene in the guise of her husband King Amphytryon, the grandson of Perseus (see p.46–47). Zeus, knowing that he had fathered Heracles, boasted that the next descendant of Perseus to be born would be a great king. So Hera, to thwart her husband, arranged for Heracles' birth to be delayed and that of his cousin Eurystheus to be accelerated. Alcmene bore two children: Heracles and, a day later, his brother Iphicles. At eight months old, Hera placed two serpents in the babies' cradle – Iphicles fled, showing himself to be Amphytryon's son, but Heracles strangled the snakes with his bare hands. Heracles spent much of his youth living with Amphitryon's shepherds, having accidentally killed one of his tutors in an argument. Then, at 18, he killed a huge lion that was decimating the flocks and soon afterwards set out upon the adventurous life of a hero.

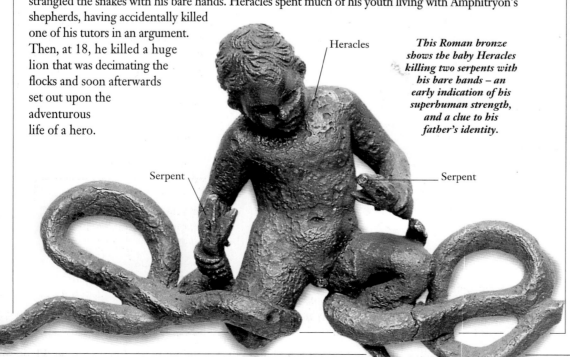

Heracles

Serpent

Serpent

This Roman bronze shows the baby Heracles killing two serpents with his bare hands – an early indication of his superhuman strength, and a clue to his father's identity.

HERACLES DID NOT KNOW where to find the garden of the Hesperides where the golden apples grew. The nymphs of the river Eridanos told him that the shape-shifting sea god Nereus knew the answer. Heracles wrestled with Nereus to force him to answer his question. The god transformed himself into all kinds of creatures, but Heracles held him fast, and at last he had to reveal the secret.

IN ONE STORY, Nereus (or Prometheus) advised Heracles to trick Atlas, who supported the sky, into fetching the golden apples. While he was away Heracles held up the sky. When Atlas returned, he refused to take up his burden again, but Heracles persuaded him to do so while he arranged a pad on his head. As soon as Atlas had the sky on his shoulders, Heracles took the apples and ran.

Golden Apples

The golden apples belonged to Hera who had been given them as a wedding present by her grandmother Gaia. Eurystheus did not believe that Heracles could win them, and when Heracles did so, Eurystheus gave them back, not wishing to incur the goddess' anger. They were returned to the garden by Athena.

HERA CHARGED LADON, the serpent, to prevent anyone from stealing the golden apples, and also to stop the Hesperides from eating them.

● GUARDIAN SERPENT
Ladon, the terrifying serpent that guarded the apples, had 100 heads (although they are not shown here) each of which spoke a different language. Like the Sphinx (see p.48), he was a child of the monsters Typhon and Echidna. When he was killed, the grief-stricken Hera set him in the sky as the constellation Draco.

● SLEEPING HESPERIDES
Sources vary as to whether there were three or four Hesperides. Those shown on the left are Aigle, Erytheia, and Hesperia. So peaceful here, the theft of the apples caused them unspeakable sorrow.

THE TWELVE LABOURS

1. Heracles strangled the Nemean lion and wore its invulnerable pelt as armour, with its head as a helmet.

2. Heracles killed the nine-headed Hydra whose heads grew back in duplicate each time one was cut off.

3. Hercules captured the bronze-hoofed, golden-horned Ceryneian hind, sacred to Artemis. He blamed the sacrilege on Eurystheus.

4. Heracles captured and killed the Erymanthian boar that had been devastating the countryside. In killing it, he also accidentally shot the centaur Cheiron (see p.39).

5. Heracles was told to clean out the filthy stables of Augeias in one day, so he diverted two rivers to run through and sluice the yard.

6. Heracles shot down the flesh-eating Stymphalian birds, which had wings, beaks, and claws of iron.

7. Heracles captured the Cretan bull, father of the Minotaur (see pp.56–57), which had gone mad.

8. Heracles captured the flesh-eating mares of Diomedes.

9. Heracles acquired the belt of Ares the war god from Hippolyta, queen of the Amazons.

10. Heracles took possession of the cattle belonging to the three-headed monster Geryon.

11. Heracles stole the golden apples of the Hesperides.

12. Heracles kidnapped Cerberus, guardian dog of the underworld.

THE GARDEN OF THE HESPERIDES
by Frederic Leighton (1830–96)
This painting shows three of the Hesperides asleep in their garden beneath the golden-apple tree guarded by the serpent Ladon. Heracles' eleventh task was to find and take these apples and give them to Eurystheus, his cousin and master.

JASON AND THE GOLDEN FLEECE

JASON, THE SON OF KING AESON who was usurped by his half-brother Pelias, was brought up by the centaur Cheiron (see p.39). When he grew up, he went to his uncle's court to press his claim to the throne. Pelias, warned to beware a claimant wearing one sandal (as Jason did, see left), agreed to name him as his heir if he fetched him the Golden Fleece belonging to Aeëtes, the cruel king of Colchis. With the help of Athena (Roman Minerva) he built a ship, the *Argo*, and and gathered a crew of 50 or so, the Argonauts, which included many of Cheiron's ex-pupils. He then sailed to Colchis, where Aeëtes' daughter, the witch Medea, fell in love with him and helped him to steal the fleece and escape. Returning home, Medea murdered Pelias, but strangely Jason did not claim the throne. Instead the couple lived in Corinth for ten years until Jason rejected Medea to marry King Creon's daughter, Glaucis. Medea avenged herself by killing Glaucis, Creon, and her own children by Jason, before fleeing. Jason died an old man, crushed beneath the falling prow of the *Argo*.

Jason, Protected by Hera
Jason sailed under the special protection of Hera. When Jason was hurrying to the court of King Pelias to lay his claim to the throne, he had to cross a flooded river. An old woman stood forlornly on the bank and begged him to carry her across. He did so, losing one of his sandals in the process. The old woman was Hera in disguise, and this small service earned Jason her devoted help.

THE GOLDEN FLEECE
The fleece had belonged to a golden flying ram endowed with reason and speech. This ram was given by Hermes (Mercury) to Phrixus and his sister Helle, the children of King Athamas of Boeotia, who were escaping from their vindictive stepmother. Unfortunately, Helle fell into the sea (now called the Hellespont) and died. Phrixus escaped to Colchis, sacrificed the ram to Zeus, and gave the fleece to Aeëtes. Aeëtes killed Phrixus and hung the fleece up on a tree guarded by a serpent.

MEDEA, WITCH AND LOVER

Medea, a witch with a fiery and ruthless temperament, was madly in love with Jason. When she thought he was plotting with her brother Apsyrtus to leave her behind, she boiled with rage, longing to set the *Argo* on fire, and hurl herself into the flames. Although Medea used her magic to help him, Jason was terrified of her. Her aid was substantial – not only did she charm the serpent that guarded the Golden Fleece, but she also restored Jason's father Aeson to his lost youth by replacing the blood in his veins with a magic potion. She even removed the usurper Pelias by persuading him she would rejuvenate him as well. But once his daughters had cut him up as she directed, she simply boiled him in her cauldron, and refused to bring him back to life. After being rejected by Jason, and taking her terrible revenge (see above), Medea married King Aegeus of Athens, where she enters the story of another hero, Theseus (see pp.54–55).

Taken from a Greek vase, this illustration shows Medea and Jason beneath the sacred oak tree on which the Golden Fleece was hung. Medea has charmed, or put to sleep, the serpent guardian and Jason, with his protectress Hera standing behind him, has taken down the fleece, which now hangs over his arm. Hermes, who first advised Phrixus to sacrifice the golden ram to Zeus (see above) stands behind Medea.

ANCAEUS
Ancaeus the steersman stood by Jason's side as the *Argo* fled. Originally a rower who shared a bench with Heracles (see pp.50–51), Ancaeus took over the wheel when the original helmsman, Tiphys, died.

ALL THE ARGONAUTS survived the dangers of the voyage except for Tiphys and Idmon the seer. Idmon had prophesied at the start that everyone would survive except himself. He was gored by a boar and died.

WHEN JASON ARRIVED IN COLCHIS, he asked Aeëtes to give him the Golden Fleece. Surprisingly the king agreed, but on two conditions: that Jason harness two fire-breathing bulls with bronze hooves and then use them to plant a field with dragons' teeth. Medea provided a salve of invulnerability that enabled Jason to yoke the bulls and defeat the warriors that sprang up. But Aeëtes then refused to keep his word so, with Medea's help, Jason stole the Golden Fleece and fled.

JASON, TRIUMPHANT THIEF
The exultant Jason yells his defiance to Aeëtes who is pursuing him. When, with the aid of Medea's spells, Jason stole the fleece from the sacred grove of Ares (Mars), we are told that he put it over his shoulders and revelled in it like a girl admiring herself when the moonlight catches her silk gown.

ADVENTURES OF THE ARGONAUTS

On the way to Colchis, the Argonauts met with many dangers, but always escaped by strength or stratagem. Early on, they benefited from the superhuman strength of Heracles who singlehandedly deflected an attack by a group of six-armed earth giants. But Heracles left the crew before reaching Colchis (although he did return later), distraught at the loss of his friend Hylas who had been pulled into a well by water-nymphs entranced by his beauty. Other dangerous challenges on the voyage included a boxing match with King Amycus (who was used to winning and slaughtering his opponents), won by Polydeuces, the inventor of boxing (see p.60); navigating the Clashing Rocks, which moved and smashed anything in their way; and resisting the perilous charms of the Sirens (see p.64), when the bard Orpheus drowned out their song with the beauty of his own music.

Passionate Love
Medea loved Jason because Hera and Athena (Juno and Minerva), whose favour he had gained, arranged with Aphrodite (Venus) and Eros (Cupid) for her to fall in love with him. As a result, Medea was consumed with such passion for Jason that she betrayed her own father and used her magic for both good and ill, to help Jason in his task.

PURSUING FLEET
The fleet of King Aeëtes failed to catch the *Argo*, largely through the wiles of Medea, who inherited her father's ruthless temperament.

DEFENDING THE SHIP
When he reached the *Argo* with his prize, Jason instructed his crew to set sail immediately. Half the crew were to row for all they were worth, two to a bench, and the other half to protect the rowers. The two parties took turns.

HELPLESS VICTIM
The bound victim here is Medea's brother Apsyrtus. According to one account, Medea cut him into pieces and threw them one by one into the sea, thus delaying her father's pursuit while he gathered together his son's scattered limbs for burial. The poet Apollonius places the murder on dry land, and says that Jason licked and spat out the victim's blood three times, to prevent the ghost from haunting him.

THE GOLDEN FLEECE
by Herbert James Draper (1864–1920)
This painting shows Jason, Medea, and the crew of the Argo fleeing from King Aeëtes, Medea's father, after stealing the Golden Fleece. Jason, holding the fleece, gesticulates to the enemy. Half the crew defend the ship, while the rest row for their lives and arrange the sails. Medea (centre) is preparing to kill and cut up her young brother, whose pieces she will scatter into the sea to delay her father.

MATCHLESS CREW
The crew of the *Argo* probably consisted originally of men of Thessaly, but became enlarged over time by the addition of heroes such as Heracles and Orpheus (see pp.30–31), as well as men from various Greek cities eager to share in the glory. Among the crew were Zetes and Calais, the winged sons of the north wind; Castor and Polydeuces, the Dioscuri; Peleus, the father of Achilles; Telamon, the father of Ajax; Lynceus, who had superhuman eyesight; and Mopsus, the seer.

THE *ARGO*
Homer writes of "the celebrated *Argo*", and the boat is almost as much the hero of the story as Jason himself. It even has a voice of its own, for its prow was cut from the speaking oak of Zeus at Dodona. It was built by Argus on the instructions of Athena. Confusingly, another Argus, son of Phrixus, who had been put to death by Aeëtes, later joins Jason's crew.

THESEUS THE HERO

THESEUS WAS ONE OF GREECE'S MOST FAMOUS HEROES. Said to have had two fathers, King Aegeus of Athens and the sea god Poseidon (Roman Neptune), he grew up unaware of who his father was. He showed heroic qualities even as a child – when Heracles (see pp.50–51) visited and caused panic among the children by throwing his great lion skin over a stool, the seven-year-old Theseus fetched an axe to confront the beast. When he was 16, Theseus' mother Aethra told him that Aegeus was his father. She led him to the Altar of Strong Zeus where Aegeus had left his sword and sandals under a heavy rock so that if Aethra bore him a son, the boy could reclaim them when he was strong enough and come to Athens. Theseus moved the rock with ease, claimed the tokens of his birth, and set out for Athens. He encountered many trials along the way (shown here), which he overcame with a skill comparable to that of his cousin Heracles. Welcomed in Athens as a hero, Theseus was invited to a banquet at the king's palace. Aegeus was unaware of Theseus' identity, but his wife, the witch Medea (see p.53), had her suspicions and tried to poison him. She failed, Aegeus recognized Theseus as his son and heir, and Medea and her son Medus fled.

THE EXPLOITS OF THESEUS
This Greek plate dates from c.440 BC and depicts several of Theseus' exploits both along the road to Athens and later in his career when he was recognized as Aegeus' son and heir to the Athenian throne.

THE CROMMYON WILD SOW
Theseus travelled to Crommyon, where he performed his third daring deed by killing Phaea, a ferocious wild sow that had been ravaging the countryside. Phaea was said by some to be one of the monstrous children of Typhon and Echidna (see p.48).

SINIS, THE PINE-BENDER
Theseus' second dangerous encounter was with Sinis, a man so strong he could bend the tops of pine trees until they touched the earth, hence his nickname, "the pine-bender". He would ask passers-by to help him hold the trees down, then let go, catapulting the unwary stranger into the air; or he would tie his quarry to two bent trees, and then release them, ripping his hapless victim in two. Theseus served Sinis in the same manner, and then took his daughter, Perigune, as his lover. She bore him a son, Melanippus.

WHEN THESEUS FIRST SET OUT upon the road to Athens, he was attacked by the bandit Periphetes who used to beat travellers to death with an iron club, thus earning himself the nickname of "Club-man". Theseus killed Periphetes, and carried his club ever after, finding it an infallible weapon.

Theseus

Iron club

Bull of Poseidon

The Bull of Poseidon
The capture of the fierce white bull of Poseidon was the first feat Theseus achieved after coming to Athens; some say he was sent by Medea, who hoped he would be killed. Since being brought over from Crete by Heracles (see p.51), the bull had become wild again, and had killed many people. Theseus seized it by the horns and dragged it through Athens to the Acropolis, where he sacrificed it to Apollo.

MINOTAUR

Soon after Theseus reached Athens, the city had to send young men and women to Crete to be fed to the Minotaur, a monster half-man, half-bull. Theseus volunteered, faced the monster and killed him (see pp.54–55).

SHORTLY AFTER HIS WIFE PHAEDRA DIED (see below), Theseus and his widowed friend Pirithous, king of the Lapiths and a son of Zeus, decided to marry again – but only daughters of Zeus would do. First they kidnapped Helen of Sparta (see p.62) for Theseus, and then they visited the underworld to abduct Persephone (Proserpine). Hades, Persephone's husband, welcomed them courteously and asked them to sit. They did so, but when they tried to stand up, they found themselves welded to their seats, unable to move without ripping their flesh. They sat in agony for four years until Heracles arrived to capture Cerberus. Recognizing his cousin suffering in mute torment, he wrenched Theseus free. But when he tried to free Pirithous, the leader of their impudent expedition, the earth began to quake and they had to leave him in eternal torment.

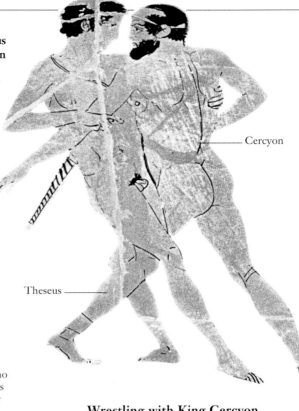

Cercyon

Theseus

Wrestling with King Cercyon
Successful in his first four encounters, Theseus came to Eleusis, where he was challenged by King Cercyon to a wrestling match. Like King Amycus, who had a boxing fight with the Argonauts (see p.53), Cercyon was used to winning, and putting the loser to death. But Theseus raised him high in the air and dashed him to the ground, and so won the throne of Eleusis, which he later added to the kingdom of Athens.

THE BED OF PROCRUSTES

Triumphant from defeating King Cercyon, Theseus came upon the giant Procrustes (Sinis' father) who lived near the road to Athens. As evil as his son, he used to offer travellers a bed for the night. But he only had one bed, and to make sure it was the right size for all comers, he stretched short men on a rack (or beat them out with a hammer) and chopped off the feet of tall men. Theseus made him lie down on his own bed and, as he was too tall, he cut off his head.

HIPPOLYTUS, THESEUS' SON

Hippolytus was the son of Theseus by either the Amazon queen, Hippolyta, or her sister Antiope. When Theseus rejected her to marry Phaedra, sister of his former love Ariadne (see pp.56–57), Hippolyta appeared at the wedding fully armed and in the ensuing battle was killed. Phaedra bore Theseus two children but then she fell madly in love with her stepson Hippolytus who, being a devotee of the virgin goddess Artemis (Diana), refused her. Phaedra, afraid lest her secret would be revealed, broke down the door of her chamber, ripped her clothes, and accused him of rape. Theseus, horrified, believed her and prayed to Poseidon to avenge her. In response, Poseidon sent a bull up from the waves to frighten Hippolytus' horses as he drove his chariot on the seashore. As planned, the horses panicked, Hippolytus fell, became entangled in the reins, and was dragged to his death. Artemis then revealed the truth to Theseus and Phaedra hanged herself in shame. Shortly afterwards, Artemis persuaded Asclepius (see p.39) to bring Hippolytus back to life; the Romans said that in gratitude he instituted the cult of Diana (Artemis) at Nemi.

The Death of Hippolytus
by Peter Paul Rubens (1577–1640)

SCIRON THE BRIGAND

Travelling near Megara, shortly after leaving Crommyon (see opposite), Theseus met a brigand named Sciron, who used to sit on a rock by a footpath high above the ocean and ask travellers to wash his weary feet. When they did so, he used to kick them to their deaths in the sea below, where they were eaten by a giant turtle that lived in the bay. When Sciron tried to trick Theseus, the hero seized his legs and the outlaw met the same doom as his victims.

THE MINOTAUR

THE **M**INOTAUR WAS THE SON OF **P**ASIPHAË, the wife of King Minos of Crete, and a white bull belonging to the sea god Poseidon (Roman Neptune). Minos had deeply offended Poseidon who, in revenge, caused Pasiphaë to fall in love with the animal. The resulting offspring was the Minotaur, a violent creature, half-man and half-bull, who ate human flesh. To hide his shame and protect his people, King Minos asked the inventor Daedalus to construct a labyrinth from which the monster would never be able to find its way out. Every nine years, to appease it, Minos gave the Minotaur a sacrificial offering of seven young women and seven young men, which he exacted as tribute from the city of Athens. One year, the hero Theseus (see pp.54–55) volunteered as a victim, intending to kill the Minotaur and rescue Athens from its terrible fate. With the help of Ariadne, the king's daughter who had fallen in love with him, he succeeded. He then set sail for Athens with Ariadne but left her on the island of Naxos, where she married the god Dionysus (see pp.58–59).

THE LABYRINTH

The labyrinth was named after the Cretan double-headed ritual axe, the *labrys*. It may be that such an axe was used in the lost Cretan religious mysteries to which the Minotaur story must relate. The maze is clearly a plan of the underworld, to which the hero (Theseus) must descend with the help of the maiden (Ariadne). The link continues when Minos, at his death, becomes a judge, deciding people's fate in the afterlife. Mazes appear on Cretan vases, coins, and frescoes, and ritual dances were probably performed in maze patterns. Homer speaks in the *Iliad* of "the dancing floor which Daedalus once built in Knossos for lovely-haired Ariadne". Also at Knossos, frescoes show youths and maidens leaping over bulls in ritual dances.

KING MINOS was the son of Europa by Zeus (see p.45); Europa later married King Asterius, who adopted Minos as his heir. When he became king, Minos prepared an altar to Poseidon and prayed for a bull to emerge from the sea to be sacrificed. A beautiful white bull promptly appeared, but it was so handsome that Minos took it for himself, and sacrificed a lesser animal in its stead. Poseidon was furious and to avenge this slight made Minos's wife, Pasiphaë, fall in love with the white bull.

ROYAL SISTERS •
Ariadne and Phaedra were the two daughters of Minos and Pasiphaë. Their brothers included Androgeus and Glaucus. It was in payment for the Athenians' murder of Androgeus that Minos required the tribute of youths and maidens.

Reel of Thread
Ariadne offers Theseus a reel of thread given to her by Daedalus, the architect of the labyrinth. Tying one end to the entrance and tracing the winding paths of the labyrinth, Theseus could find his way out again.

Thread

THESEUS AND THE MINOTAUR
by the Master of the
Campana Cassoni
This wooden panel depicts Theseus' arrival in Crete and his meeting with the royal princesses; Ariadne giving him the reel of thread to help him; his success in killing the Minotaur, and his departure with Ariadne – but the ship still carries black sails of mourning, anticipating the end of the story.

• **THESEUS**
The hero Theseus talks with Ariadne and Phaedra. It is with their help that he kills the Minotaur.

• **FOREIGN STEERSMEN**
The Athenian boat was piloted by Phaeax, and steered by Nausitheus. Neither man was a native of Athens, for the Athenians at this date knew nothing about navigation.

• **TRIBUTE SHIP**
The black ship of mourning comes into harbour with the tribute of seven youths and seven maidens, demanded by King Minos every nine years from the subjugated city of Athens.

DAEDALUS AND ICARUS

Daedalus was an Athenian inventor who had been taught his skills by the goddess Athena (Minerva) herself. However, he was eclipsed by his nephew Talos who, while still a youth, invented the saw, the potter's wheel, and the compasses. Jealous of him, Daedalus threw Talos off the roof of Athena's temple and killed him. For this, he was banished and took refuge at the court of King Minos, where he had a son, Icarus, by a slave girl. After Theseus slew the Minotaur, Minos shut Daedalus and Icarus in the labyrinth. The only way to escape from the unroofed labyrinth was by air, so Daedalus made two pairs of wings out of feathers and wax. He told Icarus neither to fly too near the sun, which would melt the wax, nor too near the sea, which would wet the feathers, and then the pair took flight. But Icarus, exulting in the freedom of the air, forgot his father's words and flew ever higher, until the sun melted the wax and he plummeted to his death in the ocean below. Daedalus arrived safely in Sicily and took refuge with King Cocalus. Minos pursued him to the island, where Daedalus, who had installed a system of hot-water pipes in the palace, scalded him to death while he was bathing.

The Fall of Icarus *(detail), by Carlo Saraceni c.1580/85–1620*

HALF-MAN, HALF-BEAST
The Minotaur, with his human mind trapped in the body of a beast, is one of the most tragic and pitiable of all the monsters of Greek mythology. He even had a human name, the same as that of Minos' foster-father: Asterius or Asterion. Both names mean "star"; Minotaur means simply "bull of Minos".

SAVAGE ANIMAL
The Minotaur, like his father the rampaging white bull, was liable to kill anyone who stood in his way – here he is shown being captured and driven into the labyrinth.

DEATH IN THE MAZE
At the heart of the maze, Theseus engages the Minotaur in single combat. According to different sources, he slayed him, either with his bare hands, a club, or with a sword that Ariadne had given him.

GUARDIANS OF THE MAZE
Ariadne and Phaedra guard the maze in which their half-brother, the Minotaur, is confined.

ATHENIAN HERO
The Athenian hero Theseus – heir to King Aegeus – makes his way to the labyrinth where the Minotaur is incarcerated, sure that the gods will help him triumph.

A LOVE BETRAYED
Theseus leaves with Ariadne after he has killed the Minotaur with her help. But he will abandon her on the island of Naxos, where she will become the bride of Dionysus.

PROMISE OF MARRIAGE
Ariadne fell in love with Theseus – perhaps at the prompting of Aphrodite (Venus) – and offered him her help in slaying the Minotaur if he would take her back to Athens with him as his wife.

PHAEDRA
Theseus later marries Ariadne's sister Phaedra, who falls in love with Hippolytus, Theseus's son by the Amazon Hippolyta.

Black Sails
When previous tributes had been paid, the ships taking the victims to Crete had set out and returned with black sails. King Aegeus was so confident in Theseus that he gave him white sails to hoist if he defeated the Minotaur. But Theseus forgot to raise them and Aegeus, seeing the black sails on the horizon, threw himself into the sea, now called the Aegean in his memory.

DIONYSUS AND ARIADNE

ARIADNE, A CRETAN PRINCESS, MARRIED THE GOD DIONYSUS (Roman Bacchus) on the island of Naxos, where she had been abandoned while sleeping by her lover, Theseus (see pp.54–55). Why he did this is unclear – he seems either to have tired of her, or feared taking her home to Athens as his bride. Some accounts say that when Ariadne awoke to discover that he had left her, she either hanged herself in her grief or, as she was pregnant, was destroyed in childbirth by the goddess Artemis (Diana), urged on by Dionysus who was furious that Theseus and Ariadne had profaned his sacred grotto on Naxos. But other sources say that Dionysus wanted Ariadne, and scared Theseus away by appearing to him in a dream, causing him to forget her. Dionysus then married Ariadne, although their first two children, Oenopion and Thoas, are sometimes referred to as fathered by Theseus.

DIONYSUS AND ARIADNE
by Johann Georg Olatzer (1704–61)
Dionysus and Ariadne celebrate their
marriage with their friends. The
painting contains plenty of references
to Dionysus' role as god of the vine.

CHERUBS
The cherubs here may represent Dionysus and Ariadne's future sons: Oenopion, Thoas, Staphylus, Latromis, Euanthes, and Tauropolus.

TREES
The yew, fir, fig, ivy, and vine were all sacred to Dionysus.

SATYRS
The satyrs were spirits with some goatlike characteristics, not least their uninhibited lust. Dionysus himself was the father of the phallic god Priapus, by the goddess Aphrodite (Venus).

MAENADS
The female devotees of Dionysus were known as Maenads, which translates as "raving women". In their ecstatic orgies they tore animals – and even humans such as Pentheus, King of Thebes – to pieces, and devoured their raw flesh.

SILENUS
Silenus, Dionysus' drunken old tutor, is his constant companion, and the leader of his revellers, made up of Sileni, Satyrs, Maenads, and Bassarids.

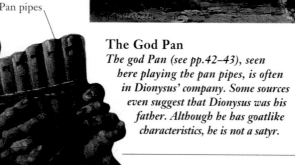

Pan pipes

The God Pan
The god Pan (see pp.42–43), seen
here playing the pan pipes, is often
in Dionysus' company. Some sources
even suggest that Dionysus was his
father. Although he has goatlike
characteristics, he is not a satyr.

MUSIC AND POETRY
Dionysus was associated, through the creative inspiration of wine, with poetry, song, music, and drama, resulting in much revelry.

REVELLERS
The orgiastic worship of Dionysus lasted until 186 BC when the Bacchanalia rites were suppressed by decree of the Roman Senate.

ARIADNE
The daughter of Minos and Pasiphaë, Ariadne is wearing a bridal wreath, given to her by Dionysus. It had belonged to his stepmother, the sea nymph Thetis (see p.25). When Ariadne died, the chaplet, a crown of seven stars, became the Corona Borealis.

MISTRESS OF THE LABYRINTH

The marriage of Dionysus and Ariadne reflects archaic mythic patterns from Minoan culture, in which Dionysus, taking the roles of both Zeus and Hades, was the chief god and often appeared as a bull. Pasiphaë's bull lover (see p.56), and the Minotaur, the offspring of this union, can also both be seen as manifestations of this god. Ariadne, as mistress of the labyrinth (which represents the underworld) is the Minoan Persephone (see pp.28-29). This interpretation explains the stories in which Dionysus is the son of Persephone, and also why Dionysus – in his role as Hades – lays claim to Ariadne. The Ephesian philosopher Heraclitus tells us that "Hades and Dionysus are one".

Temple of Dionysus
The island of Naxos (Dia) was especially sacred to Dionysus, and one ancient source tells us that he was angered when Theseus and Ariadne enjoyed sexual relations in his temple there.

CROWN OF IVY AND VINE
Dionysus was the first to wear a crown, and is rarely seen without his crown of ivy and vine. He usually holds a *thyrsus*, a rod which is also twined round with vines and ivy, topped with a pine cone (an ancient fertility symbol).

SACRED GRAPES
Vines and grapes were sacred to Dionysus, who as god of viticulture was credited with introducing the vine. His original role, however, was god of honey and the mead that was brewed from it. Under one of his Greek names, Bacchus, he became the Roman god of wine and shed most of his other roles.

WORSHIPPING MAIDENS
Maidens carrying golden baskets filled with fruits marched in the Dionysian festivals.

DIONYSUS AND THE DOLPHINS

Dionysus, drunk on wine and "as pretty as a girl", was captured while fast asleep on the island of Chios by sailors. When he awoke, he asked to be taken home to Naxos. The sailors agreed but treacherously sailed the other way. Realizing this, Dionysus pretended to weep and implored them to take pity. But they laughed at him, so the angry god, accompanied by the shadowy shapes of wild animals, stopped the boat and caused vines to sprout up the masts. The terrified sailors flung themselves into the sea, where they changed into dolphins – all except the steersman who, having taken the god's side, was protected, and later initiated into the Dionysian mysteries.

This Greek bowl, dating from the 6th century BC, depicts Dionysus and the sailor-dolphins.

DIONYSUS
The god of vegetation, wine, and ecstasy, Dionysus was the son of Zeus (Jupiter) by Semele, daughter of Cadmus (see p.49). Hera (Juno), Zeus' jealous wife, tricked Semele into demanding that Zeus make love to her in his true form, a flash of lightning, and she was burnt to death. Zeus rescued the unborn child, sewing him into his thigh until he was ready to be born; hence Dionysus was called "twice-born".

SACRIFICIAL GOAT
The slaughter of a goat was central to the worship of Dionysus. As a child, the god was temporarily transformed into a kid by the god Hermes (Mercury); goats were also associated with vines.

LEDA AND THE SWAN

LEDA, WIFE OF TYNDAREUS OF SPARTA, was another of Zeus' (Roman Jupiter's) human lovers. Walking by the river Eurotas, she was overpowered by Zeus in the guise of a swan. As a result, she laid two eggs, from which hatched four children – Helen and Clytemnestra, and Polydeuces and Castor – although only Helen and Polydeuces are considered to be Zeus' offspring. Leda is then later deified as Nemesis, the goddess of just retribution. In some early versions Leda merely finds the egg containing Helen, daughter of Zeus and Nemesis. In this story, Nemesis tries to evade Zeus by shape-shifting, turning from one animal into another in her attempts to escape. But Zeus follows suit, trumping each change with his own, until she finally turns into a goose and he mates with her in the form of a swan. She drops her egg in a marsh, where Leda finds it. Alternatively, Zeus, again disguised as a swan, pretends to be in danger, takes refuge in the bosom of Nemesis and then ravishes her. Hermes (Mercury) then throws the egg between Leda's thighs so that she "gives birth" to it.

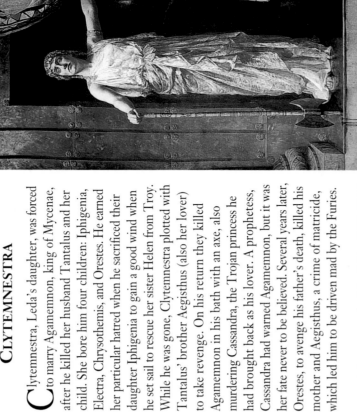

Wife of a King
Leda's husband, Tyndareus, was a son of Perseus' daughter Gorgophone; her father was King Thestius.

LEDA AND THE SWAN
by Francesco Melzi or Melzo (1493–1570)
This painting combines Leda's rape by Zeus in the form of a swan, with the hatching of the two eggs that she laid as a result – "giving birth" to the twins Helen and Polydeuces, and Castor and Clytemnestra. Helen was to become the cause of a famous ten-year war between the Trojans and the Greeks (see pp.62–63).

❝*Sing, O clear-voiced Muse, of Castor and Polydeuces, begotten by Olympian Zeus and born to great Leda beneath the peaks of Taygetos . . . Hail, O Dioscuri, riders of swift horses!*❞
HOMERIC HYMN TO THE DIOSCURI

CLYTEMNESTRA

Clytemnestra, Leda's daughter, was forced to marry Agamemnon, king of Mycenae, after he killed her husband Tantalus and her child. She bore him four children: Iphigenia, Electra, Chrysothemis, and Orestes. He earned her particular hatred when he sacrificed their daughter Iphigenia to gain a good wind when he set sail to rescue her sister Helen from Troy. While he was gone, Clytemnestra plotted with Tantalus' brother Aegisthus (also her lover) to take revenge. On his return they killed Agamemnon in his bath with an axe, also murdering Cassandra, the Trojan princess he had brought back as his lover. A prophetess, Cassandra had warned Agamemnon, but it was her fate never to be believed. Several years later, Orestes, to avenge his father's death, killed his mother and Aegisthus, a crime of matricide, which led him to be driven mad by the Furies.

Clytemnestra by John Collier (1850–1934)

NEMESIS, with whom Leda is associated, was the daughter of Night, and the goddess of divine retribution. She oversaw the distribution of wealth, looked after balance, avenged arrogance and punished any excess – even of happiness – that upset the natural balance of the world.

SHAPE-SHIFTING GOD
One of the most striking attributes of Zeus was his ability to change into any shape he chose. In his seductions or rapes of mortal women, he often enticed them by appearing in the form of some large but seemingly tame animal, and then overpowered them when they petted and caressed him.

SPARTA
In the background the city of Sparta can be seen, where Leda ruled as queen with her husband King Tyndareus. Tyndareus later made Menelaus, the husband of Leda's daughter Helen, his heir.

DECEIVED BY A SWAN
Leda, approached on the banks of a river by a gentle swan, realized too late that the bird was merely Zeus in disguise. The god overpowered and raped her.

MOTHER OF FATED GIRLS

Three of Leda's daughters – Helen, Timandra, and Clytemnestra – became victims of Aphrodite's (Venus') anger when Tyndareus overlooked her when making sacrifices to the gods. She doomed them to be "twice-married and thrice-married" and bring shame upon the marriage bed.

AFTER THEIR DEATH, the Dioscuri acquired a semi-divinity and were venerated as the twin or Gemini constellation. They were especially important to the Spartans, and later, in the fifth century BC, to the Romans. Heroic divinities, who in life had been involved in many battles and adventures, the Romans believed that they helped them on the battlefield.

COLUMBINES

Underfoot grow purple columbines representing resolution, or a desire to win. They may refer to Zeus' determination to make love to Leda. The Latin name for columbine is *aquilegia*, from the Latin for eagle. It refers to the spur-shaped petals reminiscent of talons and may be another reference to Zeus, who is often accompanied by an eagle (see p.44).

A MYTH IN TAPESTRY

The story of Leda and the swan was woven in tapestry by Arachne, who challenged Athena (Minerva) herself to a weaving competition. While the goddess wove stories of the fates of presumptuous mortals, Arachne wove those of divine scandals, including Zeus' rapes of Leda, Danaë, and Europa (see pp.44–45). Although Arachne's work equalled her own, Athena destroyed it, and drove Arachne to hang herself from shame. At the last moment, the goddess took pity and cut her down, allowing her to live in the form of a spider, with her weaving skills intact.

Polydeuces

Castor

Twin Destinies

The twin brothers were known as the Dioscuri ("sons of Zeus") and, as Castor and Pollux, became important Roman deities. When Castor was fatally wounded in a quarrel with their twin cousins Lynceus and Idas, Polydeuces begged his father Zeus not to let him outlive his brother. Taken to Olympus, Polydeuces refused to accept his immortality while Castor remained in the underworld. So they compromised, spending one day on Olympus and the next in Hades, realm of the dead.

CLYTEMNESTRA

Clytemnestra, Helen's twin sister, was first married to Tantalus of Pisa, and then forcibly married to Menelaus' brother Agamemnon (see above).

HELEN

Helen grew up to be excessively beautiful and had many suitors. After she was carried off, at the age of 12, by Theseus (after his wife, Phaedra, had died, see pp.56–57) and had been rescued by her brothers, her suitors all swore revenge if anyone tried to steal her away from her chosen husband. Helen married King Menelaus, and when she was abducted by the Trojan prince Paris (see pp.62–63), her suitors kept their promise and laid siege to Troy.

INSEPARABLE TWINS

Castor and Polydeuces were inseparable from birth, even though one was of human parentage, the other, divine. Castor was a mighty warrior and tamer of horses, while Polydeuces was a great boxer; the only way to tell them apart was by the boxing scars on his face.

BORN FROM AN EGG

Leda laid two eggs as a result of her encounter with Zeus, and the four children born from them all achieved renown. Sources differ as to the fatherhood of the individual children, but generally Helen and Polydeuces are regarded as Zeus' children, and Clytemnestra and Castor as the children of Leda's husband Tyndareus.

THE JUDGEMENT OF PARIS

PARIS WAS THE SON OF **KING PRIAM** and Queen Hecuba of Troy, the ancient city of Ilium in Asia Minor. Shortly before he was born, Hecuba dreamt that she had given birth to a burning torch from which wriggled fiery snakes. As she awoke, she screamed that Troy was burning. Hecuba's fearful dream was interpreted to mean that Paris would bring about the fall of Troy. Therefore, a shepherd was sent to expose him on Mount Ida. But five days later, the shepherd found the child unharmed, suckled by a she-bear, so he adopted him. One day, while caring for his adoptive father's flocks, Paris was visited by Hermes (Mercury) and the three goddesses, Athena (Minerva), Hera (Juno), and Aphrodite (Venus). Hermes asked him to decide which goddess was the most beautiful – an impossible choice – and to award her a golden apple. Paris chose Aphrodite because she promised to give him Helen, wife of King Menelaus of Sparta, the most beautiful woman in the world. His decision set in motion the events that led to the abduction of Helen and the start of the ten-year Trojan war.

APHRODITE
Aphrodite stands naked with Athena and Hera before Paris. They had all agreed to abide by Paris' decision, and Hermes allowed him to set the rules – so Paris required all three goddesses to disrobe.

OWL OF WISDOM
Athena was often accompanied by an owl, to signify her role as the goddess of wisdom and war.

BLUE EYES
One of Athena's names means "blue-eyed", and the eyes of her statues were painted blue. She was the patron goddess of the city of Athens.

THE GODDESS ATHENA
When the war broke out between the Greeks and the Trojans, Athena (and Hera), furious with Paris, supported the Greeks. However, Athena withdrew her support after the fall of Troy when the Trojan princess and prophetess Cassandra was violated in one of her shrines. The only Greek she continued to protect was Odysseus (see pp.64–65).

BATTLE SHIELD
Athena was the goddess of war. She had sprung fully armed from the head of her father Zeus, after he had swallowed her pregnant mother Metis, for fear she might give birth to a son stronger than himself. The motif on her shield is the head of the Gorgon Medusa, which was given to her by Perseus (see pp.46–47).

ACHILLES

This Roman drinking cup shows Priam, Hector's father, begging Achilles for the return of his son's body.

Achilles, a Greek hero of the Trojan war, was the son of Peleus and Thetis. He was invulnerable, apart from one heel, having been dipped in the River Styx as a baby. He terrified the Trojans and when he argued with Agamemnon and refused to fight, the Greeks began to lose. To help, Patroclus, his lover, wore Achilles' armour in battle. When he was killed by Prince Hector, Achilles killed Hector and dragged his body behind his chariot through Troy. Achilles died when an arrow, shot by Paris, pierced him in the heel.

GOD OF LOVE
Eros (Cupid), the impish god of love, often accompanies Aphrodite, the goddess of sexual love.

HERA, QUEEN OF HEAVEN
Hera, queen of heaven, was the goddess of marriage. Her own was a stormy one, and she often figures as a jealous and vengeful wife. For persecuting Heracles (see pp.50–51), Zeus hung her from Olympus by the wrists, with anvils tied to her ankles.

Eris, the Goddess of Strife
Eris was responsible for instigating the quarrel and competition between the three goddesses. Offended by not being invited to the wedding of the mortal Peleus with the sea nymph Thetis, she came to the feast and threw down a golden apple inscribed with the words "to the fairest", thus causing the argument that led to the Trojan war.

● HERMES, ZEUS' MESSENGER
When the goddesses began to squabble over the golden apple, Zeus refused to decide between them. Instead he asked Hermes to escort them to Mount Ida for Paris to decide which of them deserved it the most.

THE TROJAN WAR

The Trojan war is related in Homer's *Iliad* and may have its roots in a real conflict in the 12th century BC. In the Homeric tradition, the war was waged by the Greeks, led by Agamemnon, to recover Helen, his sister-in-law, who had eloped with Paris. The first nine years were inconclusive, but in the tenth, Troy fell. Fooled into thinking the Greeks had given up, the Trojans took in a huge wooden horse, left, they thought, as a religious offering. When the city gates shut, the Greeks hidden inside sprang out and sacked Troy. Aeneas (see pp.66–67), a Trojan prince, escaped and founded the Roman state. Legend tells how his great-grandson Brutus gathered and settled with the remains of the Trojan race in Britain, then inhabited by just a few giants. There he founded the city of New Troy – later known as London.

TOWARDS THE END OF THE WAR Paris was fatally wounded by Philoctetes, a Greek who had been called from the island of Lemnos after a captured Trojan prophet revealed that Troy would never fall without his aid. Armed with a bow that had once belonged to Heracles (see p.50), Philoctetes shot Paris with arrows dipped in the poison of the Hydra. Knowing he was in great danger Paris returned to Mount Ida where he begged his former wife Oenone to heal him. But Oenone, so long abandoned, refused and Paris died. She then killed herself out of grief.

● HERALD'S STAFF
Hermes' staff is called a *caduceus* – the two snakes attached themselves when Hermes found them fighting and laid his staff between them.

● PARIS, SPOILT FOR CHOICE
Paris had a difficult decision to make. Not only were the goddesses potentially dangerous, but they all tried to bribe him. Hera offered riches and earthly dominion; Athena wisdom and victory in battle; and Aphrodite offered him Helen, the most beautiful woman in the world.

● MOUNT IDA
Paris lived on Mount Ida tending his adoptive father's flocks. At this point he is married to Oenone, daughter of the river god Cebren, with whom he has a son Corythus. But he abandoned her for Helen without a second glance.

THE JUDGEMENT OF PARIS
by Peter Paul Rubens (1577–1640)
Paris, with Hermes leaning on the tree behind him, holds out the golden apple while the three naked goddesses stand before him, waiting for his decision. Eris, goddess of strife, watches overhead.

Apple of Strife
Paris holds the golden apple, not sure to whom he should give it. Apples were sacred to Hera, so she felt that she had an even greater claim than the other two. Unable to decide between themselves who should win, the goddesses had all agreed that as Paris was the handsomest of mortal men he should be the judge of their beauty and award the apple accordingly.

Golden apple

● PERSECUTOR OF TROY
Hera's fury when Paris chose Aphrodite knew no bounds, and she devoted all her energy to supporting the Greeks in the war with Troy. She even lay with Zeus under the cover of a cloud in order to allow Poseidon to assist the Greeks unobserved.

● PEACOCK OF PRIDE
The peacock was Hera's bird, as the owl was Athena's. It signifies pride and ostentation, and the eyes in its tail are those of the 100-eyed guard dog Argus, killed by Hermes in the furtherance of Zeus' love-affair with the mortal princess Io.

ODYSSEUS RETURNS HOME

ODYSSEUS (ROMAN ULYSSES), HERO AND KING OF ITHACA, sacked several cities in Thrace before sailing home after the Trojan war. Owing to the enmity of the sea god Poseidon (Neptune), his journey took ten years. His adventures included first landing on the island of the Lotus eaters, where some of the crew were trapped in a trance, and then on the island of the cyclopes (see box), where several of the crew were devoured. It was Odysseus' blinding of the cyclops Polyphemus – Poseidon's son – that angered the sea god who subsequently blew Odysseus off course, wrecked his ships, and ultimately killed his entire crew. In his travels, Odysseus indulged in two romantic interludes on the way – the first with Circe, an enchantress who had turned his crew into pigs, and the second with the sea nymph Calypso, with whom he stayed for seven years before his longing for his home and wife moved the gods to pity. Unbeknown to Poseidon, Athena (Minerva) and the other gods helped Odysseus build a raft and sail for home; but when Poseidon discovered this he was enraged and wrecked the ship. Odysseus was washed ashore where he was discovered by Nausicaa, daughter of Alcinous, king of the Phaeacians, who – at the cost of himself provoking Poseidon's anger – helped Odysseus home to Ithaca.

ODYSSEUS AND THE SIRENS
by Herbert James Draper (1864-1920)
This painting shows Odysseus and his crew as they sail past the island of the sirens, whose irresistible song lured sailors to their doom. On Circe's advice the crew stuffed their ears with beeswax so that they could not hear the false promises embodied in their seductive chant. Odysseus, wishing to hear their song, was lashed to the mast so that he could not leave the ship.

TIGHTENING THE KNOTS
When Odysseus heard the sirens' voices, he longed to join them, and begged his crew to untie him; but they obeyed his previous orders, and lashed him tighter still. The man tightening the ropes is Eurylochus, Odysseus's brother-in-law.

ODYSSEUS WAS THE FIRST man to hear the sirens' song and live. Their island of Anthemoessa was littered with the bleached bones of sailors they had lured to their deaths. Previously only Jason and the Argonauts (see pp.52-53) had passed the sirens and survived – because the minstrel Orpheus (see pp.30-31) drowned out their singing with his lyre.

LASHED TO THE MAST
Odysseus alone heard the sirens' song – for he had asked his crew to tie him to the mast so that he could listen to it.

THE CYCLOPES

The cyclopes were one-eyed giants. The poet Hesiod says that there were three of them, the sons of Uranus (Cronos) and Gaia, and that they forged Zeus' thunderbolts – these cyclopes were killed by Apollo for the death of Asclepius (see p.39). The ones Odysseus meets tend sheep and live on an island now thought to be Sicily. Landing there, Odysseus and his men were shut in a cave by the cyclops Polyphemus, who ate several of them. Odysseus – who told the giant that his name was "Nobody" – made him drunk and blinded him with a sharpened tree trunk heated in the ashes of the fire. The next day he and his crew escaped hidden under the giant's sheep as they went to pasture.

Odysseus and Polyphemus by Tibaldi Pellegrino (1527–96)
Odysseus stabs Polyphemus in the eye, which bubbles and hisses before winking out. When his neighbours call out to ask who is hurting him, the cyclops shrieks "Nobody" and they do not come to his aid.

DEAF TO ALL ENTREATIES
Odysseus had to sail past the island of the sirens, whose irresistible song lured sailors to their doom. On the advice of the enchantress Circe, Odysseus stuffed his crew's ears with beeswax, so that they could not hear the sirens' seductive chant.

PENELOPE AND HER SUITORS

Odysseus's wife Penelope was alone for 20 years, during which time a band of suitors had gathered in her palace, each hoping to marry her. She delayed, refusing to make a choice until she had woven a shroud for Odysseus' father. But each night, she unpicked her day's work, so it was never finished. By the time Odysseus came home – disguised as a beggar – Telemachus, his heir, was of age and the suitors were planning to kill him. Only recognized by his dog and his old nurse Eurycleia, Odysseus revealed himself to his son, and together they killed the suitors. He convinced Penelope of his identity by knowing the secret of their marriage bed, which was carved from a living tree and so could not be moved. When Odysseus died Penelope married Telegonus, his son by Circe; and Circe married Telemachus.

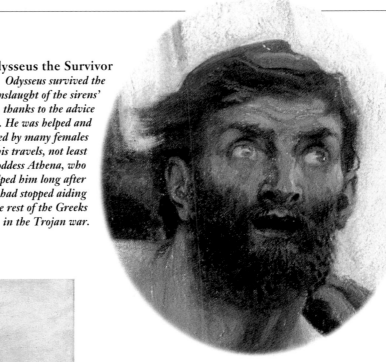

Odysseus the Survivor
Odysseus survived the onslaught of the sirens' song, thanks to the advice of Circe. He was helped and beloved by many females in his travels, not least the goddess Athena, who helped him long after she had stopped aiding the rest of the Greeks in the Trojan war.

BIRD-WOMEN
The sirens were conceived of as harpy-like creatures, part-bird, part-hag. While they were singing, they seemed like beautiful maidens – but those who succumbed to their song soon learned their true nature.

NEAR THE SIRENS' ISLAND are two further dangers – the deadly whirlpool Charybdis, and the ravenous sea monster Scylla. Steering a course between the two, Odysseus sailed too close to Scylla, and the monster snatched six sailors from his ship – one with each of her six heads.

THWARTED
Cheated of their prey, the sirens are supposed to have drowned themselves in anger and frustration. The body of one, Parthenope ("maiden-voice") was washed ashore at Naples, and the city originally bore her name.

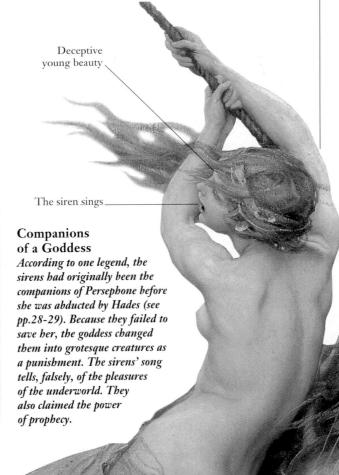

Deceptive young beauty

The siren sings

Companions of a Goddess
According to one legend, the sirens had originally been the companions of Persephone before she was abducted by Hades (see pp.28-29). Because they failed to save her, the goddess changed them into grotesque creatures as a punishment. The sirens' song tells, falsely, of the pleasures of the underworld. They also claimed the power of prophecy.

ODYSSEUS AND HIS CREW have just sailed back from the underworld, where Odysseus sacrificed a ram and a ewe to the shades of the dead. The ghosts, twittering like bats, flocked to the blood, but Odysseus held them at bay until the seer Teiresias had told him how to get home.

SAILORS' PERIL
The sirens here are depicted as mermaids, seductive maidens, half-human, half-fish, who sing to sailors of the delights of life under the sea, luring them to shipwreck.

DIDO AND AENEAS

ENEAS, A TROJAN PRINCE, was the son of Venus (Greek Aphrodite) and a
mortal called Anchises. Aphrodite told Anchises that his son would one day
found a great dynasty and, indeed, the Romans regarded Aeneas as the founder of
their race. Virgil's *Aeneid* tells how he escaped from the sack of Troy carrying his
father on his back and how, after a long journey, during which his father died, he
came to Italy and founded a settlement on the site of Rome. The most famous part of
the story is his love-affair with Dido, Queen
of Carthage. Shipwrecked by Juno (Hera),
who did not wish him to fulfil his destiny,
Aeneas and his men were brought to Dido's
court, where he and Dido fell in love. Aeneas
stayed in Carthage as her consort, until
Jupiter (Zeus) sent Mercury (Hermes) to
tell him to leave and continue his journey.
When Dido found out that he planned to
leave her, she had a funeral pyre built and,
as his ship set sail, she climbed up onto it
and stabbed herself to death with his sword.

BY TAKING AENEAS AS HER CONSORT, Dido became
a pawn in a power game between Juno and Venus.
Juno hated the Trojans (see p.62) and deliberately
wrecked Aeneas' ships at Carthage, her own city, and
encouraged a union with Dido to prevent him from
founding Rome. Venus did not trust Juno and wished
her son to fulfil his destiny. Unsure of Juno's plans
and afraid of the house of Carthage, she acted first,
making sure that Cupid (Eros) caused Dido to fall so
deeply in love with Aeneas that her allegiance to
Juno would be forgotten.

DARK CAVE •
Light shines from the cave, offering shelter from the storm.
It was here that Juno, goddess of marriage, to whom Dido
had made sacrifice, joined her with Aeneas. In doing this, she
planned to keep Aeneas in her favoured city of Carthage rather
than let him found Rome, a city that might destroy Carthage.

**DIDO AND AENEAS
ESCAPE A STORM**
by Johann Heinrich Tischbein (1722–89)
*This painting shows Dido and Aeneas about to
enter a cave to shelter from a storm that has blown
up while they have been out hunting. In
the cave, they admit their love for each other
and thereafter Aeneas is Dido's consort.*

Consumed by Love
*Dido's first husband Sychaeus, whom she had
loved deeply, had been killed by her own brother,
and Dido had sworn never to remarry. But after
Cupid kindled the fire of love in her heart for
Aeneas, she was consumed by desire for him.*

DIDO, QUEEN OF CARTHAGE •
Dido is wearing a yellow dress.
When she welcomed Aeneas and his
men to Carthage, he gave her a dress
in gratitude. It had a border woven
of yellow acanthus flowers and had
originally belonged to Helen of Troy.

DEVOTED SISTER •
Anna, Dido's sister, encouraged her
in her love for Aeneas. When Dido
built a pyre, Anna helped, thinking
she meant to practise love magic,
either to bring Aeneas back or
to free herself from his spell.

AENEAS
Aeneas follows Dido, accompanied
by Cupid. Like Dido, Aeneas had
been married but his wife, Creusa,
had died on the journey. He had a
son called Ascanius, who in Virgil's
Aeneid is almost adult.

Aeneas in the Underworld

On leaving Dido, Aeneas wished to see his dead father Anchises again, so he visited the Sybyl of Cumae. She advised him to pluck a golden bough from the sacred grove, and offer it to Proserpine (Persephone), who would guide him. Once among the dead Aeneas saw Dido, who turned silently away from his tearful words, and also found his father. But when he tried to hug him, he only embraced the air. He also saw souls drinking the water of oblivion so that they would forget their former lives and be born again. Anchises showed him a parade of souls who would be born again as great Romans, including Romulus and the Roman Emperors.

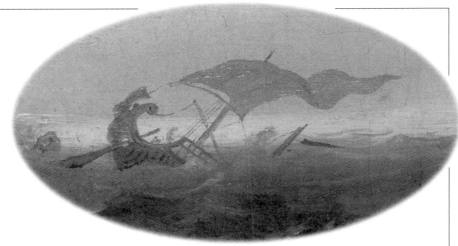

Wrecked Ships
Aeneas and his men were driven ashore at Carthage because Juno had heard that if they founded a new city it would destroy her own city of Carthage. By wrecking them there and bringing Dido and Aeneas together, she hoped to prevent this.

● **Divine storm**
While Dido and Aeneas were out hunting, they were overtaken by a storm. It was no natural gale, but one sent by Juno in order to separate them from their companions, and force them to take refuge in a cave.

The Founding of Rome

Romulus and his twin brother Remus were the sons of Aeneas' descendant Rhea Silvia, a vestal virgin, and Mars (Ares), the god of war. At their birth, their mother's evil uncle Amulius (who had deposed her father) killed her and threw the boys into the River Tiber. Luckily, they were carried ashore and cared for by a female wolf until they were found by Faustulus, one of the old king's shepherds. When the boys grew up, Faustulus told them their history and they killed Amulius and restored their grandfather to the throne. Then they decided to build a city on the Tiber. They each climbed a hill and sought omens from the gods as to which of them should rule it. Romulus, having seen 12 vultures to Remus' six, was favoured and began to plough a furrow to mark the city's limits. When Remus leaped over the furrow jeering (which was a sacriligious act) Romulus killed him. To gather a population, Romulus made his city a sanctuary, and it was soon filled with outlaws who stole their wives from the nearby Sabine tribe. Once Rome was established, Mars took Romulus away in his chariot to become a god.

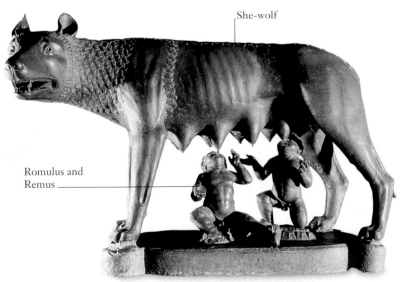

She-wolf

Romulus and Remus

This bronze statue used to stand on the Capitoline Hill in Rome, where Romulus saw the 12 vultures and began to make the city boundaries. It shows Romulus and Remus being suckled by the she-wolf. Wolves were said to have connections with the god of war, so it is possible he sent her purposefully to rescue his children. The wolf dates from the fifth century BC but the children are later additions.

● **Jealous king**
This figure may be Achates, Aeneas' armour-bearer and companion. But his glowering looks suggest that he is Iarbas, the king of Libya. Iarbas was in love with Dido but she rejected him. When he learned that she loved Aeneas, he jealously begged his father Jupiter to end their union.

● **Nymphs**
The heavens were witness to the "marriage" of Dido and Aeneas within the cave. Lightning flashed, and nymphs wailed upon the mountain tops, for they knew that this moment would lead to Dido's death.

DIDO KILLED HERSELF in grief, lamenting that Aeneas had not even left her with a child to love in his stead. But even in death she suffered for many hours before Iris, Juno's messenger, cut a lock of her hair to release her soul from her body.

THE NORSE GODS

ODIN THE CHIEF GOD, or "All-Father" of the Norse gods and his brothers, Vili and Ve, created the world from the body of the first living creature, the frost giant Ymir whom they killed. Ymir had come into being when the fiery sparks of the hot, southern land of Muspell had met with the melting ice of Niflheim, the cold land in the north. When Odin and his brothers killed him, Ymir's blood drowned all the frost giants save Bergelmir and his wife, who later bore a race of giants, forever opposed to the Norse gods (see opposite). Once he was dead, the brothers used Ymir's bones to make mountains, his skull to make the dome of the sky, and his blood became the seas. Then they set the stars, the sun, and the moon in the sky. One day, when walking along the beach, they found two tree trunks – an ash and an elm. From these, they made the first man and woman, Ask and Embla. Odin breathed the spirit of life into them, Vili gave them thoughts and feelings, and Ve gave them hearing and sight. They were given the realm of Midgard – Middle Earth – to live in (see pp.70–71). The gods lived in the realm of Asgard. There were two races of gods, the Aesir and the Vanir, who waged war against each other until they agreed to a truce. Of the three gods depicted in this tapestry, the battle god Odin and his warlike son Thor were Aesir, and Freyr, the fertility god, was one of the Vanir. Freyr went to live with the Aesir to seal the truce.

AN 11TH-CENTURY account of the heathen temple at Uppsala tells us that Odin, Thor, and Freyr were the three most important gods, and describes how they were worshipped in the form of statues, and how sacrifices of dogs, horses, and men were made to them. Much less is known about the Viking goddesses than the gods, though one primary source, Snorri Sturluson, claims that they were just as holy and powerful.

World Tree
Odin once hanged himself on the world tree, Yggdrasil, for nine days and nights. Pierced with a spear, he sacrificed himself to himself, in a magic rite, in his quest for hidden knowledge. On the ninth day, he saw magic runes below him. When he managed to lift them, they set him free and filled him with power.

MISSING EYE
Odin has only one eye. He sacrificed the other one for a single mouthful of water from the spring of wisdom, which bubbled from underneath the second root of the world tree Yggdrasil (see pp.70–71).

THE VALKYRIES

The valkyries were supernatural women who had several roles: they lived with Odin in the golden hall of Valhalla where they served ale to the shades of dead warriors; they also rode into battle in armour, wielding spears, and allotting victory and defeat – "valkyrie" literally meaning "Chooser of the Slain". Two valkyries, Gunn and Rota, chose men for death, accompanied by Skuld (necessity), the youngest of the Norns, one of the Three Fates who shaped men's lives. The valkyries may have had a special relationship with the warriors known as "berserks" who, inspired by Odin's battle fury, flung off their armour to fight with supernatural strength. Certainly the beserks were likely to die in battle, and so win a place in Valhalla, where they split their time between fighting and drinking. Valhalla was envisaged as a vast golden hall, with a roof of shields, a frame of spears, and 540 doors, through each of which 800 warriors would be able to march abreast at the last battle of Ragnarok.

The Ride of the Valkyries by Arthur Rackham

ODIN, LORD OF HOSTS
Odin had many names and many disguises, but he is most often invoked as a battle god. Here, he carries an axe, but more frequently carries the spear Gungnir; one of his epithets is Spear-Brandisher. Odin inspired warriors with battle ecstasy, and welcomed the battle dead in his paradise hall of Valhalla.

EARLY GERMANIC PEOPLES worshipped Odin as Wotan or Woden, the origin of the word "Wednesday". His wife Frigg, is the origin of Friday, Thor gives us the word for Thursday and Tiw or Tiwaz, another Germanic battle god, is the source for Tuesday. Tiw survives as Tyr in Norse mythology, but most of his functions seem to have been transferred to Odin.

EAR OF CORN
Freyr holds an ear of corn, in token of his role as the god who controls rain and sunshine. He is also a god of fertility, and some kind of ritual marriage seems to have formed part of his rites. His sister Freya, who was probably originally a fertility goddess, became regarded as a goddess of battle, love affairs, and soothsaying.

LOKI AND THE GIANT

After the war between the Aesir and the Vanir, Asgard was left without a defensive wall. One day, a man came on horseback and offered to rebuild the wall even stronger than before. But his price for the job was the sun, the moon, and the goddess Freya for his wife. On the advice of the trickster god Loki, the gods agreed but only on condition that the work was done in six months – which they considered impossible. But the man and his horse Svaldifari worked so fast that three days before the deadline the wall was almost complete. The gods were horrified, so Loki, who could change shape, disguised himself as a mare and lured Svaldifari away, leaving the man unable to finish the wall in time. At this, the man became so angry that he began to swell and revealed himself to be a rock giant, a race who hated the gods. Thor killed him with one hammer blow. Months later, Loki returned leading a strange foal – Loki's child by Svaldifari. This was Sleipnir, Odin's eight-legged steed, who could outrun anything, and bear its rider right down to Hel, the land of the dead.

VIKING TAPESTRY
This picture shows a detail from a Viking tapestry dating from the 12th century. It shows the Aesir gods Odin and Thor, and Freyr, who was one of the Vanir. It used to hang in a church in Halsingland.

ASK, THE FIRST MAN
Ask and his wife Embla were the first man and woman. They were created by Odin from logs on the seashore and are said to be the ancestors of all mankind.

RAVEN FRIENDS OF ODIN
Odin is often depicted with his two ravens, Huginn and Muninn (Thought and Memory) perched on his shoulders. He sent them flying abroad each day from his chair in Asgard, from which he could survey all of the worlds.

Thor, God of Thunder
This bronze statuette depicts Thor, the thunder god whose weapon was the hammer Mjollnir. Mjollnir was given to Thor by the god Loki (see p.71), who had tricked the dwarves into giving it to him. It could never miss its mark, and returned to the thrower's hand.

Hammer

THOR, GOD OF THUNDER
Thor the thunder god was Odin's eldest son; his mother was the earth. He was immensely strong, and famed for his enormous appetite. In a contest in the land of the giants, he drank so much of the sea at one gulp that he created the tides. He travelled in a chariot drawn by two goats.

FREYR, GOD OF FERTILITY
Freyr, a god of fertility, was originally one of the Vanir, who became subsumed in Odin's more warlike Aesir. Freyr and his sister Freya were the children of Njord, the god of the sea.

THOR'S HAMMER, MJOLLNIR, enabled the Aesir to protect Asgard against the giants. A giant did once steal it and would only return it if the goddess Freya would marry him. So Thor and Loki dressed up as Freya and her maid. When Mjollnir was placed in Thor's lap to bless the union, he discarded his disguise and killed all the giants.

THE WORLD TREE MYTH

ACCORDING TO THE NORSE POEM *The Lay of Grimnir*, "Of all trees, Yggdrasil is the best". Yggdrasil is a huge ash tree that stands at the centre of the cosmos, protecting and nourishing the worlds. The gods are described as riding out each day "from Yggdrasil" to deal out fates to mankind, and it was on Yggdrasil that the supreme god Odin willingly sacrificed himself, hanging in torment for nine long nights before he could seize the runes of power. Yggdrasil supported nine worlds, set in three layers. At the top was Asgard, the realm of the Aesir, or warrior gods, Vanaheim, the realm of the Vanir, or fertility gods, and Aflheim, the realm of the light elves. In the middle, linked to Asgard by the rainbow bridge Bifrost, was Midgard (Middle Earth), the realm of mortal men, and also Jotunheim, the world of the giants, Nidavellir, the home of the dwarfs, and Svartalfheim, the land of the dark elves. Below was Niflheim, the realm of the dead, and its citadel Hel. The ninth world is sometimes said to be Hel and sometimes the primeval fire of Muspell, which will devour creation at the end of time. Yggdrasil itself will survive, and will protect in Hoddmimir's Wood the man and woman who will re-people the world. The branches of Yggdrasil spread out over the whole world, and reach up to heaven.

THE BATTLE OF RAGNAROK

Ragnarok, sometimes called the Twilight of the Gods, is the final cataclysm that will destroy this world and the gods. After three terrible winters, a universal war will break out and the god Loki – now an enemy of the Aesir – and his son, Fenrir the wolf, will break from their bonds. Loki will then sail with an army of the dead to the final battle, in which Fenrir will swallow the sun, and kill Odin; Thor will slay the World Serpent, but die from its poison; and the gods will perish. Finally Surt, guardian of the fires of Muspell since the beginning of time, will release them and engulf the world in flame. After this world is destroyed, a new one will arise. Only Odin's sons Vidar and Vali, and Thor's sons Modi and Magni, will survive, and the gods Balder and Hod will return to life. They will sit on the new earth and talk of the world that was; in the grass they shall find the golden chess pieces of the gods. Two people, Lif and Lifthrasir, will survive in the branches of the World Tree and repopulate the earth.

This Viking stone at Kirk Andreas on the Isle of Man shows Fenrir swallowing Odin, who has one of his ravens on his shoulder.

GAG
Fenrir howled so terribly when he knew he was bound, that one of the gods stuck a sword between his upper and lower jaw as a gag.

RIVER OF SPITTLE
The drool from Fenrir's mouth runs down to form the river of Hope.

FENRIR THE WOLF
Fenrir the wolf was a son of Loki, the trickster god. He was brought to Asgard, but grew so fierce that only the god Tyr dared to feed him. Here, he is shown bound and gagged by the gods. They tricked him into letting them bind him with two chains called Laeding and Dromi by teasing him that he would not be able to escape. He did so with ease. But then they bound him with a magical chain and be was unable to escape. He will remain bound until the final cataclysmic battle of Ragnarok (see above).

MAGIC FETTER
Fenrir is bound by an unbreakable fetter called Gleipnir. It was made by the dark elves from the sound of a cat's footfall, a woman's beard, a mountain's roots, a bear's sinews, a fish's breath, and a bird's spittle. It was as soft and smooth as silk.

THE WORLD TREE
This manuscript shows Yggdrasil, the world, or cosmic, tree, which supports the nine Norse worlds. Stags and goats nibble at its twigs, its trunk rots, and the dragon Nidhogg gnaws its roots, causing it great suffering. But the tree is saved from decay by the three Norns, – Fate, Being, and Necessity – who sprinkle the tree each day with water from the well of fate.

EAGLE
A giant eagle sits at the top of Yggdrasil, with a hawk perched between its eyes. The flapping of the eagle's wings causes winds in the worlds below.

TREE OF SACRIFICE
Yggdrasil literally means "terrible horse" or "Odin's horse". Odin, when he was sacrificed on the tree to gain knowledge of the magic runes, is described as "riding" it, in the same sense that Norse poets refer to a gallows tree as a horse.

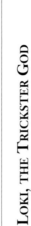

STRANGE NEW FETTERS

Fenrir was suspicious of the strange new fetter, and agreed to be bound only if one of the gods put their hand in his mouth. Tyr thrust his right hand into the beast's mouth and when Fenrir realized he had been tricked, he bit off Tyr's hand.

SPAWN OF LOKI

Fenrir was the son of Loki and the giantess Angrboda. His brothers, also fathered by Loki, were Jormungand, the World Serpent, which encircled Middle Earth, and was once fished up by Thor, and Hel, ruler of the dead.

"Three roots spread three ways
Under the ash Yggdrasil.
Hel is under the first, Frost-Giants
under the second,
Mankind under the last."
THE LAY OF GRIMNIR

ALTHOUGH IT WAS PROPHESIED that at Ragnarok Fenrir would swallow the sun and devour Odin – before being killed in turn by Odin's son Vidar – the gods refused to profane the holy ground of Asgard by killing him, so they chained him up instead.

TREMBLING LEAVES

When Ragnarok approaches, the World Tree will begin to shake and tremble.

LOKI, THE TRICKSTER GOD

Capable of good and evil, Loki is an ambiguous figure, who in later records becomes entwined with the image of the Christian devil. Although he was brought up as Odin's foster-brother, he was actually a giant. He was accepted among the gods because of his lively wit, but it is perhaps his "outsider" status that is at the root of his later bitterness and vengefulness. He plays tricks on the gods, stealing or hiding treasures such as the apples of youth (causing the gods to age), or Freyja's precious necklace, Brisingamen; but he always rescues the situation. However, he becomes increasingly malicious after he causes the death of Balder, Odin's son, the handsomest of the gods. For this, the gods catch him and bind him to a rock with the entrails of one of his sons, and a snake drops poison in his face, which his wife catches in a cup. When splashed, his writhings made the entire earth shake. He does not escape until Ragnarok (see above).

This 12th-century stone shows Loki bound to a rock for killing Balder.

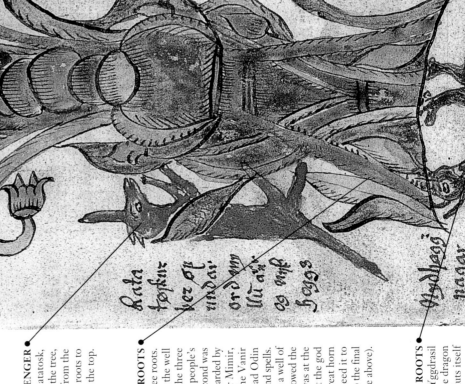

SHELTERING TREE

Yggdrasil shelters the nine worlds. At the end of the world, during the battle of Ragnarok, it will provide shelter for a man and woman, Lif and Lifthrasir, who will feed on the sweet morning dew, and be the source of new life in the age to come.

SPECIAL FRUIT

The cooked fruit of Yggdrasil ensured safe childbirth. The tree drips dew so sweet that bees make honey from it.

FOUR DEER

Four horned deer – Dain, Dvalin, Duneyr, and Durathror – lived on Yggdrasil's trunk, nibbling the fresh green shoots.

SQUIRREL MESSENGER

The squirrel, Ratatosk, runs up and down the tree, carrying insults from the dragon at the roots to the eagle at the top.

THREE ROOTS

Yggdrasil had three roots. Beneath the first was the well of fate guarded by the three Norns who control people's lives. Beneath the second was the well of wisdom, guarded by the head of the Aesir Mimir, who was killed by the Vanir gods, but whose head Odin preserved with herbs and spells. Beneath the third was a well of poison, from which flowed the rivers of Hel. It was at the well of wisdom that the god Heimdall left his great horn until he should need it to summon all creation to the final battle of Ragnarok (see above).

DRAGON AT THE ROOTS

At the bottom of Yggdrasil in Niflheim lies the dragon Nidhogg, which gluts itself on corpses. He also gnaws at the roots of the world tree, hoping to destroy it. He is at war with the eagle at the top.

SIGURD THE DRAGON-SLAYER

SIGURD, SON OF THE HERO SIGMUND and a favourite of the Norse god Odin, grew up an orphan. A valiant youth, he slew the dragon Fafnir at the behest of Regin the Smith and took his treasure (see below). But the treasure hoard was tainted by a ring that had been cursed (see box) and disaster followed. Sigurd soon married Gudrun, daughter of Giuki, king of the Niflungs and agreed to help her brother Gunnar to win Brynhild, a valkyrie who lived behind a wall of fire. Disguised as Gunnar, he won her, gave her the fateful ring, and Gunnar married her. But Sigurd's own wife Gudrun, seeing Brynhild wearing the ring, could not resist taunting her with the true story. Brynhild was furious and demanded that Gunnar and his brother Hogni murder Sigurd. She then killed herself and was burned on Sigurd's funeral pyre. After this, Gudrun married Atli, Brynhild's brother and he killed Gunnar and Hogni for her, in revenge for killing Sigurd. But Gudrun then killed her children by Atli, made their hearts as meat. Then she wine and their blood as skulls into cups, and served Atli their blood as set fire to his hall, and everyone in it.

Underwater, Beowulf fights Grendel's mother who had attacked him for the death of her son.

THE HEROIC DEEDS OF BEOWULF

Every night for 12 years, the hall of Hrothgar, king of the Danes, had been visited by a monster of the fens named Grendel, who attacked and killed Hrothgar's men. At last a hero, Beowulf of the Geats, swore to kill Grendel or die in the attempt. That night, when the monster entered the hall, Beowulf wrestled with him, tore off his arm, and the creature fled howling into the night to die. The next night, there was great feasting but unexpectedly, as the company slept, Grendel's mother descended upon the hall to take revenge for her son's death. The next morning, Beowulf tracked her to the lake where she lived, dived into the murky water, and killed her with a great sword, too heavy for anyone but a hero to wield, which he found lying on the lake bed. The waters boiled with blood and Beowulf's followers thought he must be dead – but he surfaced, holding the heads of Grendel and Grendel's mother. Beowulf became a great king of the Geats, and died in old age battling another monster – a fire-breathing dragon, which for centuries had guarded its hoard of treasure in an ancient burial mound.

THE DYING DRAGON asked Sigurd who he was. Sigurd, fearing to give such a creature power over him by telling it his name, told Fafnir his name was "Noble-beast", and that he had no father or mother: "I walk this world alone".

THE STORY OF SIGURD was developed in Norse sagas and poems and also in Germanic literature, culminating in the highly sophisticated saga of love and revenge, *The Nibelungenlied*, in which Sigurd is called Siegfried, and the story of the dragon-slaying is unimportant. Today most people know it as the basis of Wagner's opera cycle *The Ring* (see p.79).

Sigurd
Sigurd is the greatest of the Germanic heroes, hero of the Volsunga Saga, the Nibelungenlied, and of many Eddaic poems such as Reginsmal and Fafnismal.

BROTHER-IN-LAW
In a later part of the story, Sigurd's brother-in-law tries to escape from a snake pit by playing a lyre with his toes and charming the snakes.

DYING DRAGON
Before he died, Fafnir warned Sigurd to leave the treasure alone, for it would bring only misery. But Sigurd took it so that he could win Gudrun, daughter of Giuki, king of the Niflungs, as his bride.

SIGURD KILLS FAFNIR
Crouching in the pit, Sigurd stabbed upwards, slicing through the dragon's body. When Sigurd killed Fafnir, he was doused in the dragon's blood, which made him invulnerable, except for a tiny area on his back, where a leaf had stuck to his skin.

CHURCH DOORWAY

This doorway was carved in about 1200 and comes from a church at Hylestad, Norway. It shows the story of Sigurd. On the top right, Regin forges him a sword and Sigurd kills the dragon. On the left, Sigurd tastes the dragon's blood and, as a result, understands the birds, who warn him that Regin is planning to kill him. Sigurd then kills Regin.

POISON TONGUE
As the dragon returned, it spat poison at Sigurd.

A TRAP FOR THE DRAGON
Sigurd and Regin went to Gnitaheath where the dragon lived, and dug a trench for Sigurd to hide in.

TESTING THE SWORD
To test the reforged blade, Sigurd swung it down on Regin's anvil, which shattered in two. The sword was so sharp that when Sigurd put it in running water it severed a tuft of wool that drifted against its edge.

REGIN, SMITH TO A KING
Regin became smith at the court of King Hjalprek of Jutland, foster-father of the young hero of the Volsungs, Sigurd. The cruel-hearted Regin took Sigurd under his wing. He told the boy about Fafnir's hoard, and offered to make him a sword with which to slay the dragon, and win the gold.

SIGURD'S SWORD was remade from fragments of Gram, the sword that had belonged to his father, the hero Sigmund. It had been a gift from Odin, the god of battles, who had brought it himself into Sigmund's hall and thrust it into the roof-tree. Only Sigmund had been strong enough to pull it out. When Sigmund died, Odin shattered the sword.

OTTER'S RANSOM

One day the gods Odin, Loki, and Honir visited Middle Earth. They saw an otter about to eat a salmon and Loki threw a stone and killed it. Coming to a house, the gods offered the meat in exchange for a room for the night. But their host Hreidmar's smile soon faded, for the otter was his own son, Otter. Skilled in magic, Hreidmar made the gods helpless and, with his other sons Fafnir and Regin, tied them up and threatened to kill them. Instead, Odin offered to pay a ransom, so Hreidmar demanded as much gold as would fill and then completely cover Otter's flayed skin. Loki was released to search for the gold. Helped by Aegir and Ran, the sea gods, he caught the dwarf Andvari, who was hiding disguised as a fish, and forced him to hand over his treasure. Loki would not even allow him to keep a magic ring that would enable him to build up his fortune again; so Andvari cursed the ring to bring misfortune to whoever owned it. When Loki returned, he had almost enough gold to pay the ransom – one whisker was still left uncovered. So malicious Loki took out Andvari's ring, and added it to the pile, and with it, Andvari's curse.

Dragon-Slayer
When Fafnir returned, Sigurd drove the sword through him, killing him, but drenching himself with blood, thus becoming invulnerable. It is possible that originally it was Sigurd's father Sigmund who was the dragon-slayer – the eighth-century Anglo-Saxon poem Beowulf (see above) says he killed a dragon and gained its treasure.

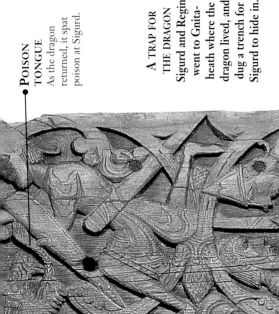

SIGURD KILLS REGIN
Sigurd had loved and trusted Regin. Warned by the birds of Regin's treachery, Sigurd, overcome by feelings of betrayal, ran him through with the sword that Regin himself had forged.

CHEATED BROTHER
Regin had been cheated of his share of Otter's ransom by his brother Fafnir, who took it all for himself. Regin fled from Fafnir, who possessed a helmet of terror, and Fafnir turned himself into a dragon so that he could lie on his hoard and protect it.

SIGURD'S HORSE
Sigurd's horse Grani, which would only carry its master, was descended from Odin's horse Sleipnir (see p.68). Here Grani is shown loaded down with the dragon's treasure – including the cursed ring of Andvari.

BIRDS IN THE TREE
The birds singing in the tree above warned Sigurd that Regin intended to trick him.

COOKING THE HEART
While cooking the dragon Fafnir's heart, Sigurd accidentally burned his thumb. When he put it in his mouth, he discovered that he had acquired the dragon's powers, and could understand the language of birds.

AFTER SIGURD HAD KILLED FAFNIR, Regin revealed the dragon had been his brother, and that Sigurd, therefore, owed him a blood-debt. However, he said that if Sigurd cut out the dragon's heart and cooked it for him to eat, he would accept that deed as payment.

SIEGFRIED AND THE NIBELUNG TREASURE

Siegfried (originally Sigurd, see pp.72–73) is a central figure of the German epic *Nibelungenlied* (c. 1203), and of Wagner's *Ring* cycle. He gained the cursed Nibelung treasure, and then wooed Kriemhild, the sister of Gunther, the Burgundian king. Gunther granted Siegfried her hand in return for his help in winning him the amazonian queen Brunhild. Siegfried defeated and subdued Brunhild, who thought it was Gunther, using his cloak of invisibility. But when the couples married, the queens quarrelled, and the trick came to light. Brunhild, vowing vengeance, enlisted the help of Hagen, one of Gunther's vassals, who discovered that the invulnerable Siegfried had one vulnerable spot on his back (see p.72). Hagen told Kriemhild to mark Siegfried's cloak at this spot as protection, but then killed him. In grief, Brunhild killed herself on Siegfried's funeral pyre. Hagen then stole the Nibelung treasure and hid it in the Rhine. Later, Kriemhild married Etzel (or Atli), king of the Huns, and they slew both Gunther and Hagen; but to the end, even at his death, Hagen refused to reveal where he had hidden the treasure.

Act II of the Opera Siegfried by Aubrey Beardsley (1872–98)

LOHENGRIN'S PROHIBITION against being questioned about his name and background recalls Cupid's warning to Psyche not to attempt to look on his face (see pp.34). Such a taboo is common in European folktales, and can be found in stories of marriage to magical swan maidens, with which the original Lohengrin story may have been connected.

• THE HOLY GRAIL
This holy object of quest and legend (see pp.80–81) hovers like a blessing as Lohengrin defends Elsa's honour. The legend of the Swan Knight was first incorporated into Arthurian legend in the *Parzival* of Wolfram von Eschenbach (c. 1200). There "Loherangrin" is said to the the son of the Lord of the Grail, Parzival, and his wife Condwiramurs. He has a twin brother, Kardeiz, who inherits Parzival's earthly thrones, while Lohengrin inherits his spiritual ones.

LOHENGRIN

LOHENGRIN THE SWAN KNIGHT is a hero of medieval European myth who was eventually absorbed into Arthurian legend, as the son of the Grail knight Parsifal (Percival, see p.80). According to the 13th-century folk epic *Lohengrin* and related sources, when the Duke of Brabant died, he urged his only child, Elsa, to marry his knight, Friedrich of Telramund. But Elsa refused Friedrich, who complained to the Emperor, Henry the Fowler, that she had broken her promise, and accused her of killing her father. Faced with these charges, and without anyone to defend her, Elsa prayed for help. This caused the bell in the Grail kingdom of Montsalvat to peal, indicating that someone needed help. Lohengrin came to her rescue, helped by a magical swan. Lohengrin defeated Friedrich in single combat, thus proving Elsa's innocence, and Friedrich was condemned to death. Lohengrin then married Elsa, and became Duke of Brabant, but only on condition that she never asked him his name or where he had come from. But the inevitable happened and Elsa was left alone and broken-hearted.

The Swan Knight
Lohengrin, the Swan Knight, is shown here as the very image of the "parfit gentil knyght". He appears in a vision to Elsa, and she becomes convinced that he is her future husband and will come to save her.

"*Lohengrin grew to be a strong and valiant man in whom fear was never seen. When he was of an age to have mastered the arts of chivalry he distinguished himself in the service of the Grail.*"

PARZIVAL, c. 1200 BY
WOLFRAM VON ESCHENBACH

LOHENGRIN
This illustration shows the end of Act 1 of Wagner's opera, **Lohengrin**. *At this point Lohengrin has mysteriously arrived and beaten Friedrich in combat, clearing Elsa of the dreadful charges made against her.*

ORTRUD

Ortrud, wife of Friedrich von Telramund, is an invention of Wagner and does not appear in the medieval sources. The evil antithesis of the pure Elsa, it is she who urges Friedrich to denounce the girl and taunts her at her wedding with Lohengrin's anonymity. In Wagner's version of the tale, Friedrich is Elsa's guardian and his accusation is that she has murdered her brother Gottfried, the true heir of Brabant, who has disappeared. Gottfried has, in fact, been turned into a swan by Ortrud's magic. He is released from the spell at the end of the opera by Lohengrin.

DUELLING SWORD

The notion that guilt or innocence could be decided in single combat by knightly champions is commonplace in medieval romance. Such a duel is not a mere trial of strength or skill for, as here, divine powers may aid the righteous.

Elsa, Heiress to Brabant

As heiress to the Duchy of Brabant, Elsa was a Princess of the Holy Roman Empire. In the year 1204 (when Wolfram von Eschenbach was probably at work on Parzival), Henry of Brabant, who had no sons, received authority from Emperor Philip to name his daughter Maria as his heir, thus giving topicality to von Eschenbach's use of the Lohengrin story.

FRIEDRICH

Here, Elsa's challenger, Friedrich, is shown humbled at the hands of Lohengrin. In keeping with his knightly courtesy, Lohengrin did not take his life; instead the Emperor condemns Friedrich to be beheaded. In Wagner's opera, Lohengrin kills Friedrich in a later combat.

HENRY THE FOWLER

The emperor Henry the Fowler was a real historical figure, the first non-Carolingian ruler of the German Reich (916–36). His wife Matilda was a descendant of Widekund, the pagan ruler who led the Saxon resistance to Charlemagne, and although after her death she was venerated as a Christian saint, she was also feared for her supposed supernatural powers.

SWAN HELM

Lohengrin's helm with swan's wings marks him as a knight, both of this world and of the spirit world.

WHEN LOHENGRIN arrives at Antwerp, drawn by the swan, he tells Elsa that if he marries her, she must never ask his name. She promises never to ask – but after some years, during which they have several children, her curiosity gets the better of her. In the original *Lohengrin* she is shamed into asking by the mockery of the Duchess of Cleves; in Wagner's opera, it is at the urging of Ortrud, Friedrich's wife. The Grail itself has decreed that when knights go out from the Grail kingdom they must do so anonymously, and that if their identity is revealed they must return. So Lohengrin must go "back to the keeping of the Grail", leaving Elsa only his sword, horn, and ring as heirlooms for his children.

DRAGON

Statues of two saints watch over the duel between Lohengrin and Friedrich. The statue of St George killing the dragon may refer to Friedrich's heroic past. Although, thwarted by the self-willed Elsa, Friedrich's sense of rejection has curdled into spite. He was originally a sound choice as a husband for her, having proved his worth by slaying a dragon at Stockholm in Sweden.

THE FAIRY MELUSINE

The Melusine legend mirrors that of Lohengrin. Melusine was said to be the daughter of Elinus, king of Scotland, and the fairy Pressina. When she grew up, she learnt that her father had seen her birth against her mother's wishes, so she imprisoned him in a mountain. Her mother blamed her for this and condemned her to become a serpent below the waist every Saturday. Wandering through the woods one day, Raymond de Poitiers, Count of Lusignan, saw her bathing. He fell in love and she married him on condition that he never visited her on a Saturday. But Raymond's brothers convinced him that she saw a lover on Saturdays. Finally he spied on her, saw her serpent's coils, and she disappeared forever.

THE STORY OF VÄINÄMÖINEN

VÄINÄMÖINEN, HERO of the Finnish epic, *The Kalevala*, was the first man on earth, and a singer and poet of magical powers. A great shaman, he was the main prophet and seer of the Finnish people, who cleared the land, planted barley, and spent his time singing songs of creation. Then, one day, a younger rival, Joukahainen, challenged him to a singing match. Angered at the boy's insolence, Väinämöinen sang him into a swamp and, despite his pleas, would not free him until Joukahainen had promised him his sister Aino in marriage. Väinämöinen was delighted, but Aino was so greatly distressed that she drowned herself in the sea (see below). Väinämöinen then went in search of another wife. Along the way, his horse was shot down in revenge by Joukahainen, and he fell into the ocean. From there he was rescued by an eagle, which carried him to the Northland, home of his enemy, Louhi the sorceress. Väinämöinen could only gain his freedom by promising Louhi the Sampo, a mysterious magic object (see opposite). Many battles, impossible tasks, and adventures later, Väinämöinen sailed towards the setting sun, never to be seen by mortals again.

❝*Old Väinämöinen was delighted to have Joukahainen's maid care for him in his old age.*❞
THE KALEVALA: THE SINGING MATCH

❝*. . . now would be the time for me to part from this world – the time to go to Death . . . down below the deep billows . . .*❞
THE KALEVALA: THE DROWNED MAID

Old Man
Väinämöinen, the eternal bard, spent 700 years in his mother's womb, and was already old by the time he was born.

AINO-MYTH
by Akseli Gallen Kallela
(1865–1931)
This tryptych shows an early episode in the Kalevala, *compiled from an oral tradition of Finnish folk songs by Elias Lönnrot (1802–84). On the left, Väinämöinen meets Aino who rejects him as her husband and runs home to find her mother in favour of the match. On the right, Aino sits naked by the sea before she drowns herself in despair. In the central panel, Väinämöinen, who has gone fishing, catches Aino who has become a mermaid. But she escapes and swims away.*

VÄINÄMÖINEN
Väinämöinen, whom Aino calls a "dodderer", approaches her as she gathers twigs in the forest. "Don't for anyone, young maid, except me, young maid, wear the beads around your neck, set the cross upon your breast, put your head into a braid, bind your hair with silk!' he cries.

AINO, ONLY GIRL
Aino's name means "only", from the Finnish word *Aiona*, meaning "only one of its kind". Here she rejects Väinämöinen, wrenches the beads from her neck, and runs home weeping.

TO AINO'S HORROR, her mother was pleased with the match and did not understand her daughter's grief. She gave Aino wedding clothes woven by Moon-daughter and Sun-daughter.

BIRCH TWIGS
When Väinämöinen approached her, Aino was gathering birch twigs for the sauna. It was to the sauna that a hare brought the news of her death to her mother.

❝*Not for you or anyone do I wear crosses upon my breast, tie my hair with silk.*❞
THE KALEVALA: THE DROWNED MAID

STRANGE FISH
Aino escapes as Väinämöinen stretches to clasp her. Taunting him, she dives into the waves. Although he searched all the waters of Finland, Väinämöinen never caught Aino again.

IN A SOURCE POEM for this story, the girl, named Anni, hangs herself rather than marry her suitor. Aino's death by drowning is more subtle and less definitive. She becomes one with the sea, comparing its water to her blood, its fish to her flesh, its driftwood to her bones, and the grasses on the shore to her hair. When her mother learns of her fate, her tears create three new rivers.

IN A SOURCE POEM for this story, the girl, named Anni, hangs herself rather than marry her suitor. Aino's death by drowning is more subtle and less definitive. She becomes one with the sea, comparing its water to her blood, its fish to her flesh, its driftwood to her bones, and the grasses on the shore to her hair. When her mother learns of her fate, her tears create three new rivers.

THE MAGICAL MILL OF PLENTY

Stranded in the Northland, Väinämöinen needed the sorceress Louhi to help him home. She agreed to help and to give him her daughter, the Maid, as his bride if he forged for her the magical Sampo, the mill of plenty, out of a swan's quill-tip, a barren cow's milk, one barley grain, and the wool of one ewe. Unable to forge it himself, Väinämöinen asked Ilmarinen, the smith who had forged the sky, to help him, promising him the Maid in return. Ilmarinen had to build a new forge to make the Sampo, and only after great labour did he create this mill, which ground out corn on one side, salt on another, and money on the third. Delighted, Louhi hid the treasure behind nine locks, and rooted it in the earth. But, despite his success, Illmarinen had to return home alone because the Maid refused to marry him. Later, after she had been wooed by other men, including Väinämöinen and Lemminkäinen, a "wanton loverboy" who was killed but restored to life by his mother, Ilmarinen did marry her. However, she died and, when attempts to forge another wife out of gold proved unsuccessful, he decided to win back the Sampo. So he sailed north with Väinämöinen and Lemminkäinen and stole it. Returning home, they were attacked by Louhi and the Sampo was lost in the sea. And, although the corn and money parts were broken, to this very day the Sampo continues to grind out salt.

Forging the Sampo by Akseli Gallen Kalela (1865–1931)

SEA VOYAGER
Väinämöinen was a great boat builder and sea voyager. Although his mother was the Daughter of the Air, he was born in the sea and his name derives from *väinä* – "river mouth".

Drowning Maid
When Aino drowns she becomes a mermaid, "the wave-wife's watery maid, Ahto's peerless child". As she drowns she identifies herself with the sea – the waters are her blood and the fish her flesh.

THE BIRTH OF VÄINÄMÖINEN

In the beginning there was only sea and air. Weary of being alone, Ilmatar, the Daughter of the Air, lay down on the sea and conceived a child. But for 700 years, she could not give birth. Eventually, a sea bird, sent by the sky god, Old Man, nested on her knee and laid six eggs of gold and one of iron. Three hatched and the rest smashed into the sea. The bottom half of the eggs became the earth, and the upper half became the heavens – the yolk was the sun, the white the moon, and the mottled shell became the stars and the clouds. Still Ilmatar did not give birth, so she began to shape the world, dividing land and sea. Her son, Väinämöinen, the first man, was born 30 years later. He floated in the sea, reaching dry land eight years later.

FORLORN FISHERMAN
When Väinämöinen learned of Aino's death, his consolation was to go fishing on the sea. There he landed a beautiful "fishy fish I never saw the like of!" He drew his knife to cut it up, but it flipped out of the boat and revealed itself to be Aino, turned into a mermaid.

CONTEMPLATING DEATH
Aino reached the sea early in the morning of the third day. Heartbroken, she took off her clothes and swam out to a boulder in the distance. There she sat until "the boulder sank down and the maid with the rock".

THE LORD OF THE BEASTS

THE EARLY CELTIC GOD CERNUNNOS was the Lord of the Beasts, and is shown as such in various reliefs, most notably on the Gundestrup cauldron (see below). He was worshipped most strongly in central France, and is often accompanied by ram-headed serpents. He wears a chieftain's torc around his neck and is sometimes shown with purses filled with coins. His name means "The Horned One", and he is evidently a god with nearly as complicated a role as the Greek Dionysus (see pp.58–59). He is predominantly a god of fertility and prosperity, but is also a god of the underworld. A coin found in Hampshire seems to show him as a sun god, with a solar wheel between his horns. In northern Britain he was called Belatucadros, "The Fair Shining One", whom the Romans associated with the war god, Mars. Although there are no surviving stories about Cernunnos, he may survive in folk belief as Herne the Hunter, the antler-horned spectral rider who leads the ghostly Wild Hunt across the sky.

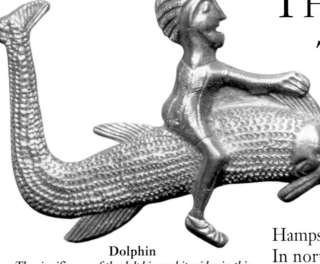

Dolphin
The significance of the dolphin and its rider in this scene is not clear, but may suggest that Cernunnos had sway over the beasts of the sea. A dolphin also appears on the sceptre found in Willingham Fen, England, which shows an unidentified sky god.

THE GUNDESTRUP CAULDRON
This image showing a horned deity with wild animals is a panel from the Gundestrup cauldron, which was found in Denmark, one of the Celtic territories, in 1891. It is made of silver-gilt embossed plates welded together and dates from the first or second century BC.

BULL

Horned bulls are often shown in association with Cernunnos, as for instance on a stone relief from Rheims, France, in which Cernunnos holds a sack from which coins flow down to a bull and a stag. Many Irish myths centre round the attempted thefts of supernatural bulls, most notably the *Táin Bó Cuailnge*, whose hero is Cuchulain, son of the sun god Lugh. The two bulls whose battle is the climax of the *Táin* are said to have originally been divine swineherds – even after undergoing many transformations, they can still reason like human beings.

Stag horns

Cernunnos, the Horned God
The horns of Cernunnos and and those of the stag are identical and show how the god was regarded as part-man, part-beast; on one British relief his legs are depicted as ram-headed snakes. It is also possible that Cernunnos was able to assume animal shape.

VEGETATION
Cernunnos was primarily a god of nature, fertility, and abundance, and is associated with fruit, corn, and vegetation, as well as animals.

TORC OF RANK
Cernunnos both wears a torc around his neck and holds another one in his hand. A Celtic chieftain would have worn a torc as a mark of rank, and warriors were also rewarded with torcs and armrings. Dio Cassius writes of the British queen Boudicca that "She wore a great twisted golden necklace". Gaulish warriors went naked into battle save for their gold or bronze torcs and armrings.

CROSS-LEGGED POSTURE
Cernunnos' posture may show a Near-Eastern origin, or may simply reflect the habitual sitting posture of the Celts who, according to classical authors, sat on the ground. His position here is strikingly similar to that of a horned Indian deity shown on a seal from Mohenjo Daro in Pakistan, who also sits cross-legged surrounded by animals; it is suggested that this Indian deity represents Shiva in his role as Lord of the Beasts (see pp.112–13).

> *After February 6th many people both saw and heard a whole pack of huntsmen in full cry. They straddled black horses and black bucks while their hounds were pitch black with staring hideous eyes. This was seen in the very deer park of Peterborough town, and in all the wood stretching from that same spot as far as Stamford. All through the night monks heard them sounding and winding their horns.*
>
> THE ANGLO-SAXON CHRONICLE, AD 1127

THE STAG'S HORNS worn by Cernunnos may have a lingering echo in the horns worn by the dancers in the Horn Dance, held for centuries each September in the Staffordshire village of Abbots Bromley. One set of the reindeer horns worn by the dancers has been carbon dated to around AD 1000.

THE MOTHER GODDESS

Celtic mythology abounds in strong women, and the worship of a mother goddess seems to have been basic to Celtic culture from neolithic times. Many dedications are to the Matres, a triple mother goddess, shown with symbols of life and abundance, but also associated with death and war, as personified, for example, by the triple Irish war goddess, the Morrigan. There are also single mother and fertility goddesses, such as the horse goddess Epona, and the Celtic "Venus" who is modelled in many pipe-clay figurines. The mother goddess is often coupled with the tribal all-father, as in the pairing of the Gaulish Sucellus, "the Good Striker", and his consort Nantosuelta, "the Winding River", or, in Ireland, the Dagda and the Morrigan. Images of the Celtic mother goddess can still be seen on Christian churches in Britain and Ireland, in the statues of women in a pose either of sexual invitation or childbirth known as *sheela-na-gigs*.

This fertility figure, known as the "Willendorf Venus", was found at Willendorf, Germany, and dates from neolithic times.

> *At the stag's call the animals came, as numerous as the stars in the sky . . . there were serpents and lions and all sorts of animals. He looked at them, and told them to go and eat, and they bowed their heads, and did him homage as vassals to their lord.*
>
> THE MABINOGION, 14TH CENTURY

THE CAULDRON OF THE DAGDA

Another important Celtic god was the *Dis Pater* (Underworld Father), from whom, Julius Caesar said, "The Gauls all assert their descent . . . and say that it is the Druidic belief". This all-father god, both creator and ruler of the underworld, was known in Gaul as Sucellus, but in Ireland as the Dagda. The Dagda was essentially a tribal god and the Irish warriors in the Ulster Cycle swear "by the god to whom my tribe swear". His ritual mate was either the triple war goddess, the Morrigan, or Boann, the goddess of the river Boyne. The Dagda was the chief of the ancestral Irish tribe known as the Tuatha de Danann, "the people of the goddess Danu". They had four magic talismans: the stone of Fal, which shrieked under a lawful king; the spear of Lugh, which ensured victory; the sword of Nuadha, from which none could escape; and the cauldron of the Dagda, from which none would go unsatisfied. This cauldron is one of the origins of the Holy Grail (see pp.80–81). In the Welsh myth cycle of the *Mabinogion* it appears as a cauldron of regeneration, bringing dead warriors to life. The Dagda had a club with the same property: one end killed the living, the other end revived the dead.

• RAM-HEADED SERPENT
Cernunnos is often shown with serpents (both with and without ram heads) symbolic of death and fertility. It has been suggested that the incident in the Irish *Driving of Fraich's Cattle*, in which the hero Conall Cernach meets a fierce serpent, reflects a memory of the god whose name the hero bears. The horns are a curious addition to the serpents, and may show their close identification with the god himself.

• BOAR
Boars had cult significance for the Celts from early times. One Gaulish god is actually called Moccus, "pig", and a boar and serpent accompany depictions of the north British god Veteris. A boar was the first convert of the Irish St Ciaran, followed by a fox, a badger, a wolf, and a stag. It has been suggested that this shows the old mythology being assimilated into the Christian tradition.

• WILD ANIMALS
These two sparring animals are not usually identified, but their paws and manes suggest that they may be lions. These animals incongruously appear in some Celtic stories, such as the early Welsh "Lady of the Fountain", in which they are associated with a divine herdsman.

THE HOLY GRAIL

DEPENDING ON THE SOURCE, the Holy Grail was either the dish that Christ used at the Last Supper, or the vessel used to catch his blood at the Crucifixion. According to tradition it was brought to England, with the lance that was used to pierce Christ's side, and left in the care of the Grail-keeper, or Fisher King. Legend tells how the wounding of the Fisher King's father, usually referred to as the Maimed King, caused the land to become barren; he could only be cured and prosperity restored if a purehearted knight found the Grail and asked the right questions. The Quest, which becomes a test of each knight's purity and worth, is initiated when a vision of the Grail appears to King Arthur and his knights. Although Christian, this legend is built on a sub-structure of Celtic mythology, which abounds in horns of plenty and cauldrons (including one that restores life) and in quests in which the hero must venture into the otherworld to win some precious prize. It is, therefore, no surprise that there are several versions of the legend. But they all agree that Arthur never went on the Quest and that only one knight (in later versions, Sir Galahad) finally proved worthy of finding this most precious object.

SIR PERCEVAL, EARLY HERO

In the later versions of the Grail legend, Sir Galahad finds the Grail. But the earliest Grail hero was Sir Perceval. Brought up by his mother in Wales, in ignorance of the world, Perceval is inspired by a group of armed knights, whom he takes for angels, to set out to seek his fortune. He comes to the Grail castle, where he fails, out of politeness, to ask the vital questions about the Grail and the lance. Later, he reaches King Arthur's court, and an old woman curses him for this failure, which has caused the land to become barren. The second time Perceval goes to the Grail castle, he asks the right questions: whom does the Grail serve? and why does the lance drip blood? In one of the most poetic Grail narratives, the *Perlesvaus* or *High Book of the Grail*, Perceval takes the Grail on a magic boat and comes to the Isle of Plenty, where he is to be king. Beneath the Isle of Plenty is the Isle of Need, whose people will be fed by the Grail.

ANGELS
When the knights approached the Grail chapel, they saw visions of angels, a sign that they were about to be granted an otherworldly experience.

Fruitful Earth
When the quest for the Grail came to an end, the land became fruitful once more.

SIR PERCEVAL
Sir Perceval was the hero of several early Grail romances (see above), but in the later French *Quest of the Holy Grail*, and Malory's *Morte d'Arthur*, he merely accompanies Sir Galahad, the purest of all the knights, when he succeeds in the Quest. Sir Perceval dies shortly afterwards.

SIR BORS
Sir Bors was Sir Galahad's other companion at the end of the Quest, and the only knight to survive and return to Camelot. He was Sir Galahad's uncle, and had been granted a vision of the Grail years earlier when he prayed that the boy might become as good a knight as his father, Sir Lancelot.

Sir Galahad
The pure and saintly Galahad is the knight who finds the Grail, asks the relevant questions and frees the land from misery. He was the son of Sir Lancelot by Elaine, the daughter of King Pelles, the Fisher King. Lancelot had been made drunk, and led to believe that Elaine was his true love, Queen Guinevere (see p.85).

Sir Galahad has cast aside his helmet and weapons to worship the Grail.

IN ONE VERSION OF THE GRAIL LEGEND, the Fisher King is named as Bron. This connects him with Bran the Blessed, legendary king of England in the Welsh *Mabinogion*. Bran possessed both a horn of plenty and cauldron of rebirth. After he was wounded with a spear, his head was cut off and buried beneath the Tower of London, to protect the land; but King Arthur dug it up to show that Britain needed no other protection other than him.

Holy Spear

One of the angels is shown holding a spear. A spear that drips blood into the Grail is a feature of many Grail stories, and is identified with the lance of the mythical Longinus, which pierced Christ's side on the cross. However, the concept is probably derived from the lightning spear of the Irish sun god Lug. Galahad uses the blood from this spear to cure the Fisher King's father, the Maimed King, whose injuries have caused the land to become barren.

SON OF SIR LANCELOT

Sir Galahad was the son of Sir Lancelot, who had come very close to ending the quest for the Grail. But, although Lancelot was the bravest and most skilful of King Arthur's knights, he was judged unworthy of success because of his adulterous love for Queen Guinevere (see p.85). When he dared approach the Grail chapel, he fainted and remained as if dead for 24 days.

THE ROUND TABLE

The Round Table was a gift to King Arthur from his future father-in-law, King Leodegrance, who had received it from Arthur's father, King Uther Pendragon (see p.84). Other sources say King Arthur himself had it made to prevent quarrels about seating arrangements. The Round Table had seats for 150 knights, and when a knight proved worthy to sit at it, he found his name set miraculously on his chair in letters of gold, by the magic of Merlin the wizard. Only one seat, the so-called Siege Perilous, would remain empty, until either Sir Perceval or Sir Galahad – depending on the source – arrived to claim it. In some versions it is by sitting in this danger seat that the Grail hero dooms the land, thereby requiring the Grail Quest to put things right. This recalls the Welsh story of Pryderi, nephew of Bran, who brings desolation on Dyfed by sitting on a perilous mound after a banquet.

This 15th-century illumination shows the vision of the Grail appearing to Arthur and his knights the day that Sir Galahad arrives in Camelot and sits in the Siege Perilous.

THE ATTAINMENT
designed by Sir Edward Burne-Jones (1833–98)

Based on the legend as told by Thomas Malory in Morte d'Arthur, *printed in 1483, this tapestry shows Sir Galahad, Bors, and Perceval, before the Holy Grail.*

THE END OF THE QUEST

Kneeling before the Grail, Sir Galahad asks the ritual questions, "What is the Grail? Whom does the Grail serve?", thus bringing the quest to an end. The lilies surrounding Sir Galahad indicate his pure and saintly character.

GRAIL CHAPEL

The Grail chapel is in the castle of Corbenik belonging to the Fisher King, who is often called King Pelles. Corbenik can be translated as the "Castle of the Blessed Horn" or the "Castle of the Sacred Host". Galahad, Perceval, and Bors are fed from the Grail by Christ himself.

THE HOLY GRAIL

The Holy Grail is variously described as a cup, a plate, and even as a stone. Its likely origin is in Celtic stories of a horn of plenty. A platter that provided "whatever food one wished" was one of the Welsh Thirteen Treasures of Britain, and the Grail also provided King Arthur's knights with whatever food and drink that they desired.

DIARMUID AND GRANIA

The love of Diarmuid and Grania is a key tale in the Irish cycle of stories about the hero Finn MacCumhal and his warrior band, the Fianna. It shares many features with Tristan and Iseult, and Welsh storytellers evidently adapted it to fit in with the legend of the Pict, Drust. Grania, the High King of Ireland's daughter, was betrothed to Finn but at the wedding fell in love with his nephew Diarmuid who had a love spot on his forehead that made him irresistible to women. Grania imposed magic bonds on Diarmuid so that he followed her, and the two eloped and became lovers. After a long pursuit, Finn found Diarmuid dying, gored by a boar. Finn had the power to save him, for as a boy he had burnt his thumb on the salmon of knowledge and, as a result, could make anyone who drank from his hands young and healthy again. Twice he filled his hands with water and let it trickle away. The third time he carried the water to Diarmuid but it was too late: he was dead. Unlike Iseult, the passionate Grania did not die for love, but was reconciled with Finn.

TRISTAN AND ISEULT

TRISTAN WAS A YOUNG KNIGHT in the retinue of his uncle, King Mark of Cornwall. One day, when a swallow dropped a fair hair at the king's feet, he declared that he must marry its owner. Tristan embarked on the quest and arrived in Ireland, where he slew a marauding dragon and claimed the hand of Iseult, the king's daughter, for she was the girl he sought. Taking her back to King Mark, fate intervened when the pair accidentally drank a love potion intended for Iseult and the King. Even so, Iseult married King Mark, keeping Tristan as her lover. Endings vary: in one tradition, King Mark slays Tristan whose dying embrace also kills Iseult, and the pair are buried side by side (see below); another tells of Tristan's banishment and marriage to another Iseult, Iseult of the White Hands. As Tristan lies dying, having sent for the first Iseult to come and heal him, his wife tells him that the ship sent to fetch her has black sails indicating that she has refused his request. At this, he dies, heartbroken. But Iseult does arrive, and she too dies of grief.

Love Potion
After Tristan won Iseult's hand for King Mark, they set sail for Cornwall. Iseult's mother prepared a love potion for Iseult and Mark, and entrusted it to Iseult's maid, Brangain, who mistakenly served it to Tristan. He, unwittingly, shared it with Iseult.

THE STORY OF TRISTAN AND ISEULT
designed by Dante Gabriel Rossetti (1828–82)
These four stained-glass windows relate the story of Tristan's defeat of Morholt, his love for Iseult, and his madness and death.

KING MARK
In the background, the artist has placed a figure of King Mark shaking his fist at the lovers. But he did not discover the truth until after his marriage. Even on his wedding night Mark was deceived when Iseult's maid Brangain slipped into his bed instead of Iseult. Later, Iseult, desperate to preserve the secret, tried to have Brangain killed, but she relented when Brangain still refused to betray her.

THE KISS
Tristan has drunk the potion and kisses Iseult's hand – their fate is sealed.

THE VERY FIRST Tristan-figure was Drust, son of Tallorc, a Pictish king of the eighth century, whose story (partly preserved in the Irish "Wooing of Emer") developed in Irish, Welsh, and Breton legend into the Tristan story as we know it.

TRISTAN
When Tristan arrived at his uncle's court he did not reveal his identity, but waited for an opportunity to prove himself. When King Mark refused to pay the Irish their customary tribute, they sent their champion Morholt to exact it, but Tristan fought and defeated him.

MORHOLT
When Morholt died, his sister, Iseult's mother, found in his skull a fragment of Tristan's sword. Iseult later recognized Tristan by his damaged sword. In the 13th-century French prose *Tristan*, the basis for later versions, Tristan takes Morholt's seat at the Round Table.

JEALOUS KING

King Mark has just slain Tristan. Mark is an ambiguous figure in the Tristan legend, but also a jealous and at times vindictive one. By the time of the French prose *Tristan*, the character of King Mark has become blackened. Now a villain, and enemy of King Arthur, he murders Tristan as he plays his harp to Iseult, and she also perishes.

FATED LOVERS

Iseult clasps the dying Tristan, and dies heartbroken. The fact that Tristan and Iseult have no choice in their passion, being bound together by the love potion, is an important element of their story. Even after death, the potion retained its power. Trees sprang up from their graves and intertwined, and although King Mark cut them down three times, they always grew again.

This medieval manuscript illumination shows Sir Bertilak's wife trying to seduce Sir Gawain.

SIR GAWAIN AND THE GREEN KNIGHT

Gawain and the Green Knight is a poem dating from c.1400, which tells how Sir Gawain's courage and virtue were tested. One New Year's Day, a huge green knight challenged Gawain, one of King Arthur's knights, to cut off his head. When Gawain did so the green knight calmly picked it up and told him to come to the Green Chapel a year later, to receive a blow in return. After a long journey towards certain death, Gawain spent three days at the castle of Sir Bertilak, preparing to meet his doom. During this time, Sir Bertilak's wife tried, and failed, to seduce him. But she did succeed in making him accept a magic girdle – a gift that he concealed from his host. Next day at the Green Chapel, the green knight inflicted a minor wound with his axe – a rebuke for taking the girdle. He then revealed himself as Sir Bertilak, given this terrible form by the enchantress Morgan le Fay (see p.85) to test the honour of King Arthur's knights. Sir Gawain, convinced he had failed, left in shame, but the other knights of the Round Table wore green girdles from then on in his honour.

LIKE KING MIDAS

(see pp.40–41), King Mark was said to have the ears of an animal. Only his dwarf knew, but when the responsibility became too great, the dwarf confided the truth to a hawthorn bush: "King Mark has horse's ears". Mark means "horse" in all Celtic languages.

TRISTAN IN DISGUISE

Tristan returned briefly to Cornwall disguised as a minstrel, Tantris. By pretending to be mad, he was able to see Iseult and remind her of their love.

TRISTAN AND ISEULT

are the archetypal lovers of medieval romance. Although the story has become entwined with that of King Arthur (in some stories Tristan becomes a knight of the Round Table) it is essentially Celtic in origin, and the action takes place in Cornwall and Ireland.

JEERING MOB

Jeering shepherds mocked Tristan in his apparent madness, as he played his harp in the forest, chasing him and shouting "Look at the fool!" Such threatening groups appear several times in the Tristan legends, most strikingly in the *Tristan of Beroul*, in which King Mark, having condemned Iseult to be burnt at the stake, commutes the sentence and hands her over to a group of a 100 lepers instead – a fate from which she is saved by Tristan.

Mad for Love

Tristan and Iseult's love affair continued under the influence of the love potion, despite King Mark's jealous suspicions. On various occasions, the pair only just escaped being found out. Eventually Tristan was banished to Brittany, where he married Iseult of the White Hands. But be continued to languish for love of Iseult. Therefore, disguised once more as the minstrel Tantris, he went back to Cornwall and, pretending to be mad, managed to see her again; in some versions of the legend he does go mad.

THE DEATH OF KING ARTHUR

KING ARTHUR AND HIS KNIGHTS were the model for medieval chivalry – pure in heart and deed and defenders of the weak against the strong. Arthur lived in Camelot with his queen, Guinevere, surrounded by his noble knights. But even they had failings, and that of Sir Lancelot – to fall in love with Guinevere – was Arthur's downfall. Told of the affair by Sir Agravain, one of his knights, Arthur condemned Guinevere to die. Lancelot rescued her, but in doing so, killed Agravain's brothers Gareth and Gaheris. Another brother, Sir Gawain (see p.83), insisted Arthur follow Lancelot to France to fight. Arthur left Mordred, his son by his half-sister Morgause, as regent. But Mordred turned traitor, and Arthur had to come back to face him at the battle of Camlann. Here, Arthur ran him through; but Mordred, with superhuman effort, hauled himself the length of the lance, and dealt Arthur a fatal blow. Taken from the battle, and knowing his fate, Arthur asked Sir Bedivere to cast Excalibur, his magical sword, into the lake where a hand arose to take it. As Arthur breathed his last, a barge appeared to take him to the mystical isle of Avalon.

A TOMBSTONE was raised to King Arthur, with the inscription, *Hic iacet Arthurus, rex quondam rexque futurus*: "Here lies Arthur, the once and future king." Folk belief says that Arthur and his knights lie asleep under a hill, ready to awaken and lead Britain in its hour of deepest need.

Merlin the Enchanter
Merlin was Arthur's mentor, and a caster of spells and reader of dreams. It was he who enabled Arthur's father, King Uther Pendragon, to take on the appearance of the Duke of Cornwall and lie with Cornwall's wife Igraine. But he required the resulting child as payment for his help.

LADY OF THE LAKE
Nimue, a lady of the lake, talks with Merlin. She was the reason Merlin was not with Arthur in his last troubles. Beguiled by her charm and beauty, Merlin had told her his magical secrets, and she had then used them to imprison him in a rock (or hawthorn tree).

THE SWORD IN THE STONE

Arthur grew up as the son of Sir Ector, a knight into whose family Merlin had placed him anonymously at birth. Several years later, King Uther Pendragon died leaving no heir, and the realm fell into disarray. But soon afterwards, Merlin placed a sword thrust through an anvil into a stone in a London church, with the words "Whosoever pulleth out this sword of this stone and anvil, is rightwise king born of all England". Every English knight tried, and failed, to remove it, including Arthur's brother, Sir Kay, who had lost his own sword while travelling, and sent Arthur to find another one. When Arthur returned with the magic sword, Kay recognized it at once, and falsely claimed his own right to kingship. But Sir Ector was suspicious and uncovered the truth, so Arthur became king, and Sir Kay his seneschal.

KING ARTHUR, SLAIN BY HIS SON
It was Sir Mordred, Arthur's son by his sister Morgause, who struck the king's death blow. Arthur had, at Merlin's instigation, tried to kill Mordred as a baby – casting adrift all children born that May day. But when the ship foundered, Mordred alone was saved; for even King Arthur could not escape his own fate.

DRAGON
The dragon on Arthur's breast is the crest of his family, the Pendragons.

MAGICAL BARGE
Magical boats appear miraculously to carry Arthurian knights from place to place, especially in the quest for the Holy Grail. This one appears to take Arthur to the isle of Avalon.

THE HOLY GRAIL
Although King Arthur himself never took an active part in the great quest for the Holy Grail, the artist here depicts the Grail appearing to the dying king, with a promise either of renewed health or resurrection.

THE ISLE OF AVALON is thought by some to be Glastonbury. But it is probably a Celtic isle of the blest, such as the land of youth, Tir na n'Og. In Tennyson's *The Passing of Arthur*, the island lies in the west, the direction of the setting sun.

LE MORTE D'ARTHUR by James Archer (1824–1904)
This picture shows Arthur's last moments before he is taken to the isle of Avalon. It is based on the poem The Passing of Arthur *by Tennyson. The four women directed by Morgan Le Fay, Arthur's half-sister, are tending to him and other important elements of Arthur's life, such as Merlin and the Holy Grail, are also included.*

LANCELOT AND GUINEVERE

This detail from a French manuscript, L'ystoire Lancelot du Lac *shows Lancelot and Guinevere, and dates from* c.1470.

The illicit love of Lancelot and Guinevere is one of the strongest threads in Arthurian literature. A fine knight, with great integrity, Lancelot was bitterly ashamed of his love and fought against it; even, at one point, going mad. But their love was preordained and could not be resisted. As a result, Lancelot could not approach the Holy Grail (see p.80) and after his rescue of Guinevere, Arthur's knights split into warring parties, giving Mordred the opportunity to betray and kill his father. After the battle of Camlann, Lancelot went back to England and saw Guinevere once more. She told him she was resolved to enter a convent, "for through our love that we have loved together is my most noble lord slain" (*Le Morte d'Arthur*, Thomas Malory). Lancelot entered a hermitage, only leaving it when he learned in a vision that Guinevere was dying. By embracing the religious life, Lancelot finally redeemed himself.

WEEPING QUEENS
The dying king was attended by three weeping queens, who accompanied him to the isle of Avalon. Only Morgan le Fay is named but they must all have been at home in the fairy realm as well as the human one, as the name "le Fay" suggests.

Morgan le Fay
The enchantress Morgan le Fay was a daughter of Igraine of Cornwall and, therefore, Arthur's half-sister. Morgan le Fay is depicted as Arthur's implacable enemy, but she is also identified as one of the three queens who came to take him to the fairy realm of Avalon. Her sister Morgause was married to King Lot of Orkney, by whom she had four sons, all of whom became knights of the Round Table: Gawain, Agravain, Gaheris, and Gareth. When Arthur was declared king, King Lot declared war on him, and Morgause seduced him, giving birth to her son Mordred as a result.

Book of spells

ESHU THE TRICKSTER

ESHU IS THE TRICKSTER GOD of the Yoruba people of West Africa. He acts as a messenger and mediator between gods and men, and he is a key player in divination, "the cornerstone of Yoruba culture", a ritual that resolves and balances the conflicting forces of the world. Full of human contradictions and a lover of mischief, Eshu looms larger in Yoruba myth than either the supreme god, Olodumare, or the creator, Obatala who, with the other *orisha*, or benevolent gods, created dry land and human beings. The *orisha*, such as Shango, god of thunder (see below), Ogun, god of iron and war, and Ifa, god of divination, are opposed by the *ajogun* or malevolent gods, such as Iku (Death) and Arun (Disease). In the endless cosmic struggle between good and evil, one of Eshu's key roles is to trick the *ajogun*. But like the Norse god Loki (see pp.69), Eshu is related to the *ajogun* as well as the *orisha*, forming a link between them; and like Loki, he has sometimes been wrongly identified with the Christian devil. The wrath of the *ajogun* can be turned aside by sacrificing to Eshu, and his role might be best expressed as god of Fate.

Tester of Humanity
Eshu tests human beings to discover their true nature. If they resist temptation, he rewards them; if they give in, he punishes them.

LIGHTNING
The decoration here may represent lightning; the lightning bolt was Eshu's gift to Shango, the thunder god.

TRANSFORMATION
Eshu can assume 256 different forms, and the most constant thing about him is his changeability. He can appear as a giant or as a dwarf; as a cheeky boy or as a wise old man. He can speak all languages.

ESHU STATUETTE
This wooden carving of Eshu is part of the costume of an Eshu priest and is designed to be worn hooked over the shoulder. It shows Eshu dressed as a priest with an Eshu statuette (like itself) over its left shoulder. Eshu's contradictory nature is shown by the fact that the carving has two faces, the second one at the back of the phallic headdress (see above). One face looks into the spirit world, and the other into the world of men. Also, each side of the carving is different.

Double-headed axe – a symbol of thunder

SHANGO, GOD OF THUNDER

Shango was the fourth king of Old Oyo, and only later became the god of thunder and lightning. His reign on earth ended when he was banished from Oyo by the superior power of the hero Gbonka. Shango hanged himself in the forest in shame, but rather than dying, he returned to his place in the sky. From here, he keeps an eye on humanity, and still sends his thunderstorms. Shango had three wives: Oya, Oshun, and Oba. Oya is the goddess of the Niger River, into which she stepped when Shango's life on earth came to an end. Shango is often depicted with a ram's head and horns. The sound of thunder is said to be the sound of a ram bellowing. Because he is thought to punish the guilty by striking them with his thunderbolts, Shango is regarded as the god of justice and fair play. The double-headed axe shown here symbolizes the thunderbolt. It signifies "My strength cuts both ways", meaning that no one is beyond the reach of his authority. Devotees of Shango, possessed by the god, hold a staff representing the god's thunder-axe as they dance to the sound of the bata drum – said to have been invented by Shango to terrify his opponents. A very powerful god, Shango nonetheless is subordinate to Eshu in terms of authority.

A Shango staff

> **"***Eshu throws a stone today And kills a bird yesterday* **"**
> YORUBA POEM

ESHU is said to haunt gateways and crossroads where he can divert humans from their planned course.

"Eshu turns right into wrong, wrong into right."
YORUBA POEM

TWO SIDES, ONE MAN
Eshu's headdress differs on both sides, indicating his changeability. In one story, Eshu breaks up a firm friendship between two men by wearing a hat which is white on one side and black on the other, causing them to quarrel irreconcileably about the colour of his hat.

ESHU'S EYES
When Eshu is angry, he internalizes his emotions and weeps tears of blood, or hits a stone until it bleeds.

ESHU FIGURE
Eshu is holding a small statue of himself, much as one of his priests would do. His ability to introduce chance and accident into life means that he is widely respected. He is known for helping people only if they offer him sacrifice, a ritual presided over by a priest.

"Eshu supports only he who offers sacrifice."
YORUBA SAYING

THE WILY TRICKSTER, HARE

Many stories are told in Africa of animal trickster figures. One such is Hare (who in America became Brer Rabbit). One story tells how Hare owes money to both Elephant and Crocodile. To placate them he tells them that he will repay them with interest – all they have to do is pull on a rope of liana and they will recover a treasure chest. So without realising it, they engage in a tug-of-war, each unaware that the other is pulling at the far end of the rope. Of course, in the meantime, Hare escapes. In only one story of the many that reveal his wily character, is he completely outwitted. This is the story of the race between Hare and Tortoise, in which Tortoise, instead of racing Hare, simply positions members of his family along their circular racecourse, and sits waiting to greet Hare at the finishing line.

Hare's ears

Hare

This headpiece belonged to the Yoruba people in Nigeria and was used in ceremonies to impersonate the trickster Hare.

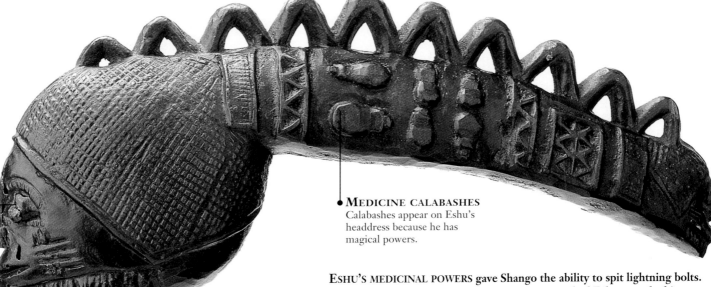

MEDICINE CALABASHES
Calabashes appear on Eshu's headdress because he has magical powers.

ESHU'S MEDICINAL POWERS gave Shango the ability to spit lightning bolts. One day, Shango, wanting even more power, asked Eshu to make him a medicine that would help him to terrify his enemies. He paid Eshu by sacrificing a goat, and his wife Oya went to collect the medicine. But the packet was so small that she doubted its strength and tasted it. Arriving home, she greeted Shango and fire suddenly flashed from her mouth. Furious, Shango tried to kill her with his thunderstones, but she hid. When his anger cooled, he forgave her, and tried the medicine himself. So much flame leaped from his mouth that the whole city of Oyo was burned to the ground.

"Death, Disease, Loss, Paralysis, Big Trouble,Curse, Imprisonment, Affliction They are all errand boys of Eshu."
YORUBA SAYING

ANANSI THE SPIDER

Anansi the spider is a trickster figure belonging to the West African Ashanti tribe. Among the Zande tribe he is known as Ture. One of the best-known myths is the one in which Anansi asks the sky god Onyankopon (also called Nyame) if he can buy the stories for which he is famous. "What makes you think that you can buy my stories?" asked the god. "I have refused them to the great and powerful and you are no-one important." But Anansi insists on a price, so Onyankopon tells him to bring him Onini the python, Osebo the leopard, Mmoboro the hornet swarm, and Mmoatia the spirit – creatures that he considers impossible to catch. But Anansi, with his wife's help, traps them all, adding his own mother for good measure! The sky god is so impressed that he gives Anansi his stories with his blessing. Since then, they have been called spider-stories. Anansi or Nancy stories are now commonly told in the West Indies as well as Ghana.

Orb-web spider

THE COSMIC SERPENT

THE FON PEOPLE OF AFRICA tell how the cosmic serpent, Aida-Hwedo, was brought into being at the beginning of time by the Creator, an androgynous god with two faces: Mawu the female moon and Lisa, the male sun. Aido-Hwedo helped with the creation by carrying the Creator in his mouth as the world was shaped. But when the work was done, the Creator saw that there was too much weight for the earth to bear – too many trees, too many mountains, too many elephants, everything. So he asked Aido-Hwedo to coil himself into a circle and lie underneath the overburdened earth like a carrying-pad. As Aido-Hwedo does not like the heat, the Creator made the ocean for him to live in. But the earth chafes on Aido-Hwedo, and when he shifts to ease himself, he causes earthquakes. Aido-Hwedo eats iron bars that are forged for him by red monkeys that live beneath the sea. When the iron runs out, hunger will drive him to eat his own tail. Then the earth with all its burdens will overbalance, and tip into the sea. A second Aido-Hwedo, the rainbow serpent, lives in the sky and sends the thunderbolts of the gods to earth.

GU, THE GOD OF IRON

Gu, the god of iron, is one of the 14 children of Mawu and Lisa. The first three were: Da Zodji, the chief of the Earth pantheon; So, the chief of the Thunder pantheon; Agbe, the chief of the Sea pantheon. Other key figures include Agè, the god of the hunt, Djo, the god of the air, and Legba, the trickster and mediator, the Fon equivalent of Eshu (see pp.86–87). Gu is the god of iron and, therefore, also of war, weapons, and tools. As a god of war he is sometimes known as Ebo. Gu is said to be made of iron or, alternatively, to have a body of stone and a head like an iron sword. The notion that Gu's head was shaped like a sword relates to a myth in which Lisa is sent by Mawu to use Gu as a tool to clear the forests and teach men how to build shelters and dig the ground. Ever since, the cutlass that Mawu-Lisa gave to mankind has been called *Ali-su-gbo-gu-kle*, The-road-is-closed-and-Gu-opens-it. But as well as being personified in the first cutlass, Gu is also regarded as an important deity. As the god of smiths, he himself is thought of as a smith, always at work in his forge. For this reason his shrines never have a roof, for if they did, they would burn down.

An iron statue of the god Gu

PAINTED WOODEN BOWL

This painted wooden bowl from West Africa shows the world and a man, woman, and snake. The Fon believe that the first man and woman came to earth in the company of Aido-Hwedo, the Cosmic Serpent. Aido-Hwedo is also said to have helped the Creator to shape the world like a great calabash. In the mythology of the Fon sky-cult, the Creator parent, Nana-Buluku, is revered as the creator of the world, which Mawu then shaped and peopled. But like many African supreme gods, Nana-Buluku is scarcely remembered today; the name Mawu has come to mean "God" in Fon.

AFTER THE WORLD WAS MADE, the Creator is said to have made the first people from clay and water. He prepared the mixture in the same way as preparing building materials for a house.

AIDO-HWEDO can be seen as a personification of creative power – a power that can still be seen in the rainbow, in water, in the ebb and flow of the sea, and in the dance of the stars.

• **AIDO-HWEDO**
The name Aido-Hwedo means either "You were created before the earth and before the sky" or "You are both in the earth and in the sky". Aido-Hwedo in the earth supports the earth and everything on it; Aido-Hwedo, the rainbow serpent in the sky, sends thunderbolts to earth. The second crack of thunder, the recoil, is the sound of Aido-Hwedo's tail whipping back after flinging the bolt to earth. The two Aido-Hwedos are sometimes regarded as twins.

• **SERPENT'S HEAD**
Aido-Hwedo carried the Creator in his mouth as the world was being shaped; that is why the world curves and winds as it does. The Creator pressed the earth together and made it into the shape of a calabash, and Aido-Hwedo then coiled around it. There are said to be 3,500 snake coils above the earth, and 3,500 below.

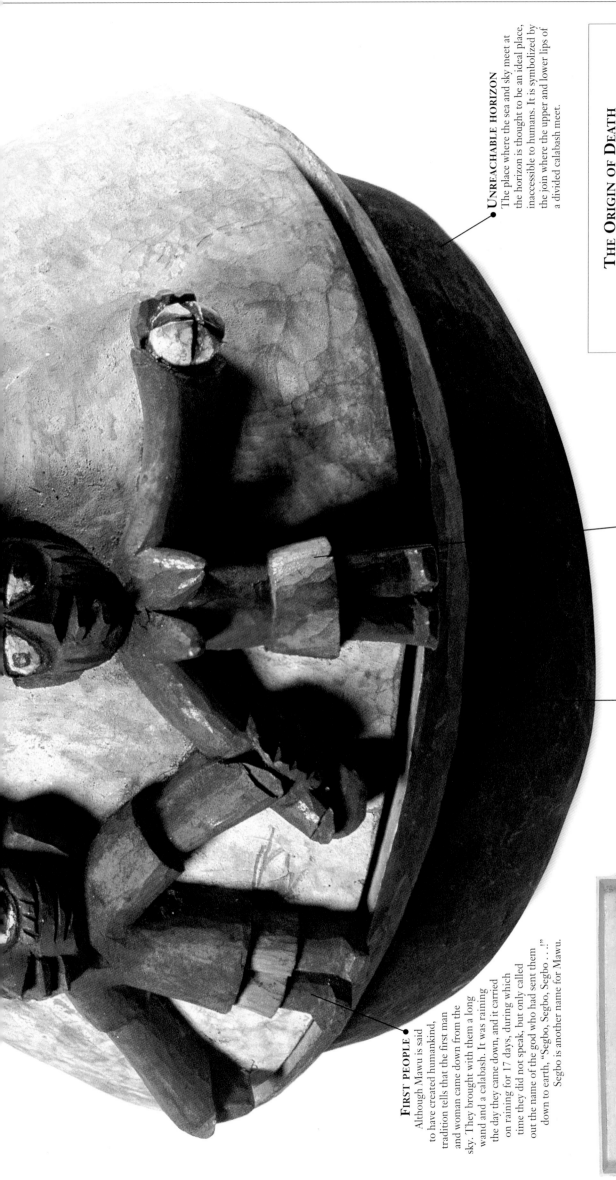

UNREACHABLE HORIZON

The place where the sea and sky meet at the horizon is thought to be an ideal place, inaccessible to humans. It is symbolized by the join where the upper and lower lips of a divided calabash meet.

THE ORIGIN OF DEATH

Many African cultures contain a myth explaining the origin of death: the Zulus tell how the Creator sent the chameleon Unwabu to tell humankind that it would not die, and Intulo, the lizard, to tell it that it must. The chameleon lingered on the way, but the lizard ran straight there, so his message arrived first. The Hottentot version tells how the moon sent an insect to say, "... as I die, and dying live, so shall they". On the way to deliver this message, the insect met the hare. On hearing his commission, the hare said that as he was the faster runner, he would go. When he reached the earth, he told humankind that the moon's message was, "As I die, and dying perish, so you shall die and come wholly to an end". When the hare returned and told the moon what he had said, she was angry and struck him on the nose. Since then, the hare's nose has been slit; but people still believe what the hare told them.

WORSHIPPING THE GODS

The first man and woman, who are sometimes named Adanhu and Yewa, established the worship of the sky gods Mawu and Lisa, and of the lesser gods their children, such as Gu, the god of iron, and Age, the god of hunting.

WORLD LIKE A CALABASH

The world is said to be round like a calabash, a gourd which, when empty, can be used as a waterpot or turned into a rattle. Fon temples contain carved and decorated calabashes that house small offerings to the gods.

Aido-Hwedo

This bas-relief from the palace of King Ghezo of Dahomey shows Aido-Hwedo with his tail in his mouth (see above). Aido-Hwedo is also known as Da Aido-Hwedo. "Da" is the word for snake but as "Da" Aido-Hwedo it means the living quality of everything that is flexible, sinuous, and moist, such as the rainbow, smoke, the umbilical cord, even the nerves. "Da" also means wealth, good fortune, and all desirable things that tend to slip from one's grasp.

AIDO-HWEDO is said to have existed before any of the children of Mawu, "created by whoever created the world". A statement that Aido-Hwedo "came with the first man and woman of the world" may allude to the snake's phallic quality, or to the way in which snakes have come to be identified by the Fon people with the life force. In some stories, the snake teaches the first man and woman the mystery of procreation.

FIRST PEOPLE

Although Mawu is said to have created humankind, tradition tells that the first man and woman came down from the sky. They brought with them a long wand and a calabash. It was raining the day they came down, and it carried on raining for 17 days, during which time they did not speak, but only called out the name of the god who had sent them down to earth, "Segbo, Segbo, Segbo..." Segbo is another name for Mawu.

THE VOODOO GODS

THE VOODOO GODS OF HAITI (and their counterparts in the *Candomblé* and *Santería* cults of Brazil and Cuba) derive from West African mythologies, but are also shaped by slavery and the influence of Catholicism in the New World. The word *vodu* is the African Fon word for "god"; and *lou*, meaning spirit, is a Congolese word. Voodoo is a religion with many *loas*, who are dedicated to serving humans as long as they are welcomed and well fed. But there is little formal mythology in the sense of a creation narrative or heroic exploits of the gods. This is because the gods are actors in the lives of their worshippers – even possessing them during Voodoo rites. Thus the characters and attributes of the gods as living beings are seen as more important than their histories. This is borne out in the story of a gang of Ghedes besieging the presidential palace (see right), showing that Voodoo gods can be a potent political force in shaping Haiti's present and future.

Erzulie Freda
Erzulie Freda is one of the aspects of Erzulie (or Ezili), the goddess of love. She is the consort of Agwé, the god of the sea, but also dallies with Damballah Wedo, the god of thunder, with Ogoun, the god of war and iron, and with Ghede (Gedé) in his role as Ghede Nimbo, the gravedigger.

ALL THE VOODOO GODS are identified with Catholic saints: Erzulie with the Virgin Mary, Legba with both St Peter and Lazarus, Ogoun with St James the Greater, Damballah Wedo with St Patrick, Azaca with St Isidore, Baron Samedi with St Expedit, and so on.

GHEDE, THE LORD OF DEATH AND LIFE

Ghede, the master of the underworld, is also a lord of life, strongly associated with erotic activity and with the protection of children. He is a glutton for both food and drink, stuffing food into his mouth with both hands and washing it down with great swigs of fiery spirit. Yet he is also elegant and sophisticated. He brooks no questioning of his authority. Earlier this century, a crowd of Ghedes (Voodoo priests possessed by his spirit) marched on the palace of President Borno in Port-au-Prince, singing "Papa Ghede is a handsome fellow". Each was dressed in Ghede's best clothes: top-hat and tail-coat, smoked glasses, a cigarette or cigar, and a cane in his hand. When they arrived they demanded money, and the President, who knew that no man is stronger than Death, gave it to them. Ghede wears dark glasses because he spends so much time underground that his eyes are sensitive to the sun. With his left eye, he surveys the entire universe; with his right eye, he keeps an eye on his food.

Altars to Baron Samedi, such as this one, always show a cross, at least one skull, a hat, sunglasses, and rum.

THE VOODOO GODS INCLINE TOWARDS THE FATE OF HAITI
by Cameau Rameau
This painting reflects the widespread belief that the gods are involved in the politics of the island, often helping to elect or get rid of a president. It shows the major deities of Rada Voodoo (one of the gentler forms of Voodoo) in council over Haiti's future.

• **MOUNTAIN ORIGIN**
The Petro voodoo cult, which grew out of the rage of the slave experience, was born in the hills of Haiti, among escaped slaves known as Maroons. In 1791 a Petro ceremony, led by a Voodoo priest, Boukman Dutty, sparked off an uprising for independence.

• **GRAVE**
The cross on this tomb, the symbol of Baron Samedi, is the crossroads of death. An offering of rum to Ghede stands at its base.

• **OGOUN**
Ogoun, god of war, fire, and patron of ironworkers, rides up on his white horse. In his role as a military leader, Ogoun has also acquired many political skills; the conference of the gods on the future of Haiti cannot start without him.

• **WORSHIPPERS**
The worshippers following Ogoun hope to be possessed by a *loa*, in Voodoo rites. The *loa* displaces the worshipper's soul, or *gros-bon-ange* (big-good-angel), which will survive mortal death to become one of *les Invisibles*, the spirits.

ERZULIE DANTO

Erzulie is seen here in her happier guise, identified with Notre Dame de Grace (Our Lady of Grace), sometimes called *La Sirène* (the Siren). She takes this form when she is Agwé's consort in the sea. Erzulie can also appear as an old woman, Gran Erzulie, and, in a rage of grief and despair, as Erzulie Ge-Rouge.

BARON SAMEDI

Ghede (Gédé), the god of death, is shown here in his most authoritative role as Baron Samedi. He must be kept informed of everything going on in life. Jaunty and often irresponsible, Baron Samedi has a skull and crossbones on his hat in case anyone amused or offended by his actions forgets that his life force comes from his mastery of death.

VOODOO MYTHOLOGY

derives mainly from the Fon in Nigeria (see pp.88–89). Legba, Aido-Hwedo, Agbè and Gu retain many of their Fon characteristics, although Gu has taken the name of the Nagos god of war, Ogoun. The harsher Petro rites, forged in anger and adversity in the New World, have Congo, Bomba, and Limba roots.

CANE

Ghede's cane is both a phallic symbol, appropriate to a god whose actions are often obscene, and a balance on which the lord of death may weigh souls.

PAPA LEGBA

Papa Legba, the god of the crossroads, is depicted as a frail old man, although he is celebrated as the lord of life. A prayer at childbirth begs Legba to "open the road for me . . . do not let any evil spirits bar my path". Legba straddles all the worlds, and all prayers must pass through him.

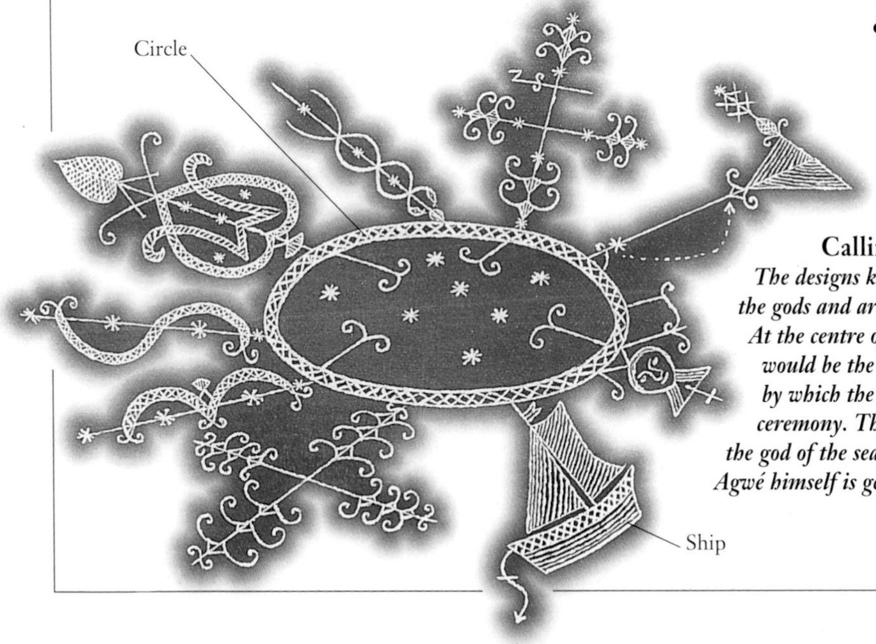

COCKEREL

The black cockerel is a bird of sacrifice, waiting to be slaughtered to Ghede.

JAR OF SPIRIT

The jar probably contains fierce alcohol – perhaps Ghede's special drink of crude rum steeped in hot spices, which only he can bear to swallow.

SNAKE

The snake twined around Legba's walking stick, the symbol of his old age, represents Damballah and Ayida Wedo (Aido-Hwedo, see p.88), the male and female rainbow snakes who embrace the world, across the sky and beneath the sea.

AZACCA

Azacca (or Azaka), dressed in peasant clothing and carrying a straw satchel, is the patron of farming and all agricultural work. He probably derives from the maize culture of Haiti's original Indian population, rather than from African roots. Azacca is said to be the younger brother of Ghede (see above); but where Ghede is sophisticated and worldly, Azacca is simple and naive.

ERZULIE FREDA

Erzulie Freda is identified here with the Christian Virgin of Sorrows. She often cries for the loss of her only child, by Ogoun, a girl called Ursule who drowned.

CHILD

The child in Erzulie Freda's arms almost certainly represents the twin children of Voodoo mythology, the Marassa. They are of great importance to Voodoo belief and ritual and their feast, once held at harvest time, has been assimilated with Christmas, in association with the Christ child.

C. Rameau

PAPA GOD AND GENERAL DEATH

A Haitian folktale tells how Papa God and General Death were walking together one day. General Death pointed to a house from which he had taken a soul the day before, and another he was due to take one from the next day. "You always take, while I always give," said Papa God. "That is why people prefer me." But General Death did not agree. So they decided to each visit the man whose soul General Death would take the next day. When Papa God asked the man for a cup of water, he refused him. "I have to walk ten miles to fetch water," the man said. "But I am Papa God," Papa God replied. "I still don't have any water for you, but I would give some to General Death." "Why?" asked Papa God. "Because unlike you, who give me no water while others are swimming in it, General Death has no favourites. All are alike to him." And indeed, when General Death asked, the man let him drink his fill of cool clear water. General Death was so pleased that next day, he did not stop at the man's house after all.

Calling the Gods

The designs known as vevers are used to call the gods and are drawn on the earth in flour. At the centre of the circle in a Voodoo ritual would be the poteau-mitan, the centre-post by which the gods make their entrance to the ceremony. The ship symbol stands for Agwé, the god of the sea and formal consort of Erzulie. Agwé himself is generous, faithful, and strong.

Ship

Circle

MOUNTAINWAY

ONE DAY, Reared-within-the-Mountain, a young Navajo man, was captured by some Ute warriors. Shut in a lodge on the edge of a ravine, he called on Talking God, grandfather of the gods, and god of the dawn and the eastern sky, to rescue him. So Talking God appeared through the lodge smoke-hole as a flash of lightning, and they escaped. On his way home, the young man met many animals and people, including the Holy People, who made him as beautiful as they were and taught him the shamanistic secrets of the Mountainway ceremonies. The sandpainting here is part of these ceremonials and relates to the young man's night in a cave with four bears. The bears unrolled this picture for him on a sheet of cloud. It shows the Holy People of cultivated plants. When Reared-within-the-Mountain first saw the bears, they were lying by a fire in the same positions as the Holy People in the picture. Eventually Reared-within-the-Mountain arrived home but he hated its smell. So, after teaching his family the secrets of Mountainway, he returned to live with the Holy People.

CHANGING WOMAN

Changing Woman is the most important goddess of the Navajo. Daughter of Long Life Boy and Happiness Girl, she was brought to life by Talking God from a turquoise image, and brought up by First Man and First Woman. She is crucially involved in the creation, and is identified with the essence of life, growing old and becoming young again in an endless cycle of regeneration. Her sister is White Shell Woman. Changing Woman married (but did not live with) Sun God, who carries the sun on his back and hangs it on the west wall of his lodge each night. Their sons, the hero twins, Monster Slayer and Born-for-Water, aided by Spider Woman (see opposite), located their father who helped them to make the earth safe by destroying the monsters that ruled it. But despite killing many evil creatures, they could never slay Old Age, Cold, and Hunger.

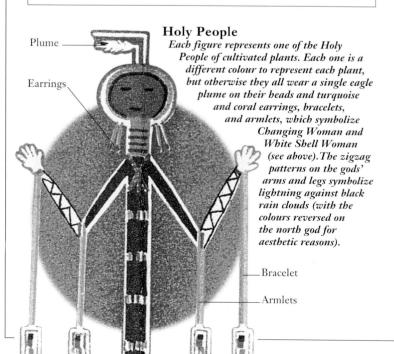

Plume

Earrings

Holy People
Each figure represents one of the Holy People of cultivated plants. Each one is a different colour to represent each plant, but otherwise they all wear a single eagle plume on their heads and turquoise and coral earrings, bracelets, and armlets, which symbolize Changing Woman and White Shell Woman (see above). The zigzag patterns on the gods' arms and legs symbolize lightning against black rain clouds (with the colours reversed on the north god for aesthetic reasons).

Bracelet

Armlets

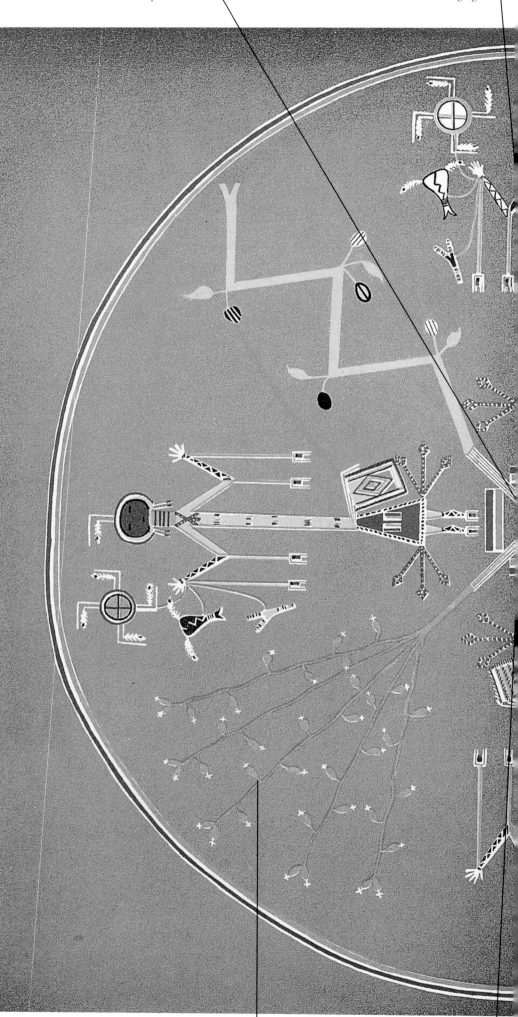

BOWL OF WATER •
A bowl of sacred water sits in the centre of the painting, sprinkled over with special charcoal, and surrounded with sunbeam symbols.

SKIRTS OF SUNLIGHT •
Each Holy Person wears a skirt of red sunbeams. Mountainway songs invoke figures such as Daylight Boy and Daylight Girl in tracing the beautiful journey from the house of dawn to the house of evening light.

CULTIVATED PLANTS •
Each plant relates to the Holy Person to the left of it. Clockwise from top right (north-east), they are a tobacco plant, a stalk of corn, a beanstalk, and a pumpkin vine. Their colour reflects the body of the Holy Person, and their roots are in the sacred water in the centre.

SUNBEAM RAFTS •
The Holy People are standing on sunbeam rafts. They are placed in each of the four cardinal directions, which are crucial to the rituals of nearly every Native American culture.

THE BEARS IN THE STORY lay around a fire that was burning without any wood – the flames were issuing from four coloured pebbles. The bears taught Reared-within-the-Mountain how to make the bear *kethawns*, sticks to be sacrificed to the bear gods.

• RAINBOW GODDESS
Talking God bridged a canyon by breathing out a rainbow, which led Reared-within-the-Mountain to the bear cave. This represents Rainbow Woman, goddess of the rainbow.

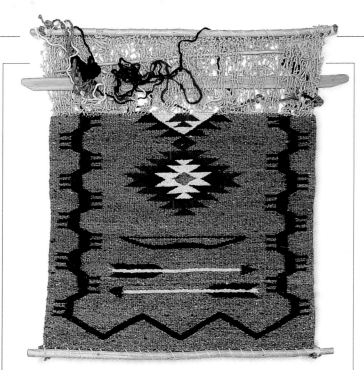

Navajo woven blanket

SPIDER WOMAN

Spider Woman is an important figure in the mythologies of the American Southwest and plays various roles, including assisting at the creation. In Navajo myth, she is a helpful old woman. She helps the hero twins, Monster Slayer and Born-for-Water, and it is she who taught the Navajo how to weave. This is why Navajos must never kill spiders, which also help humans by catching insects, flies, and mosquitos. Any child who kills a spider is expected to have crooked second teeth because Spider Woman is said to have needle-sharp teeth that slant backward to stop her prey from escaping. To encourage Navajo girls to become tireless weavers, spiders' webs are rubbed on their arms. And when a Navajo woman uses Spider Woman's knowledge to weave a rug, she must weave a break into the pattern at the end, so that her soul can come out, back to her.

MOUNTAINWAY is one of many Navajo chantways, ceremonies that express myths through song, prayer, dance, ritual, and sand-painting, usually for healing purposes. The painting is created and destroyed as part of the ritual and the sand transferred to the body of the person who is being sung over. The sand painting here is one of the first to be recorded in a fixed medium, with the approval of the singer; some argue that to make a permanent record is to abuse its meaning.

• BIRDS OF DAWN
These blue birds are known by the Navajo as the heralds of dawn and relate to Talking God, the god of dawn and the eastern sky who makes a distinctive sound, "hu'hu'hu'hu", as he approaches.

• POUCHES
Each god carries a pouch covered with porcupine quills. These pouches were precious to the Navajo because they traded for them with nations such as the Ute. When Reared-within-the-Mountain makes his escape, Talking God instructs him to take with him two bags filled with embroideries, as well as tobacco, which he later offers to the bears.

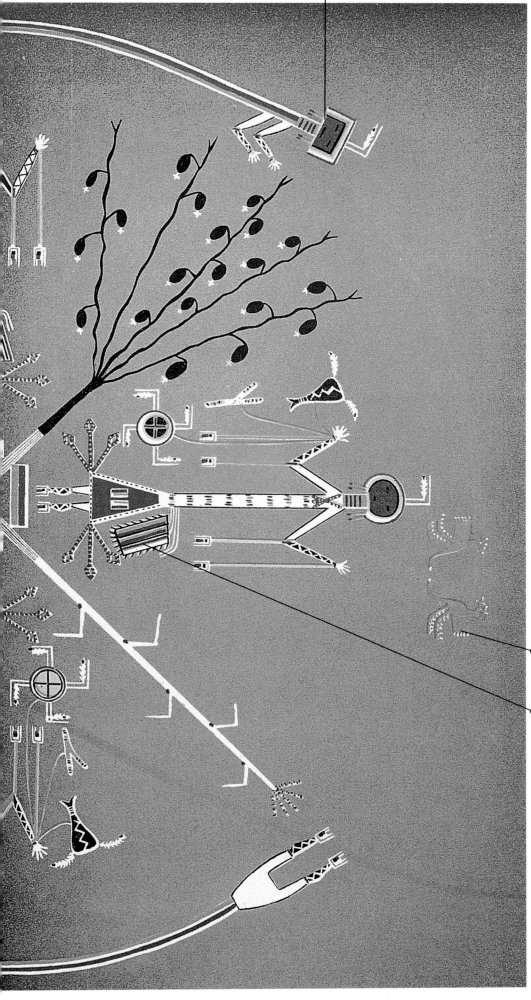

NAVAJO SAND PAINTING
This painting is a representation of the painting that Reared-within-the-Mountain saw in the bears' home. Sand paintings such as these are sacred. Their Navajo name means "place where the gods come and go".

WHEN REARED-WITHIN-THE-MOUNTAIN left his home to live with the Holy People, he told his brother, "You will never see me again – but when the showers pass and the thunder peals, you will say, 'There is the voice of my elder brother' ".

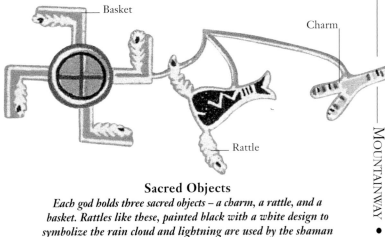

Basket

Charm

Rattle

Sacred Objects
Each god holds three sacred objects – a charm, a rattle, and a basket. Rattles like these, painted black with a white design to symbolize the rain cloud and lightning are used by the shaman in the Mountainway ceremony. The baskets, shaped in the ancient sun-symbol of the swastika, are dressed with eagle plumes and face anticlockwise.

LONE MAN

IN THE BEGINNING, says the Native American Mandan creation myth, the earth was covered in water, and darkness reigned. Then First Creator and Lone Man, walking on top of the waters, saw a mud hen and asked her what she ate and she fetched them a grain of sand. First Creator and Lone Man took the sand and from it they made the land. First Creator made the hills, and the animals that lived there, and Lone Man the flat country. They both thought that their own creation was the best, but agreed that time would tell. Then Lone Man created people and decided to live with them to protect and guide them. So he became a corncob, and a young Mandan girl ate him and became his mother. Lone Man grew up pure and good and travelled in a magic canoe with 12 men, performing miracles. When it was time for him to leave, he told the people to set up a cedar trunk painted red in the centre of the village, and to burn incense and offer it sacrifices. He said, "This cedar is my body, which I leave with you as a protection from all harm". He told them to build a barricade around the cedar as a protection – if the water rose again, it would rise no higher than the first hoop, and then subside.

Sacrifices
The Mandans made sacrifices of costly cloth to the Great Spirit. Four of these stood on poles outside the medicine lodge. They may represent spirits of the four cardinal points.

THE BUFFALO DANCE
by George Catlin (1794-1872)
This painting shows the Mandan Indians, who lived on the upper Missouri River, performing part of the annual Okeepa ceremony. It celebrated the subsiding of the waters after the deluge in the Mandan flood myth; Lone Man was the only survivor, landing his Big Canoe on a high mountain to the west, where he still lives. If the ceremony was not performed, the Mandan believed the flood would rise again to destroy the human race once more.

BUFFALO DANCERS
Eight dancers dressed in buffalo skins danced outside the medicine lodge during the Okeepa, in order to ensure plentiful supplies of buffalo for the coming year.

The Evil Spirit
O-ke-hée-de (the owl or Evil Spirit) appeared on the fourth day to disrupt the dance, creating alarm or fear. The medicine man pacifies him with the sacred pipe – but he is finally vanquished by one of the women. This woman then takes the lead in the celebratory feast that night. She is said to hold the power of creation and of life and death, and be the mother of the buffaloes.

Evil Spirit's body is covered in black grease. In the Okeepa ceremony the woman throws yellow dirt at him and it sticks.

Evil Spirit's wand is broken by the woman.

MEDICINE LODGE
The medicine lodge was sacred and only used during the Okeepa ceremony. It was the largest lodge in the village.

PART OF THE OKEEPA CEREMONY was to initiate boys into manhood. While the tribe danced outside, the initiates stayed in the medicine lodge, neither eating nor sleeping. On the fourth day, they underwent physical tortures.

WILLOW BOUGHS
Each dancer carries willow boughs on his back to represent the willow twig brought back to Lone Man by a dove as the waters began to subside. The ceremony took place when the willow leaves were full grown along the river bank.

MORNING RAYS
Four dancers, each bearing a staff and a rattle, naked except for a kilt and headdress of eagles' quills and ermine, accompany the four pairs of buffalo dancers. Two, painted red with white stripes, were called the Morning Rays.

TURTLE DRUMS
Four sacred drums in the shape of turtles were beaten during the dance by four Mandan elders. They represent the four turtles that support the earth.

ALMOST EVERY ASPECT OF THE OKEEPA incorporated the Mandan belief that they lived at the very centre of the world. Their own name for themselves was simply Numakaki - "people". In the Bel-lohk-na-pick, the Buffalo Dance, the eight buffalo dancers separated into four pairs, dancing to the north, east, south, and west.

BIG CANOE
This barrel-shaped object made of planks and hoops stood in the centre of the village. It was the shrine containing the cedar post that Lone Man left behind in his place. In the context of the Okeepa ceremony, it represented the ark of the Mandan flood myth, which by the 1830s had incorporated various elements of the biblical flood.

EARTH LODGES
The Mandan lived in earth lodges, consisting of a timber frame, thatched with willow boughs, covered with a foot or two of clay and gravel. The roofs became so hard that the inhabitants – 20 or 30 per lodge – could sit out on top of them.

THE LEGEND OF MADOC
The echoes of Christianity in Mandan mythology and culture, and the similarity of the circular Mandan "bull boat" to the Welsh coracle, struck George Catlin who lived among the Mandan. He suggested that the Mandan were descended from a lost expedition of Welshmen under the command of Madoc, a prince who sailed from North Wales to America in 1170 and founded a colony there. However, the Madoc legend is dubious and seems to have been a Tudor construct to confound Spanish claims to the Americas. Nonetheless, it has led to 15 Native American languages being identified as "Welsh", of which Mandan has remained the most popular choice. Indeed, the story has begun to infiltrate the beliefs of the few Mandan that remain, some of whom say that Lone Man was a white man who brought the Mandan people across a great water in his Big Canoe and landed them on the Gulf of Mexico.

THE ADULT DANCERS EACH SANG their own "medicine songs" – sacred and personal song-poems. The words were simple and direct. A song collected by Frances Densmore from Wounded Face of the Black Mouth Society of the Mandan translates in its entirety: "earth always endures".

ANTELOPES
The Mandan boys were painted yellow to play the part of antelopes in the dance. They alternately chased and were chased by adult men dressed as bald eagles, wolves, swans, rattlesnakes, vultures, and beavers.

TURTLE MYTH
The four sacred drums of the Mandan were buffalo skins sewed together in the shape of large turtles. They were filled with water said to have been gathered from the four corners of the earth as the flood subsided. The Mandan believed that the world rested on four turtles. The world flooded when each of these turtles made it rain for ten days each, and the waters covered the earth. Whether this flood happened before or after Lone Man and First Creator made this earth is not clear. Originally, the Mandan flood myth was set after the emergence from the world below, and does not seem to have involved Lone Man, whose story seems to have been influenced by that of Noah as well as Christ. Myths of a great flood are common among Native American peoples, as is the idea that the world rests on the back of either one or four turtles.

This Cheyenne shield shows the turtle in the "earth-diver" role taken by the mud hen in the Mandan creation myth.

CRYING TO THE GREAT SPIRIT
During the dance the chief medicine man leans against the Big Canoe, with the sacred pipe in his hand, crying to the Great Spirit for help in the coming year.

GRIZZLY BEARS
Two men dressed as grizzly bears sit by the Big Canoe, threatening to devour anyone who comes near them, and generally disrupting the ceremony. Women bring them dishes of meat to appease them.

THE NIGHT
Two of the four individual dancers, painted jet black with charcoal and grease, and covered with white spots called stars, were called the Night.

THE OKEEPA WAS AN ANNUAL CEREMONY lasting four days. It began with Lone Man entering the village and smoking a pipe to the initiation of young men and calling to the Great Spirit to give them the strength to succeed. Outside, the buffalo dance, shown above, was performed to ask the Great Spirit to continue his influence in sending buffaloes as food every year. It was last performed in 1836/37 just before a smallpox outbreak wiped out almost the entire tribe.

MYTHS OF THE ARCTIC CIRCLE

THE HARSH CLIMATE OF THE ARCTIC has forged an equally harsh mythology, in which such key figures as Sedna, mistress of the sea beasts (see below), enact stories of primal violence. The sealskin painting shown here depicts this disturbing world in which spirits and humans share the same air, and there is a constant lurking awareness that any creature may be about to change itself into another. To contain the whole world in a sealskin combines a sense of confinement with its opposite – a feeling of boundless space and freedom. Just such a contradiction is found in the widespread Inuit myth of the two couples who set out to discover the full extent of the world. They took their sledges and went in opposite directions, travelling for years across the ice. Finally, having grown old along the way, they came full-circle, back to where they first started. "The world is big!" said the first man. "Even bigger than we thought!" said the second. And with that they die.

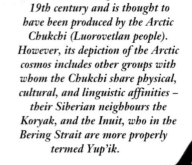

ARCTIC COSMOS
This sealskin was painted in the 19th century and is thought to have been produced by the Arctic Chukchi (Luorovetlan people). However, its depiction of the Arctic cosmos includes other groups with whom the Chukchi share physical, cultural, and linguistic affinities – their Siberian neighbours the Koryak, and the Inuit, who in the Bering Strait are more properly termed Yup'ik.

Igloo
Inuits are shown building an igloo out of blocks of ice. The myth of the Inuit who travelled round the world (see above) shows that the world is round, like an igloo. The neighbouring Chukchi live in tents.

SEDNA, INUIT GODDESS OF THE SEA

Sedna was an Inuit girl who encountered her father's wrath when she refused all human suitors, married a dog, and gave birth to puppies. Horrified, her father threw her into the sea and cut off her fingers when she tried to climb back into his boat. So Sedna sank to the seabed where she became a powerful spirit, and her severed fingers became the first seals. As mistress of the sea, Sedna is vital to human survival. But her father's harsh treatment has made her capricious and if not constantly placated, she shuts the sea beasts away and humankind starves. When this happens, a shaman must make the terrifying trip to her house, face its terrible guardians, and appeal to Sedna face-to-face. Here, because all the sins of humankind fall into the ocean and collect in her hair as grease and grime, he must clean Sedna's hair and dress it in two thick braids because, without fingers, she cannot clean it herself. Then the grateful goddess frees the beasts, and humankind can eat again.

Sedna *by Germaine Arnaktauyok*
Sedna sinks to the ocean-bottom, her severed fingers becoming the first seals.

ENDLESS FOREST
On the other side of the sea, the Chukchi say that there is an endless forest. The spirits of this forest come to trade with humans, but their presence is only indicated by the fox or beaver skins that they carry; they are mere shadows. They like to be paid in tobacco for the skins.

THE GIRL WHO MARRIED A WHALE
A Chukchi girl married a whale, who carried her far from home. But her brother followed her, persuaded her to sing her husband to sleep, and stole her back. The whale followed, but when it came to shore the people speared it to death. However, the wife gave birth to a little whale. First she kept him in a bowl of water, then in a lake, and finally she freed him into the sea. There, he led other whales in for the people to hunt, until he himself was killed by a stranger.

GULL-MAIDEN
A Chukchi lad stole the clothes left on the shore by a bathing gull-maiden, and married her. They had two children, but the gull-wife hankered for the freedom of the air. When a flock of gulls flew by, they plucked their wings and stuck feathers on the wife and children, and they flew away. But the husband travelled to the country of the birds and won his wife back. He anointed her with reindeer blood (the most important rite of Chukchi marriage) and she ceased to be a bird and became truly human.

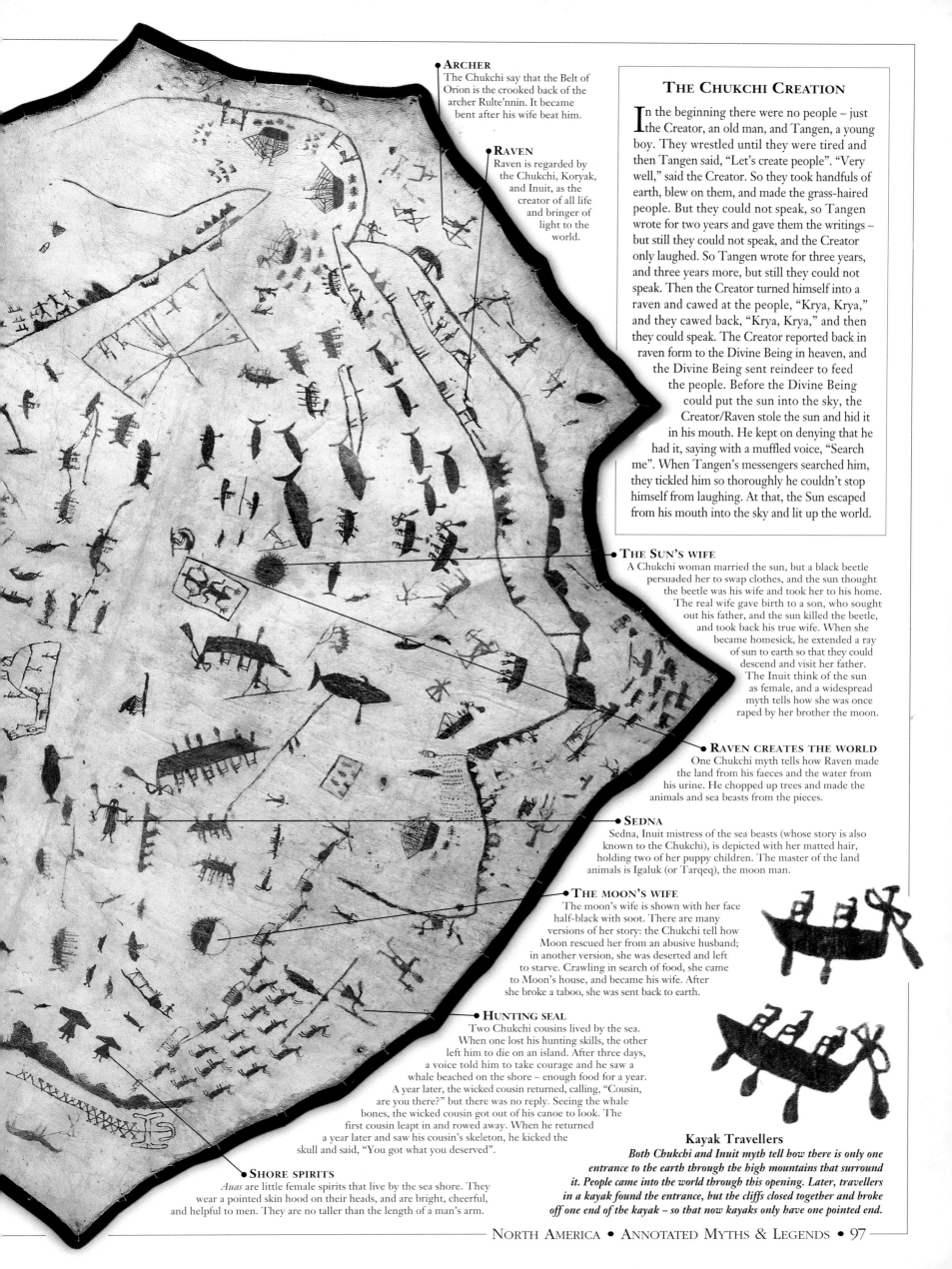

ARCHER
The Chukchi say that the Belt of Orion is the crooked back of the archer Rulte'nnin. It became bent after his wife beat him.

RAVEN
Raven is regarded by the Chukchi, Koryak, and Inuit, as the creator of all life and bringer of light to the world.

THE CHUKCHI CREATION

In the beginning there were no people – just the Creator, an old man, and Tangen, a young boy. They wrestled until they were tired and then Tangen said, "Let's create people". "Very well," said the Creator. So they took handfuls of earth, blew on them, and made the grass-haired people. But they could not speak, so Tangen wrote for two years and gave them the writings – but still they could not speak, and the Creator only laughed. So Tangen wrote for three years, and three years more, but still they could not speak. Then the Creator turned himself into a raven and cawed at the people, "Krya, Krya," and they cawed back, "Krya, Krya," and then they could speak. The Creator reported back in raven form to the Divine Being in heaven, and the Divine Being sent reindeer to feed the people. Before the Divine Being could put the sun into the sky, the Creator/Raven stole the sun and hid it in his mouth. He kept on denying that he had it, saying with a muffled voice, "Search me". When Tangen's messengers searched him, they tickled him so thoroughly he couldn't stop himself from laughing. At that, the Sun escaped from his mouth into the sky and lit up the world.

THE SUN'S WIFE
A Chukchi woman married the sun, but a black beetle persuaded her to swap clothes, and the sun thought the beetle was his wife and took her to his home. The real wife gave birth to a son, who sought out his father, and the sun killed the beetle, and took back his true wife. When she became homesick, he extended a ray of sun to earth so that they could descend and visit her father. The Inuit think of the sun as female, and a widespread myth tells how she was once raped by her brother the moon.

RAVEN CREATES THE WORLD
One Chukchi myth tells how Raven made the land from his faeces and the water from his urine. He chopped up trees and made the animals and sea beasts from the pieces.

SEDNA
Sedna, Inuit mistress of the sea beasts (whose story is also known to the Chukchi), is depicted with her matted hair, holding two of her puppy children. The master of the land animals is Igaluk (or Tarqeq), the moon man.

THE MOON'S WIFE
The moon's wife is shown with her face half-black with soot. There are many versions of her story: the Chukchi tell how Moon rescued her from an abusive husband; in another version, she was deserted and left to starve. Crawling in search of food, she came to Moon's house, and became his wife. After she broke a taboo, she was sent back to earth.

HUNTING SEAL
Two Chukchi cousins lived by the sea. When one lost his hunting skills, the other left him to die on an island. After three days, a voice told him to take courage and he saw a whale beached on the shore – enough food for a year. A year later, the wicked cousin returned, calling, "Cousin, are you there?" but there was no reply. Seeing the whale bones, the wicked cousin got out of his canoe to look. The first cousin leapt in and rowed away. When he returned a year later and saw his cousin's skeleton, he kicked the skull and said, "You got what you deserved".

SHORE SPIRITS
Auas are little female spirits that live by the sea shore. They wear a pointed skin hood on their heads, and are bright, cheerful, and helpful to men. They are no taller than the length of a man's arm.

Kayak Travellers
Both Chukchi and Inuit myth tell how there is only one entrance to the earth through the high mountains that surround it. People came into the world through this opening. Later, travellers in a kayak found the entrance, but the cliffs closed together and broke off one end of the kayak – so that now kayaks only have one pointed end.

LEGENDS OF QUETZALCOATL

QUETZALCOATL WAS ONE of the most important Aztec gods – a creator god, also credited with the gift of maize to men and the teaching of many arts and sciences, including measuring time. Also god of the air, he acted as roadsweeper for the life-giving rain gods. In this guise, in which he is called Ehecatl (meaning Wind), he descended to Mictlan, the underworld, to steal the bones of mankind from his father Mictlantecuhtli, the god of death (see below). However, as he fled, he dropped the bones, and a quail nibbled them. As a result, when Quetzalcoatl scattered his own blood upon them to create human beings, the new race of revivified men were of different sizes and doomed to die again. Quetzalcoatl's great rival was his brother Tezcatlipoca, a war god, who managed to get rid of Quetzalcoatl by tricking him into drinking the intoxicating *pulque* and sleeping, while drunk, with his sister Quetzalpetlatl. Ashamed, Quetzalcoatl sailed away to the east on a raft of serpents, promising to return. In 1519, when the Spaniard Hernando Cortés landed in Mexico from the east, the Aztecs believed him to be Quetzalcoatl returned.

AZTEC GODDESSES

The Aztecs worshipped a number of important goddesses. Coyolxauhqui takes a particularly active role in Aztec mythology as the evil older sister of Huitzilopochtli, the supreme god who was associated with the sun and with fire. When Coyolxauhqui discovered that her mother Coatlicue was pregnant, she slew her in a fit of jealousy, with the aid of her 400 brothers. In her death throes, Coatlicue gave birth to Huitzilopochtli, and the supreme god, who emerged fully armed, dismembered his treacherous sister. This primal battle provided the mythic charter for Aztec human sacrifice. Other goddesses, such as Xochiquetzal, the goddess of youthful attraction, were less fierce. Although Xochiquetzal was also associated with pregnancy and childbirth, she shared this role with Chalchiuhtlicue, the goddess of lakes and streams, who is often depicted with two children issuing in a stream from beneath her jade skirt. Other important goddesses include Chicomecoatl, the goddess of maize, and Tlatzeotl, the goddess of purification and curing.

Ritual Staff
The ritual staff with bells is made of bone and known as a chicahuaztli.

WIND SIGN
This is the day sign for wind and resembles Quetzalcoatl in his guise as the wind god.

GOD OF DEATH
Mictlantecuhtli, shown as a skeleton, is covered in blood and wears an eyeball-necklace. Every 260 days, a man representing the god was sacrificed at night in the temple of Tlalxico, "the navel of the world". The victim may have then been eaten by the priests, in an act of communion.

GLYPHS
The glyphs running down the sides of this image are a calendar for the 260-day ritual year, the *tonalpohualli* or "book of the days", which was broken up into 20 x 13-day periods. This ritual calendar expressed the Aztec understanding of the complex interrelation of the world of men and the world of the gods. It ran alongside a 365-day solar calendar (not adjusted for leap years), and the two calendars coincided once every 52 years, an occasion for much rejoicing.

CONICAL HAT
Quetzalcoatl's conical hat, the *copilli*, is one of his most distinguishing features and his temple in the sacred precinct of Tenochtlican had a conical roof, reminiscent of his headdress. One of the reasons why Cortés was taken to be Quetzalcoatl was the high-crowned hat that he wore.

GOD AND KING
In some documents Quetzalcoatl is described solely as a god, but others refer to a human incarnation as king of the legendary city of Tollan. All of the Aztec kings modelled themselves on him.

QUETZALCOATL is known as the Feathered or Plumed Serpent, because he was half quetzal bird and half rattlesnake. Quetzal means "bird of paradise" and Coatl means "serpent". Quetzalcoatl was also associated with the sun.

GOD OF THE WIND
Quetzalcoatl is seen here in his character as Ehecatl, the wind god. He wears a pectoral of shaped conch shell, known as the "wind jewel", and a red bird-beaked mask (based on a duck's beak with fierce incisors. The Aztecs believed that the sun only moved because it was blown by Quetzalcoatl's breath.

"Quetzalcoatl came to the kingdom of the Dead, to the Lord and Lady of the Dead, to the Kingdom of the Dead. He said, "Behold why I have come. You are concealing the precious bones. I have come to collect them"

LEGEND OF THE SUNS

DEER

The deer is the third period of 13 days in the Aztec calendar. Starting at alligator (below), the calendar is read alligator, jaguar (opposite), deer, flower, reed, death, rain, grass, serpent, flint, monkey, lizard, movement, dog, house, vulture, water, wind, eagle, rabbit.

DAY DISCS

These 12 dots represent the second to thirteenth days of each "month". The alligator on the right is the first day of the first "month", the first dot is the second day, the second dot the third day and so forth. The first image on the left side is the first day of the next "month" and the dots are then read right to left to arrive at the deer, then right to left to the flower and so on to the rabbit in the top left-hand corner.

THIS DEPICTION OF THE TWO OPPOSED GODS shows them almost as two aspects of the same person. A sense of the duality of opposites (life and death, day and night) is central to Mesoamerican religious thought. The highest heavens were ruled by Ometeotl, the god of duality, who was both male and female. Quetzalcoatl was accompanied on his descent into Mictlan by his "double", the coyote god Xolotl, which means twin.

AZTEC BOOK OF SECRETS

This illustration from an Aztec ritual screenfold manuscript, now known as the Codex Borgia, depicts Quetzalcoatl in his guise as Ehecatl, the wind god, and Mictlantecuhtli, the god of death, standing back-to-back on an upturned skull. The manuscript would have been used by an Aztec priest for divination of the future; many pages, including this one, incorporate calendars.

BLOOD SPOTS

The Aztecs believed they owed a blood-debt to the gods because they had drawn their own blood to generate the new race of humans. They repaid the gods with their own blood.

DEATH

This is the day sign for Death, and resembles Mictlantecuhtli, the god of death.

SKULL

The gods are supported by a schematic skull, which may be symbolic of the earth.

SACRIFICIAL VICTIM

This hieroglyph, *chalchuitl*, was used to mark a sacrificial victim, or a place of sacrifice.

TLALOC, THE RAIN GOD

Tlaloc was the Aztec god of rain and lightning. He is distinguished by his "goggle eyes" and jaguar teeth. His jaguar heritage derives from the Olmec civilization, whose rain god was depicted as a were-jaguar. Some scholars believe that the basic Olmec creation myth told of the copulation of a woman and a jaguar, making the Olmecs "the people of the jaguar". Tlaloc was known as "the provider", for the rain that made the maize grow was his gift. He was the ruler of the weather and mountain spirits.

In this stone carving, Tlaloc is shown upturning one of his nine rain buckets.

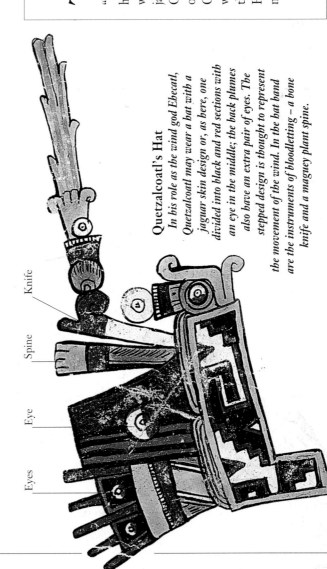

Quetzalcoatl's Hat

In his role as the wind god Ehecatl, Quetzalcoatl may wear a hat with a jaguar skin design or, as here, one divided into black and red sections with an eye in the middle; the back plumes also have an extra pair of eyes. The stepped design is thought to represent the movement of the wind. In the bat band are the instruments of bloodletting – a bone knife and a maguey plant spine.

Eyes

Eye

Spine

Knife

THE HERO TWINS

THE HERO TWINS, Hunahpu and Xbalanque, were Central American Mayan gods venerated for ridding the world of the earth giants and other monsters. In the story below, they rescue their father and uncle from Xibalba, the gloomy underworld. Years before they were born, their father Hun Hunahpu and uncle Vucub Hunahpu were challenged by One Death and Seven Death, the lords of Xibalba, to a game of *tlachtli*, the Mayan ritual ball game. But they were tricked, sacrificed, and buried under the ballcourt. When the twins grew up and learned of their father's fate, they travelled into the depths of Xibalba past many dangers to wreak vengeance. When they arrived, they defeated the lords of Xibalba at *tlachtli* and were thrown into the House of Lances where they were stabbed at by demons. They escaped, but were then shut up in the Houses of Cold, Jaguars, Fire, and Bats. Surviving all these, the twins boasted that they were immortal and, to prove it, were sacrificed and had their bones ground like flour. When they came back to life, their enemies were so impressed that they wished to experience death and rebirth themselves. So the twins killed them but, as planned, did not revive them. Instead they brought their father and uncle back to life and went home.

Water-lily Jaguar
Water-lily Jaguars drooling blood form two corners of the temple; the other two (one is hidden) show Xocfish Monsters. The Water-lily Jaguar is a form of the underworld Jaguar God, who represents the sun in the underworld.

THE HERO TWINS
This image is taken from a vase and shows the Hero twins in disguise, in the presence of One Death, the chief lord of the underworld. This story is told in the Popol Vuh, or "Council Book", a record of Mayan mythology.

AXE
Hunahpu is shown in act of sacrificing a man to demonstrate his powers. He is wielding the sacrificial axe of Chac-Xib-Chac, a god associated with the sacrificial death dance.

SACRIFICIAL VICTIM
The man's role as ritual victim is proclaimed by the akbal, "darkness", signs on his back and leg.

HUNAHPU
Hunahpu is wearing a jaguar-pelt skirt, and the headband of the Jester God. Mayan kings wore jade head ornaments of the Jester God; a court jester is a suitable disguise for Hunapu here, as he performs magic tricks to amuse the gods of Xibalba.

SERPENT
A Vision Serpent emerges from the victim towards Xbalanque. It is a symbol of rebirth and generated by bloodletting. Vision Serpents are often shown rearing up from a blood offering, belching out gods and ancestors.

XBALANQUE
Xbalanque, like his brother, is disguised, but his identity is made clear by the jaguar-paw on the nose of his mask. Xbalanque often had jaguar markings on his face, arms, and legs.

THE PRINCIPAL INCA GODS OF PERU

The Incas of Peru worshipped Inti, the sun, as their ancestor; his sister-wife was Mama Kilya, the moon. Two chief gods, the fire-and-earth god Pachacamac and the rain-and-water god Viracocha, came to be regarded as their sons. Viracocha, whose sister-wife was the sea mother Mama Cocha, was also regarded a creator god. The first world he created was a world of darkness, peopled by giants he had made from stone. But they were disobedient and he punished them by sending a great flood. Then he made humans out of clay and lit the world by sending the sun, moon, and stars up into the heavens from his abode in Lake Titicaca. After he had taught the people how to live in the world he sailed away like Quetzalcoatl (see p.98).

THE HERO TWINS first sacrificed a dog and revived it; then a man; then Xbalanque sacrificed Hunahpu and revived him. One Death and Seven Death pleaded, "Do it to us!" but after killing them, the twins refused to revive them and then humiliated the other lords of Xibalba, curbing their power.

THE STORY OF SNAKE-WOMAN

This two-headed heaven snake from Peru recalls the spirit snakes with human heads who are among the servants of the Pillan, the thunder god of the Amerindians of Chile. Sky spirits such as this may be invoked by a shaman in initiation, healing or magical ritual. The cloth's precise mythology is not known, but it may depict a myth such as the Peruvian Sharanahua story of Snake-Woman. Snake-Woman was lured out of her lake by a man who wished to seduce her. But when he grabbed hold of her, she became huge, reaching right up to the sky. Then she shrank back to his size, coiled around him, and dragged him to her underwater home. The man thought his new wife very beautiful, but when he drank the hallucinogenic *shori*, he saw her in her true form and was terrified. Although Snake-Woman calmed him, he was not happy and her brother took pity on him and led him home.

This cloth found in an ancient Peruvian tomb shows a two-headed heaven snake.

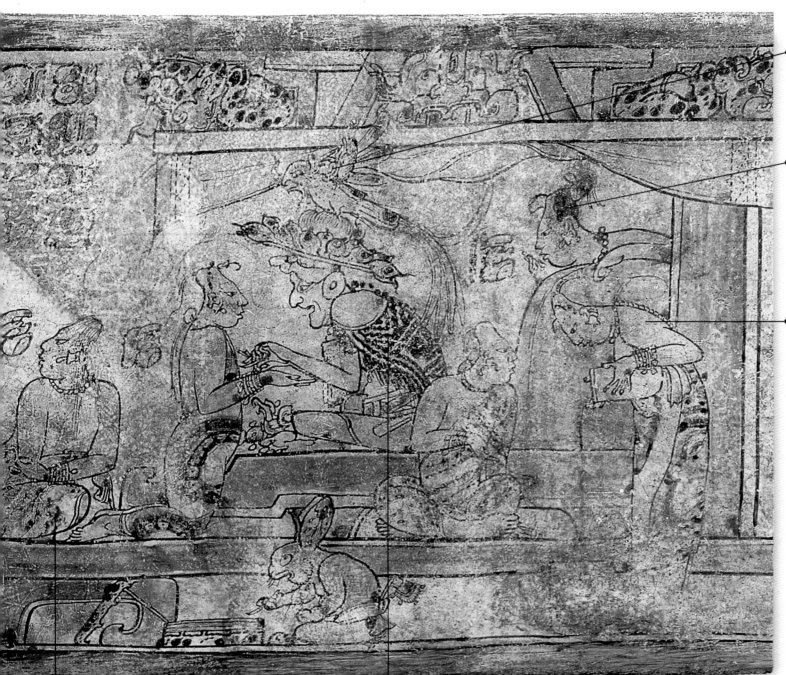

MACAW OWL
The Macaw Owl, the messenger of Xibalba, perches on One Death's hat. The messenger owls act as guides down to the underworld.

POINTED FOREHEADS
In Mayan culture, long pointed foreheads were considered beautiful. Babies had their heads bound at birth so that their skulls were squashed to achieve this effect.

BALD-HEADED GODDESSES
One Death is tended by five bald-headed goddesses, who are depicted as noble and beautiful ladies. This one is shown pouring liquid into a cup – probably *pulque*, an alcoholic drink.

THE HERO TWINS are shown masked and in disguise, having brought themselves back to life after being sacrificed by One Death and Seven Death.

DRAWING ATTENTION
One of the goddesses taps another on the foot to draw attention to the sacrifice being made by the disguised Hero Twins. In the land of death, the Hero Twins' powers of resurrection must have seemed doubly miraculous.

ONE DEATH
The chief lord of Xibalba, One Death, sits on his throne in an underworld temple, surrounded by goddesses; he is shown tying on the wrist cuff of the one who kneels before him. Two others sit cross-legged at his feet, while a fourth pours him a drink and a fifth leans over his back pillow.

Rabbit Scribe
A rabbit scribe writes in an open codex bound with jaguar pelt. A rabbit helped the Twins at the start of the ballgame – Hunahpu had his head cut off by a bat and the underworld gods decided to use it as the ball. To allow Hunahpu to fix his head back on, the rabbit pretended to be the ball and ran away with the Death Gods in pursuit. Mayan art sometimes shows a rabbit stealing the regalia of One Death. The usual Mayan scribes are the Monkey twins, Hun Batz and Hun Chuen, the Hero Twins' half-brothers.

THE UNDERWORLD, Xibalba, was a dreadful hell, whose name means literally "place of fright". Only those who died a violent death went to heaven, all others were consigned to Xibalba. It lay to the west, and could be entered through a cave, or through still, standing water.

THE DREAMING LIBRARY

THE "DREAMING" OF AUSTRALIAN ABORIGINAL MYTHOLOGY is often referred to as the *Altjeringa*. It is the time of the creation of the world, but it is not regarded as lying in the past, but rather in an eternal present, which can be accessed in ritual. Stories known as "Dreamings" tell of the exploits of Ancestor beings, who do for the first time something of which all future actions are mere copies. The Dreaming tracks of the Ancestors are encoded in song lines, and inscribed in paintings, which form a mythological map of the Australian landscape – a web of sacred memories whose heart is at Uluru (Ayers Rock). The Dreaming Ancestors are regarded as beings who slept in the primal world; but then they awoke and shaped human beings and a landscape in which they could live. The painting below tells the story of the *Fire Country Dreaming*, a myth that belongs to the Warlpiri people of Central Australia. In it, two ancestors from the *Jangala* clan are persecuted by their powerful shaman father because they accidentally kill a kangaroo, which is sacred to him, and give it to him to eat. In revenge, he sends a magical fire to pursue them wherever they go. It burns them from head to foot and they die.

GOANNA DREAMING

Many myths are about animals in the Dreaming, and one of the most important is Goanna, the monitor lizard, who among other things was responsible for inventing the canoe. The people of the Murrumbidgee river tribe tell how all the animals decided to intermarry and the male goannas had to marry magpies or teals. For some reason, the goannas, who were originally vegetarian, began to eat the flesh of their own young and also baby porcupines – a diet that made them lazy and dishonest. Then one year, there was a drought and all the animals suffered except for the goannas who had a secret supply of water. Their new wives begged them share their water with the emus and the porcupines who were dying of thirst, but they refused. So the wife of the chief goanna found the secret reservoir and, with the help of bush spirits, caused it to flow into the Murray river in a torrent that separated the goannas from their wives. Since then, the teals have refused to marry the goannas.

Goanna Dreaming by Kaapa Tjampitjinpa (c.1920–89)

FIRE COUNTRY DREAMING 1988 by **Dolly Nampijinpa Daniels and Uni Nampijinpa Martin**
The story of Fire Country Dreaming is a major myth of the Warlpiri people. The version here is taken from the oral account given by Uni Nampijinpa in 1990. The Warlpiri word for the Dreaming is Jukurpa.

TWO SONS
The old man's two sons, the *Jangala*, are described as beautiful young men, who suffered pain and hardship in order to look after their father. They gave him the best of everything to eat, such as the tail of the kangaroo.

HUNTING TRACKS OF THE SONS
The hunting tracks of the sons lead to Kirrkirrmanu, where they killed the kangaroo sacred to the old man.

SPEARS
The old man, like his sons, has his spears at the ready; the oval object to the left is his spearthrower.

BLUE-TONGUED LIZARD MAN
This is the old man, Blue-tongued Lizard. He pretended to be blind so that his sons hunted for food for him. But when they left the camp, he used to take weapons and catch his own meat, which he did not share with them.

CAMPFIRE
Two campfires mark the camp belonging to the two *Jangala* and their aged father. The two sons went out hunting, leaving their father in the warm.

EVIL SPELL
This black mark is the evil spell used by the old man to create a fire to follow and kill his sons.

BUNJIL, SUPREME CREATOR

Bunjil the eaglehawk is the supreme creator deity of the Koori peoples of Victoria. He had two wives and a son, Binbeal, the rainbow. Bunjil made the mountains and rivers (including Port Phillip Bay), and the flora and fauna, and taught humankind how to live. Then he asked Bellin-Bellin the crow, his opposite and rival, to open his bag and let out some wind. When Bellin-Bellin opened the bag, a whirlwind swept out that ripped trees from the earth. Still Bunjil called for more wind, and Bellin-Bellin opened his bag even more, until Bunjil and his family were lifted up to the sky world. The Koori believed the sky was held up by four props. Soon after the first white men came, word was passed that the eastern sky prop was rotting. Shortly afterwards, the sky fell.

Continually Igniting Fire
The Jangala are chased by a fire "always present, always present ... As they put it out ... it ate at their feet, their knees, their heads, until their skin was covered in burns." (Uni Nampijinpa Martin, 1990)

Flames re-igniting

DEATH SITE
This is Ngarra, a salt lake, where the two *Jangala* stopped, too exhausted to go any further. It is a sacred site, where only men may go. The two vertical lines below it are the bodies of the two dead sons.

EMU TRACKS
These arrows represent the tracks of an emu with a broken leg. Another Warlpiri myth tells of an emu that travels across the Fire Dreaming country eating bush food and laying eggs. This sacred landscape records its tracks.

THE SONS' CAMPS
These circles mark spots where the sons camped. The horseshoe-shapes indicate the sons. When they slept at night, the fire died down; when they rose, so too did the fire.

FLIGHT OF THE SONS
These tracks show the path of the sons' flight from the fire. They had both been badly burnt, from their feet to their heads; they were in agony and near to death.

BORDER
Here is the border with the country of the Pitjatjantjara people; the part of the story that involves what happened during the time that the fire drove the *Jangala* brothers across this border belongs to the Pitjatjantjara.

POWER OVER FIRE IS AN ATTRIBUTE of aboriginal shamans, or "men of high degree". Among the Kattang-speaking people who occupied the northern shore of Port Stephens, the initiation ceremony involved a process of death and rebirth, during which the initiate was thrown onto a fire and then lifted up and held over it until it was burned out.

Footprints

Snake cave

Tracks of the Old Man
The hunting tracks of the old man lead to Ngama, the Snake Cave. It is from the Rainbow Snake (see p.105) that the old man derived his magical powers.

THE KILLING OF LUMALUMA

LUMALUMA WAS A WHALE who came out of the sea in the shape of a man at Cape Stewart, near Milingimbi, in central coastal Arnhem Land, Australia. Once on dry land, he acquired two wives and made his way west, taking with him the important religious rituals known as *mareiin*, *ubar*, and *lorgun*, as gifts to humanity. But Lumaluma was greedy and abused his sacred role – for whenever he saw delicious food, such as sweet wild honey, or succulent yams, he declared it *mareiin*, sacred, and thus only he could eat it. But at the same time he was demonstrating the rites, clapping together his special sticks and saying, "It's good, all of it!" He came to one place where people had set up camp and he could hear them cutting down trees. Seeing their fires burning and their food prepared, he ran towards it and declared the meal sacred. He ate all the big pieces of food and left only the scraps for the people of the camp. This happened many times until, finally, he began to eat the bodies of dead children. This was the final insult and the Arnhem Land people took their spears, sticks, and spear-throwers and put him and his wives to death.

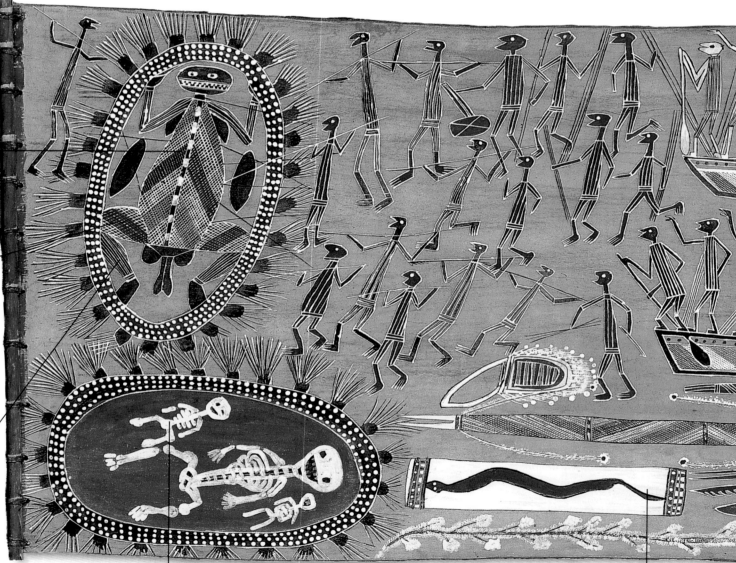

Lumaluma
The angry people of Arnhem Land, pushed beyond endurance, killed Lumaluma with their spears and sticks. After killing him, they left the body seated against a tree on the beach, with string tied around the torso and neck to hold it in place.

SHADE HUTS
Lumaluma is enclosed by the branches of a shade hut that was built over his body. Such huts are built over sacred ground in the performance of rituals learned from Lumaluma.

SACRED DESIGNS
Lumaluma's body is covered with designs that he cut into his skin before his death to demonstrate the *mareiin* ceremony. These criss-cross ochre designs tell sacred stories of each man's ancestral country. Other elements of Lumaluma's teachings were sacred dances and chants used in religious ceremonies.

DYING LUMALUMA
When the men began to spear him, Lumaluma told them to slow down, so that he had time to teach them once more how to transform themselves in the *mareiin* ceremony, when they go to their sacred place.

WIVES
When Lumaluma emerged from the sea, he stole two wives while the men were all out fishing. These wives travelled with him and shared in his death; their skeletons lie next to their husband's. Like Lumaluma, they continued to teach the religious rituals as they were speared to death and were responsible for teaching the women's religious ceremonies.

LOG COFFIN
This log coffin depicts a water python on one side and a goanna on the other (hidden from view). Above it is a long tom fish also carved by Yiridja clan members. These traditional designs are also used in body painting, ground sculptures, and bark paintings.

MOIETIES

In Arnhem Land, everything in the universe is classified as belonging to either the Dua or Yiridja moieties, according to a division laid down in the dreamtime. The myths of the Djanggawuls – two eternally pregnant sisters and their brother – belong to the Dua, while those of Barama and Laindjung belong to the Yiridja. It was these ancestors who brought the moieties their sacred objects and designs; like Lumaluma, they taught the people many sacred rituals.

LUMALUMA IS DESCRIBED as having been accompanied by the Rainbow Snake. If his attackers had buried him, Lumaluma would have died forever. But as they left his body on the beach, he was able to slip back into the sea, and come back to life as a sea creature "like a Rainbow Snake". But he never came back to land.

THE STORY OF LUMALUMA was told to anthropologist Catherine H Berndt in 1950 by Mangurug, one of the most senior women of the Gunwinggu (or Kunwinjku) people of Western Arnhem Land, who regard Lumaluma as their sacred Ancestor. The artist is a man of the Born clan of the Gunwinggu.

THE KILLING OF LUMALUMA, 1988, by Djorlom Nalorlman

This picture shows the death of Lumaluma, an important Ancestor, who brought certain religious rituals to humankind. Painted on bark, in earth pigments on a plain yellow ochre ground, the picture shows the climax of the Lumaluma myth as a frieze to be read from right to left. Along the top, men of the Dua and Yiridja moieties (see below, right) are shown embarking in their canoes; on the left, they kill Lumaluma; his skeleton and those of two wives are shown bottom left. Various sacred objects are depicted to the right of the skeletons.

THE RAINBOW SNAKE

The Rainbow Snake, an important figure in Aboriginal mythology, is said to have emerged from a waterhole (much as Lumaluma came from the sea) during the Dreaming, the time of creation, which can still be accessed in religious ceremonies. As he travelled the country, his movements created the hills and valleys and particularly the waterways of the ancestral landscape, which are now among some of the holy places of Aboriginal culture. The great snake now arches above the land as the rainbow, and can be seen in the reflection of light in water – on the sea at night, in pools of water, or in the sparkling droplets of a waterfall – and in substances such as quartz crystal and pearl shell. It is from the Rainbow Snake that the Aboriginal shamans, or "men of high degree", obtain the powers that they manipulate through quartz crystals. The name of the Rainbow Snake varies. To the Gunwinggu people he is Ngalyod and features as several Rainbow Snakes, rather than a single creature. One story tells how the Gunwinggu killed a Ngalyod that had swallowed an entire community because it was infuriated by a child's constant crying.

Snake Dreaming, 1989, by Keith Kaapa Tjangala (b.1962)

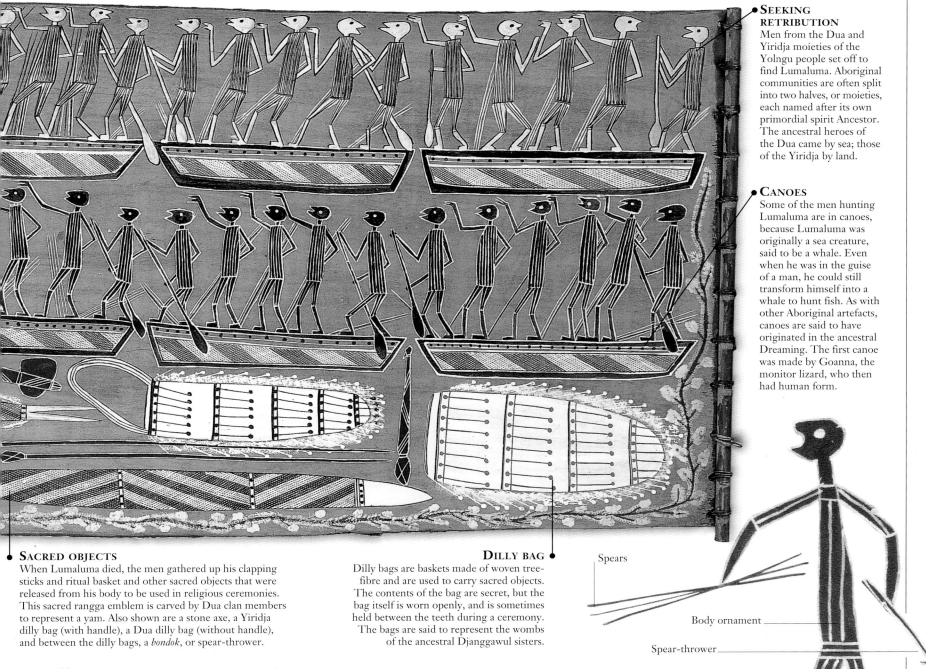

SEEKING RETRIBUTION
Men from the Dua and Yiridja moieties of the Yolngu people set off to find Lumaluma. Aboriginal communities are often split into two halves, or moieties, each named after its own primordial spirit Ancestor. The ancestral heroes of the Dua came by sea; those of the Yiridja by land.

CANOES
Some of the men hunting Lumaluma are in canoes, because Lumaluma was originally a sea creature, said to be a whale. Even when he was in the guise of a man, he could still transform himself into a whale to hunt fish. As with other Aboriginal artefacts, canoes are said to have originated in the ancestral Dreaming. The first canoe was made by Goanna, the monitor lizard, who then had human form.

SACRED OBJECTS
When Lumaluma died, the men gathered up his clapping sticks and ritual basket and other sacred objects that were released from his body to be used in religious ceremonies. This sacred rangga emblem is carved by Dua clan members to represent a yam. Also shown are a stone axe, a Yiridja dilly bag (with handle), a Dua dilly bag (without handle), and between the dilly bags, a *bondok*, or spear-thrower.

DILLY BAG
Dilly bags are baskets made of woven tree-fibre and are used to carry sacred objects. The contents of the bag are secret, but the bag itself is worn openly, and is sometimes held between the teeth during a ceremony. The bags are said to represent the wombs of the ancestral Djanggawul sisters.

Spears

Body ornament

Spear-thrower

"*Lumaluma stayed alive for a while. But then he was a very big man: he didn't die quickly. He gave them all that sacred ritual. He asked them, 'Did you get it all . . . ? Did you get it all, that sacred information I gave you? Tell me!' And those people, those real people, answered him, 'We have it all'.***"**
MANGURUG, SENIOR WOMAN OF THE GUNWINGGU PEOPLE

Yiridja Warrior
A warrior of the Yiridja moiety attacks Lumaluma. He carries his spears and his bondok, or spear-thrower, and his body is painted with traditional designs in yellow ochre. The Gunwinggu learned their ritual body designs from Lumaluma. The intricate patterns represent the ancestral landscape.

MAUI-OF-A-THOUSAND-TRICKS

IN POLYNESIAN MYTHOLOGY, the creation of the world is credited either to the sky-father Rangi and the earth-mother Papa or to the sea god Tangaroa (see right). However, it was the hero Maui (shown here), who fished up the islands of Polynesia from the bottom of the sea using a great fishing hook. His mother, often called Hina, which simply means "girl" or "young woman" (as, confusingly, are his wife, sister, and grandmother), became pregnant by mysterious means (usually by putting on a man's loincloth), and gave birth to Maui in the form of a foetus. He grew up an heroic figure, clever and strong, and earned himself the name of "Maui-of-a-thousand-tricks". He could do anything, except conquer death (see below) and improved the world for mankind: among other things, he pushed up the heavens, stole fire from the underworld for mankind, and snared the sun. He thought it moved across the sky too quickly and to slow it down, Maui lassooed it with a rope made of coconut fibre, but the sun burnt it to a cinder. So he made another rope from the sacred hair on his sister's head and waited by the eastern edge of the sea. At dawn he flung his rope and captured the sun by the throat. And although it begged and pleaded, Maui would not let it go until it had agreed to give long days in summer and short days in winter.

> *From the conception*
> *the increase,*
> *From the increase*
> *the thought,*
> *From the thought*
> *the remembrance,*
> *From the remembrance*
> *the consciousness,*
> *From the consciousness*
> *the desire.*

MAORI CREATION CHANT

HORRIFIED at the sight of his mother's first grey hairs, Maui tried to conquer death by forcing himself upon the sleeping goddess of death, Hine-nui-te-po. But the birds in the trees found the sight so funny that they laughed and woke the goddess, who crushed Maui to death.

SHELL-BORN GOD
Tangaroa was the first god. He lived in a shell that was round like an egg. Nothing existed but the shell and the void. Finally Tangaroa broke his shell and called out, "Who's there?" But there was nothing there.

MAKER OF ALL THINGS
As Tangaroa was born into emptiness, he made the world from both his shell and his own body. The top half of the shell became the sky, and the bottom the rock and sand. His backbone made a mountain range, his entrails made the clouds, his flesh made the earth. Even his fingernails and toenails made the scales and shells of the fish in the sea. He is often described as a god of the sea.

FATHER OF THE GODS
Tangaroa created a family of gods from within himself. Here, the newborn gods crawl over his body.

Tangaroa Gives Birth to the Gods
This wooden statue of Tangaroa (A'a) shows him giving birth to the gods who crawl all over his body. There is an opening at the back of this statue and inside there is a loose group of more god figures; a woman's womb was compared to the shell of Tangaroa.

A MORE COMMON CREATION MYTH than the Tangaroa story is that the sky, Rangi, and the earth, Papa, lay together to create the gods. They were then separated by their son and Tangaroa's brother. In Maori myth this son is called Tane (see box), although his name varies. Some Polynesian creation chants are abstract and philosophical; others so detailed in their account of the creation that they even celebrate the birth of the dust in the air from the union of "Small thing" and "Imperceptible thing".

TOP-KNOT
Many Polynesians call Maui by the name Maui-tikitiki-a-Taranga. This is a reference to the myth in which his mother, here named Taranga, cradled his premature foetus in the top-knot of her hair, and sent it out to sea. As only men wear the top-knot, and other sources name Maui's father as Ataranga, the mystery of Maui's birth deepens.

TATTOOS
Maui's tattoos are typical of Polynesian culture. A version of the widespread Maui legends from Manihiki says that his father was called Manu ahi whare and his mother was Tongo i whare, and they were the offspring of the god Tangaroa-of-the-tattoed-face. In Raratonga, Maui was said to be Tangaroa's son.

THE FOUNDING OF EASTER ISLAND

Mysterious stone heads on the slopes of Easter Island

Easter Island, the most secluded Polynesian island, is thought to be the mythical navel of the world. It was discovered, according to local lore, as the result of a dream. Faraway in the west, a tattooist called Haumaka dreamt that he went across the sea to a land with beaches of fair white sand. He told his master Hotu matua (one of two men contending for the throne in their land) who sent six men in search of it. These men set off across the water, taking with them breadfruit, yams, coconuts, and other things to plant and, after a long journey, came to Easter Island, an open land of grasses that waved like the sea. They explored the land but rejected it as uninhabitable because there was no fresh water. But as they came back to the beach, they saw two canoes – one belonging to Hotu matua, the other to Tu'u ko ihu, the priest. Hotu matua landed first, and his son Tu'u ma heke was born on the beach. The priest cut the child's navel cord with his teeth, put the cord in a gourd, and sent it out to sea. Then the people came ashore – in their hundreds – to settle the new land with Hotu Matua as king.

TANE, THE FOREST GOD

Tane, the forest god, was born with his brothers Rongo, the god of cultivated plants; Tangaroa, the god of fish and reptiles; Haumia, the god of wild plants; Tu, the war god; and Tawhiri, the storm god, from the union of Rangi and Papa, the sky and the earth. But so closely did Rangi and Papa cling to each other that the gods could not leave the earth womb and Tane had to wrench his parents apart. Although generally a peaceful god, Tane was in constant conflict with his brother Tangaroa, the sea god, because he gave human beings the wood and plant fibre to make equipment for fishing. Tane's name means "Man" and he is credited with a key role in the creation of human beings and their mortality. It is said that he created his own wife, Hine-hau-one, out of sand, and breathed life into her nostrils. Later he married their daughter, Hine-titama, Hina-the-dawn-maiden, but when she learned that he was also her father, she fled from him and became Hine-nui-te-po, the death goddess. Before this event death did not exist.

MAUI HAULS UP THE ISLANDS

This carving shows the myth in which Maui hauls up the islands of Polynesia (shown here as a fish). The carving is probably a house post, a structure holding up the walls and ceiling which would be made from woven grasses, and materials. It shows Maui with three-fingers. The first carving with this typical Maori three-fingered motif was said to have been brought from Tangaroa's house on the floor of the ocean, by an ancestor called Mutu who had a missing finger.

WATCHING EYES

The eyes on this carving represent Koururu the owl, who was sacrificed by the agriculture god Rongo (Hawaiian Lono) and placed under the far wall of his house. Now Koururu's eyes glare protectively from many house carvings.

FISH HOOK

The name of Maui's fish-hook, Manai-a-ka-lani, means "Come-from-the-heavens". It was given to him by his mother, Hina, and is a magic fish-hook that once belonged to Kuula, the god of fishing.

FISHING UP THE ISLANDS

Maui is shown in the act of fishing up the islands of Polynesia. As he hauled on the line, he teased his brothers by asking them to guess what kind of fish he had caught.

GREAT FISH

Maui's catch, which is really land from below the sea, is described as various kinds of fish – sometimes an *ulua*, sometimes a *baha kahaki*. Either way, it was too heavy for Maui's fragile fishing line, and he could not raise it entirely from the sea. Hence there are many islands, rather than one landmass, because the fish's body broke through the water in several places but could not be hauled up completely.

THE CHURNING OF THE OCEAN

ONE DAY, THE INDIAN GODS gathered on Mount Meru, the navel of the world, to discuss how to gain the *amrita*, or elixir of immortality, which was hidden deep in the ocean. At the god Vishnu's suggestion (see pp.110–11), they decided to try to churn it out, using Vasuki the snake as a rope, and Mount Mandara, set on top of a giant tortoise, as a paddle. The Devas, the gods friendly to humankind, seized Vasuki at one end, and the Asuras (or anti-gods) seized him at the other. As each side pulled, the paddle turned this way and that, churning the ocean, which soon became milky and turned into butter. The gods continued churning and gradually "fourteen precious things" came forth, including the sun, the moon, Vishnu's wife Lakshmi, and finally, Dhanvantari, the god's physician, carrying the *amrita*. The Devas and the Asuras clamoured to taste it but Vishnu tricked the Asuras out of drinking it, and only Rahu, "the grasper", a monstrous demon, had a sip. To prevent the whole of him from achieving immortality Vishnu cut off his head. This remained immortal and declared war on the moon god, Soma, alternately swallowing and regurgitating him, in an attempt to find more of the immortal elixir (also called soma).

COSMIC OCEAN
In the beginning, according to the holy book *Rig Veda*, there was neither Being nor non-Being, just "darkness swathed in darkness". This is usually described as a primal ocean, on which the world egg floated.

LAKSHMI
Lakshmi, sitting near a conch shell, a symbol of Vishnu, has already been pulled from the ocean. The female in front of her is busy pulling out Chandra the moon (who is also called Soma).

DURGA AND THE BUFFALO

This Indian ivory shows Durga killing the buffalo demon.

Durga, the warrior goddess, is a form of the Indian mother goddess, Mahadevi. Other forms include gentle Parvati, wife of Shiva (see pp.112–13). Durga was created by the gods when they were deposed by the Asuras from their home on Mount Meru. Arising from the flames of their fury, she rode into battle on a lion, killing every demon in her path, until she faced their leader, Mahisha, the demon buffalo. After a terrible fight, Durga defeated him and, her foot on his neck, forced the spirit from his mouth, and cut off his head. As he died, all the gods, and all the creatures in the world shouted "Victory!", and a great lamentation arose from the demon hordes.

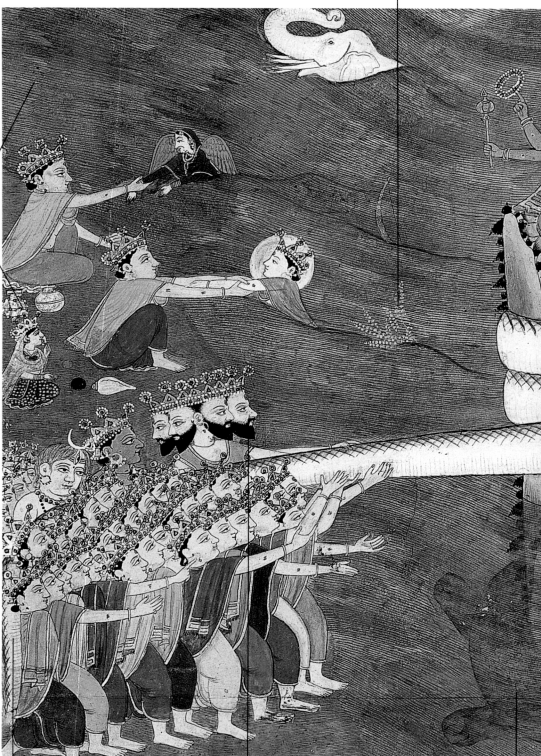

GIFTS OF THE OCEAN
The ocean yielded many gifts including the sacred parijati tree, which perfumed the whole world with its blossoms, and Airavata, the colossal white elephant (on the left), the mount of the god Indra.

DEVAS
The Devas, holding onto the tail of the snake Vasuki, are the gods. There are usually said to be 33 of them. Their home is on Mount Meru.

BRAHMA
Brahma, one of the major gods, has four heads. He used to have five, but Shiva cut one of them off when Brahma claimed to be his superior.

TORTOISE
Vishnu took the form of the tortoise Kurma to help the gods retrieve lost treasures from the ocean; hence he is present at both the top and the bottom of the churning stick. Brahma, too, took tortoise shape to make the world. The name of Kasyapa, the father of the Asuras, also means "tortoise". In Hindu mythology, the world rests on a giant tortoise.

Vishnu

Vishnu, seen here directing the churning of the ocean, is recognizable by his four hands, holding his **kaumodaki**, *or mace, his* **sudarshana**, *or discus, his* **padma**, *or lotus, and his* **shankha**, *or conch. His wife Lakshmi, is the goddess of good fortune. Also known as Padma, the lotus, she is one of the beings born from the churning of the ocean. Others include Chandra, the moon god, and Varuni, the goddess of wine.*

Discus

Lotus

Golden mace

Conch

CYCLES OF CREATION

There are many Hindu creation myths, the earliest ones involving an act of incest between father and daughter to produce, in one way or another, all living things. A later myth involves the god Brahma who, from a union with his daughter Vak, "the word", creates the first man, Manu (see p.110). Brahma is responsible, every *kalpa*, or 4,320,000,000 human years, for creating the world. Each *kalpa* is a day and night of Brahma; in the day, Brahma creates the universe but at night it reverts to chaos. At night Vishnu sleeps on the snake Ananta, on the cosmic ocean. At dawn, a lotus grows out of his navel, which contains Brahma, who creates the world anew.

ONE THOUSAND MOUTHS

Even the endless energy of the Asuras was sapped by the heat and flames issuing from Vasuki's 1,000 mouths. Whenever one of them yawns, it causes an earthquake. At the end of the world, the snake will belch forth the poison that will burn up creation.

ASURAS

The anti-gods known as Asuras were the enemies of the gods, or Devas. The two groups are locked in constant warfare, but neither side can triumph. "Asura" originally meant "god", but mutated to mean demon.

IN THE HOLY BOOK, *Rig Veda*, it is said of amrita (or soma), **"We have drunk soma, we have become immortal, we have entered into the light, we have known the gods."** Soma was a plant-based hallucinogen.

WORLD SNAKE

The serpent Vasuki, with which the gods churned the ocean, is the king of all the serpents or Nagas. He is also known as Shesha and Ananta. He lives in the primal ocean, wrapped around the earth, and serves as a bed for the god Vishnu.

THE SUN

Uccaihsravas, the white horse of the sun, was born from the ocean of milk.

PHYSICIAN OF THE GODS

Dhanvantari, the divine physician, is the last to be born from the ocean, bearing a jar of amrita, one of the precious things that for some reason had not been automatically recreated at the beginning of the new age.

Cheated Demons

The Devas persuaded the Asuras to help them churn by the ocean by promising that they too would share in the elixir of life – but this was a trick, and only one of the Asuras, Rahu, got so much as a sip. For this, Vishnu sliced off his head with his discus.

UPTURNED MOUNTAIN

The gods uprooted Mount Mandara to use as their churning stick. Afterwards, when the Devas had beaten the enraged Asuras in battle, the gods replaced the mountain in the Himalayas.

SACRED COW

Surabhi, the cow of plenty, is the mother of all cattle, which are sacred to Hindus. When Purusha, the first being, who is often identified with Brahma, took the shapes of all the animals to bring them into being, he first became a bull and a cow.

Dhanvantari appears from the ocean

The Asura Rahu, hauls Dhanvantari, the physician of the gods, from the ocean.

THE AVATARS OF VISHNU

VISHNU IS ONE OF THREE important Indian gods, of which the other two are Brahma and Shiva. Each has a role: Vishnu is the protector and restorer of the world, Brahma the creator, and Shiva the destroyer. Confusingly, although Brahma created the world, both he and Shiva were born from Vishnu, Brahma emerging from Vishnu's navel, and Shiva springing from his forehead. Vishnu is also called the "wide-strider" because he can cross the whole world in three strides. There are endless stories about Vishnu, of which the most important relate to his incarnations, or *avatars*, in which he has come to earth, in animal or human form, to help humankind. In theory, there have been nine *avatars* and a tenth is yet to come, although many stories exist that detail other appearances. Lakshmi, Vishnu's wife, has always accompanied him in his incarnations – for example, as Prince Rama's wife Sita (see p.114–15), or as Krishna's lover Radha, and his wife, Rukmini. That Lakshmi can be incarnated twice in the Krishna story and that other *avatar* stories exist is indicative of the way in which myths grow, appropriating elements from different sources at different times, often resulting in a varying versions of a common theme.

VISHNU AND LAKSHMI

Vishnu and Lakshmi are shown riding the sacred bird Garuda, who is linked with fire and the sun, up to their heaven of love. The marital devotion of Vishnu and Lakshmi extends through all of Vishnu's incarnations. Lakshmi was born from the ocean at the churning of the sea of milk (see pp.108–9), which provides her with a garland of fresh flowers every day. One of her names, Padma, the lotus, identifies her with the perfection of this flower. The holy river Ganges is at her service, and two elephants shower her with its water when she bathes. Also known as Shri, prosperity, Lakshmi is the goddess of good fortune, and also of growth and fruitfulness.

This illumination dating from 1770 shows Vishnu and Lakshmi on Vishnu's vehicle Garuda.

VARAHA, THE WILD BOAR
In his third incarnation as Varaha the wild boar, Vishnu rescued the world after it had been swamped by the flood and taken over by the demon Hiranyaksha. Varaha slew the demon and raised the earth up again with his tusk.

KURMA, THE TORTOISE
Kurma the tortoise, Vishnu's second *avatar*, held up Mt Meru and helped the gods reclaim 14 treasures from the sea of milk (see pp.108-9).

VAMANA, THE DWARF
Vishnu's fifth *avatar*, Vamana the dwarf, was born to curb the power of another demon king, Bali. When he begged Bali for only as much land as he could cover in three strides, the king laughed and granted his wish. He was horrified when Vamana covered the whole world, leaving Bali only the kingdom of Patala, underneath the earth.

MATSYA, THE FISH
Vishnu's first *avatar* was Matsya the fish, a form he took to protect Manu, the first man, from the deluge. When Manu found the tiny fish, it told him, "Look after me, and I will look after you." But then the fish grew too large, so Manu released it into the sea. The fish warned him that there was going to be a flood, and told him to build an ark. When the flood came, the fish grew a horn, to which Manu fastened his ship, using Ananta, the world snake, as the rope, and the fish towed him to safety.

NARASIMHA, THE MAN-LION
Once, a demon king called Hiranya-Kashipu ruled the world. He was cruel and wicked, and invulnerable to men, animals or gods, inside or outside his house, by day or by night. One day, as a joke, Hiranya-Kashipu struck a pillar in his palace, and asked if Vishnu was in there. To his amazement, Vishnu emerged, roaring, as a ferocious man-lion (his fourth *avatar*), and tore the demon to pieces at twilight on the veranda of the palace.

KRISHNA

Krishna, the eighth *avatar*, is pre-eminently Vishnu in his role as lover. He loved Radha and the story of their love is a favourite theme in Indian art and literature. However, Krishna did go to war and the philosophical conversation he had with Arjuna, his charioteer, became the *Bhagavad Gita*, one of Hinduism's holy books.

KALKIN, THE WHITE HORSE

At the end of this era of the world, when humankind has become totally degenerate, Vishnu will come in his tenth incarnation, riding a white horse and wielding a flaming sword to destroy the wicked and renew the world.

The Buddha

The Buddha, the ninth avatar shown here with the attributes of Vishnu, was an historical figure. He taught humankind how to free itself of desire, and the illusion of this world, and its endless reincarnations. The Buddha's previous incarnations are recounted in the Jataka Tales.

Vishnu's discus, symbol of the mind and the sun

Vishnu's mace, associated with the power of the mind

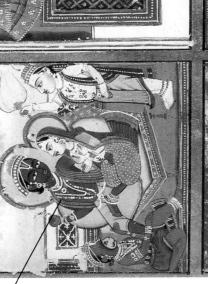

RAMA, THE GENTLE

As Rama, his seventh *avatar*, Vishnu was born to slay the demon Ravana. King Dasharatha prayed for a son, and Vishnu gave him a bowl of divine nectar to share between his three wives.

As a result, four sons were born: Rama, who received half the divine essence, Bharata, who received a quarter, and Lakshmana and Satrughna, who received an eighth each. Therefore, all four brothers shared in Vishnu's divine nature.

PARASHU-RAMA, THE AXEMAN

In this sixth incarnation, Vishnu was born into the Brahman caste, or class, of scholars. At this time, the warrior caste, the Kshatriya, dominated the world, but the gods thought it better that the Brahmans should rule. So Parashu-Rama (who was also a warrior) destroyed the warriors with his axe, and slew their 1,000-armed king, Kartavirya.

THE AVATARS OF VISHNU

This 18th-century picture from Rajasthan in northern India, shows the ten official avatars of Vishnu. In the centre Vishnu is shown as Krishna, accompanied by his lover Radha and two cowgirls. The other nine incarnations – five human, four animal, and one composite – run around the edge.

Krishna and the Gopis

Krishna is shown playing his flute, attended by Radha, his favourite gopi, one of the young women of his adoptive tribe who were all in love with him. The stories of Krishna are so extensive that, like Rama, he can be considered as a god in his own right, although he is a manifestation of Vishnu. His name means "black" and, with his flute, may suggest a tribal origin for this avatar.

THE GOD KRISHNA

During her eighth pregnancy, Krishna's mother Devaki was imprisoned by her evil brother King Kamsa because it was prophesied that her eighth child would kill him. But Devaki smuggled out the baby, Krishna, and he was placed in a family of cowherds. Although he was evidently a god (his mother saw the universe in his mouth and, as a baby, he killed the ogress Putana, who fed him poisoned milk), Krishna was playful, and many stories tell how he stole butter and teased the girls. With Balarama, his brother, he has many adventures, killing King Kamsa and winning his bride, Rukmini. Although it is said that Vishnu put one black and one white hair from his head in Devaki's womb to create the brothers, Balarama is clearly an *avatar* of Ananta, the world serpent, for the snake comes out of his mouth when he dies. Krishna himself is killed after a long life by a hunter, who shoots him by accident in the sole of his foot, his only vulnerable spot.

Radha

Krishna

SHIVA AND HIS FAMILY

THE GOD SHIVA LIVED ON MOUNT KAILASA with his wife, the gentle goddess Parvati, and his two sons Skanda (or Kartikeya) and Ganesh. Skanda, his oldest son, was originally six children created by Shiva alone, but one day, Parvati cuddled the children together too much and they merged into a single body with six heads. Skanda, who was the Hindu god of war, grew into a handsome young man, quite the opposite of his fat little brother, the elephant-headed Ganesh. As soon as he was old enough, he killed the demon Taraka who had been oppressing the gods. Ganesh, on the other hand, was born from the dirt Parvati had washed off in her bath. Stories vary as to how he acquired his elephant head: in one Parvati tells him to stop anyone from disturbing her in her bath, and when he refuses to let Shiva in, Shiva burns off his head with his third eye; in another, Shiva, who has been away, does not recognize his son and sears off his head thinking he is paying court to Parvati; yet another tells how the planet Saturn, while babysitting Ganesh, forgets the power of his glance, and burns off his head by accident. In each story, Ganesh's human head is replaced with that of an elephant.

AGNI, GOD OF FIRE

The fire god Agni, a god of sacrifice, is born anew whenever a fire is lit. One of the chief Vedic (early Indian) gods, his role gradually diminished, as many of his attributes were taken over by either Shiva or Skanda (with whom Agni was briefly and agonizingly pregnant during Skanda's highly complicated conception and gestation). While Shiva's fire will devour the world at doomsday, Agni's both consumes and purifies the dirt and sin of this world; for this reason Hindus burn the bodies of their dead. The purifying power of Agni's fire was granted him by the sage Bhrigu. Bhrigu abducted another man's wife, and the injured husband asked Agni, who knew all homes, where she was to be found. Agni told him, and Bhrigu was so angry that he cursed Agni to eat everything in his path, whether pure or impure. Agni argued that as a god he had to tell the truth, so Bhrigu granted him the power to purify everything he burnt. Agni has two heads, a fire-red body, and seven tongues that greedily lick up the butter used in sacrifices.

Dangerous Child
Parvati cradles Skanda, the god of war, who later restored peace to heaven and earth after he defeated the demon Taraka. He is identified with the planet Mars.

PEACOCK
The peacock is the vehicle of Skanda, the baby on Parvati's lap.

PARVATI, SHIVA'S WIFE
Parvati is the daughter of the Himalaya mountain himself. Like Durga and Lakshmi (see p.108), she is an aspect of the great mother goddess, Mahadevi.

NANDI THE BULL
Nandi, Shiva's milk-white bull, is the guardian of all four-legged creatures. Rudra, Shiva's name in the earliest Hindu holy books, was the ruler of the beasts.

GANESH
Ganesh, the remover of obstacles, must be propitiated at the start of any enterprise. He is also a god of wisdom and learning, and was the scribe of the holy book, the *Mahabharata*, using one of his tusks as a pen.

CRESCENT MOON
Shiva wears the moon of wisdom in his hair.

THIRD EYE
The third eye on Shiva's forehead blazes with the fire of ten million suns, and can consume any creature with flame. Shiva was so angry when Kama, the god of love, pierced him with desire for Parvati while he was meditating, that he opened his eye and reduced him to ash. So Kama is now *ananga*, "bodiless".

SHIVA
Shiva wears a leopard (often tiger) skin to represent his mastery over feelings of aggression and greed. Vasuki, the cobra (see p.109), is wrapped around his neck.

GANESH'S STEED
Ganesh's companion and steed is a rat. But Ganesh is lazy, and will not travel unnecessarily. Once he made a bet with Skanda that the first to travel round the world should win Siddhi (success) and Buddhi (intelligence), as their brides. A man of action, Skanda, made the long journey, but Ganesh simply stayed at home and read; when Skanda returned, Ganesh was waiting to tell him all the wonders of the world, and so won the bet.

LORD OF THE DANCE

Shiva, called "the destroyer", is shown as a family man; as a holy man with matted hair and an ash-smeared body; as Bhuteswara, lord of the ghosts, wearing a skull necklace; and as here, as lord of the Tandava, the universal dance in which he dances the creation and destruction of the world, trampling the dwarf of human ignorance. By the ferocious concentration of this dance, Shiva reveals the cosmic truth. He dances in a circle of flames, cupping in one hand the flame of destruction, and in another the drum of creation. The holy men who saw him dancing hailed him thus: "We behold you dancing, source of the world, lodged in our own hearts! By you does this wheel of Brahma turn. You, sole guardian of the world, are filled with Maya. We take refuge in you! We adore you! You are the soul of Yoga, the master of consciousness who dances the divine dance!"

This 11th-century bronze shows Shiva as Lord of the Dance.

TIGER OF SHIVA

As Rudra, "the howler", Shiva is revered as lord of the beasts. He is often shown wearing a tiger skin and is god of the forest and of hunting.

MOUNT KAILASA

Mount Kailasa means "the Silver Mountain". From it, the great river Brahmaputra springs, flowing through Tibet before turning south to join the holy Ganges in Bengal and Bangladesh.

SHIVA AND HIS FAMILY ON MOUNT KAILASA

Shiva and his family are shown here on Mount Kailasa with a deputation of gods and holy men at the base of the mountain. They may be worshipping the holy family or, despite the presence of Skanda, they may be asking Shiva to help them destroy the demon Taraka – for which purpose Skanda was born.

BAND OF WORSHIPPERS

Rishis, Brahmin priests, gather at the bottom of Mount Kailasa to listen to Shiva's teachings.

> The brahmins saw Rudra (Shiva) dancing in the sky, that supreme liberator who instantly releases people from their ignorance, who is kind and benevolent to his devotees.
>
> KURMA PURANA

SURYA

Surya is the sun god and is usually seen travelling across the sky in a chariot drawn by seven mares.

CHANDRA

Chandra, or Soma, the moon god, married 27 sisters, but then preferred his first wife. His wives then complained to their father, who cursed Chandra with leprosy. Horrified, they begged their father to lift the curse, but he could only soften the blow. Thus, Chandra, the moon, gradually becomes grey-skinned, and then recovers his original silver colour in an endless cycle.

> Great god, supreme lord, what are you doing inside there? All of us, the gods, have come to you for refuge, for we are tortured by Taraka; protect us.
>
> SHIVA PURANA

BRAHMA

Brahma, the creator, made the sun and the moon and placed them in the sky, and created Agni (fire), Vayu (wind), and Varuna (water).

VISHNU

Vishnu, the preserver, led the gods to petition Shiva to forsake loveplay with Parvati and help them slay the demon Taraka; Skanda was born to vanquish the demon.

Hanuman, the Monkey God

Standing aside from the other gods is Hanuman, the monkey god, the general of Rama in the Ramayana (see pp.114–15). He was the son of the wind god Vayu, was capable of changing shape, and was immensely strong. He is regarded as the epitome of loyalty.

Hanuman, the loyal monkey general

RAMA AND SITA

KING DASHARATHA OF AYODYA IN INDIA was childless and made a special sacrifice to the gods, hoping that they would give him sons. Meanwhile, the gods begged their lord Brahma to help them against Ravana, the demon king. So Brahma asked the god Vishnu to vanquish the demon. Vishnu agreed and was born, in his seventh incarnation, as Rama and his three brothers Bharata, Lakshmana, and Shatrughna. Unaware of their divinity, the brothers grew up as the sons of King Dasharatha and his three wives and married. Rama married Sita, an incarnation of Vishnu's wife Lakshmi, and was made his father's heir. However, owing to the intrigues of one of his father's wives, he left the city with Sita and Lakshmana, to live in the forest. There, they lived a quiet life for ten years, until one day Ravana tricked the brothers into leaving Sita alone, and abducted her. Rama and Lakshmana, helped by Hanuman, general to the monkey king Sugriva, searched everywhere until Hanuman finally found her, shut up on the island of Lanka. With an army of monkeys and bears, Rama killed Ravana in a huge battle, was reunited with Sita, and returned to Ayodya where he became king and ruled for 11,000 years.

FOREST EXILE
Rama was exiled to the forest for 14 years because his step-brother Bharata's mother wanted her son to succeed to the throne. King Dasharatha agreed because she had once saved his life and he had promised to grant her two requests. Grief-stricken, he died, and Bharata, horrified by his mother's actions, begged Rama to return. But he refused, so Bharata put Rama's golden sandals in charge, venerating them until Rama returned.

LAKSHMANA
Lakshmana, whose name means "lucky-omened", had one eighth of Vishnu's divine essence and was always at Rama's side. He even married Sita's sister, Urmila.

SITA
The name Sita means "furrow". When her father King Janaka of Mithila was ploughing his fields, she sprang up from a furrow, and he adopted her as his daughter.

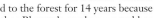

Journey Through the Sky
As Sita was carried through the sky by Ravana, she saw five monkeys sitting on a mountain. She cast down her jewels and her gold veil, in the hope that this would help Rama to find her.

SCENES FROM THE RAMAYANA
This 19th-century illustration shows scenes from the **Ramayana,** *the story of Rama's life. It shows the episode in which Rama hunts a magical deer, leaving Sita in the care of Lakshmana. However, the demon Ravana tricks Lakshmana into leaving Sita, then whisks her off, fighting any creature that tries to stop him.*

SILENT WITNESSES
As Sita was abducted, she called to the forest and the trees to bear witness to Rama that she had been stolen away against her will.

THE DEMON RAVANA
Ravana specialized in ravishing the wives of other people. To abduct Sita, he disguised himself as a wandering yogi, or holy man. When he asked her to go with him, she rejected him utterly, whereupon he revealed himself in his grotesque true form, and kidnapped her.

FIVE MONKEYS
These monkeys – Sugriva, the exiled monkey king, and his generals – saw Sita and Ravana fly overhead. Later, they met Rama, who helped Sugriva vanquish his usurper brother Valin, and in return, they helped Rama to search for Sita. Hanuman finally tracked her down.

THE SIEGE OF LANKA

At the siege of Lanka, Rama and his monkey army, led by Hanuman, fought the *rakshasas*, or demons, led by Ravana. These included such terrible adversaries as Lightning-Tongue, Smoke-Eye, Death-to-Men, and Big-Belly. All of these were vanquished in turn, but Rama could not conquer Ravana himself until he had worshipped the sun, and borrowed the chariot and charioteer of the sky god Indra. With this divine aid, Rama pursued his enemy, though every time he cut off one of Ravana's ten heads, another grew in its place. Finally, he shot the demon with an arrow forged by Brahma – it flew like the wind, struck like the sun, passed through Ravana, cleaned itself in the sea, and returned to Rama's quiver. The gods rejoiced, and the sun shone down on the field of battle.

This 19th-century illustration shows the cross-fire between Ravana and Rama during the battle of Lanka.

A SAD END

Rama rejected Sita after he rescued her because he believed she was defiled. Sita, unable to bear the slander, wanted to die but the gods would not allow it. They testified to her purity and told Rama he was an *avatar* of Vishnu (see pp.110–11). Rama and Sita lived happily for 10,000 years until Rama, told that his subjects still considered Sita impure, sent her into exile where she gave birth to his twin sons. Years later, Rama saw his sons and asked Sita to come back. But her heart was broken and she sank into the earth. Rama ruled sadly for another 1,000 years before he also returned to the gods. In the Thai version, Sita reappears from the underworld to be Rama's wife once more.

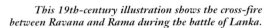

● RAMA, AVATAR OF VISHNU
Rama's blue skin marks him as an *avatar* of Vishnu. Rama, or Rama-Chandra, is "moon Rama" or "gentle Rama", in contrast to Vishnu's previous *avatar*, the warrior Parashu-Rama. Rama shares his divine essence with his brothers, though he, with half of Vishnu's divinity, has the chief role.

Rama killed the magical deer with an arrow

● IN PURSUIT OF RAMA
Lakshmana, tricked by Ravana into imagining he heard Rama crying for help, left Sita (at her insistence) and ran to his brother's aid.

● CAPTIVE PRINCESS
Sita, who refused to yield to Ravana, was taken to the golden city on the island of Lanka. When Hanuman found her there – having changed shape and leapt across the sea in a single bound – he showed her Rama's ring as a token and promised to return. As he left he was caught, but escaped and managed to set fire to the city.

● JATAYU
Jatayu, king of the vultures and son of the legendary bird Garuda, attacks and wounds Ravana with his beak. But Ravana killed him and Jatayu's soul went up to Heaven at the request of Rama.

Demon in Disguise
The golden deer was a demon in disguise called Maricha, who had been asked by Ravana to entice Rama and his brother away leaving Sita defenceless. Ravana was avenging his sister Surpanakha whom Rama had rejected. In a fit of jealousy she had attacked Sita, and had her nose and ears cut off by Lakshmana.

THE TEN SUNS OF HEAVEN

IN THE BEGINNING, there were ten suns, the sons of Di Jun, Chinese Emperor of the Eastern Heavens, and his wife Xi He, goddess of the sun. They lived in a giant mulberry tree that grew up from the waters of the Heaven Valley – waters that were always boiling hot because the suns all bathed there. Each morning, the suns took it in turns to shine in the sky, leaving the others resting in the tree. But one day, bored with their orderly life, they all rushed up into the sky at once and ran round wildly having fun. Their tenfold strength began to scorch the earth but when their parents told them to behave and come down they would not listen. So Di Jun sent his archer, Hou Yi, to teach his sons a lesson. Yi then shot down nine of the ten suns. Di Jun was devastated and he stripped Yi and his wife Chang E of their immortality and banished them from heaven.

Gates of heaven

Jade symbol of status and moral rectitude

Lady Dai

Upturned bell

Altar

THE FUNERAL BANNER OF LADY DAI
China, second century BC
This funeral banner divides into four sections. The top rectangle depicts deities in heaven. The section below, from the heavenly gates to Lady Dai, shows how mortals ascend to heaven to become immortals. The third section, below the upturned bell, shows the mourning people who have survived the deceased, and the fourth, below the altars full of food, is a reproduction of the afterlife.

HARE IN THE MOON
When Chang E arrived in the moon, she found she was not alone. Her companion in the moon is a hare, which sits beneath a cassia tree (the tree of immortality) pounding herbs in a mortar to make the elixir of life. An old man is said also to live in the moon; he spends his time trying, in vain, to chop down the cassia tree.

TURNED INTO A TOAD
When Chang E gulped down the elixir that Hou Yi had won from the Queen Mother of the West, she began to float up to the moon. As she ascended, she tried to call out, but found she could only croak. To her horror, although she had indeed become immortal, she had also been turned into a toad.

HEAVENLY GATE
The heavenly gates are guarded by two soldiers. Above them, a bell is rung by two heavenly beasts, to report that the soul of the deceased is passing through.

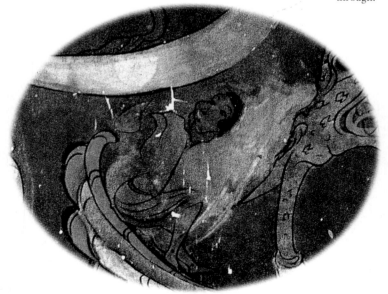

Chang E Flees to the Moon
Here, Chang E, Hou Yi's wife who lost her immortality when her husband did, travels up to heaven. After his disgrace, Hou Yi travelled to the Kun Lun Mountains to bring back a potion of immortality. There was enough for one person to return to heaven and live as an immortal, or for two to become immortal. Hou Yi had planned to share it with Chang E, but she stole all of it and floated into the sky to live in the temple of the moon.

PAN GU CREATES THE WORLD

In the beginning, the universe was contained within an egg, inside which the vital forces of *yin* (dark, female, and cool) and *yang* (light, male, and hot) interacted with each other. Inside the egg, Pan Gu, formed from these forces, slept for 18,000 years. When he awoke, he stretched and broke the egg. The heavier elements inside the egg sank to form the earth, and the lighter ones floated to form the sky. Between the earth and the sky was Pan Gu. Every day, for another 18,000 years, the earth and sky separated a little more, and every day Pan Gu grew at the same rate so that he always filled the space in between. At last the earth and sky reached their final positions, and exhausted, Pan Gu lay down to rest. But he was so worn out that he died. His torso and limbs became the mountains. His eyes became the sun and moon, his flesh the land, his hair the trees and plants, and his tears the rivers and seas. His breath became the wind, and his voice the thunder and lightning. Finally, Pan Gu's fleas became humankind.

Pan Gu holds the Yin-Yang symbol.

NÜ WA

The goddess Nü Wa was the first god to appear after Pan Gu created the world (see right). She had the body of a snake and could change shape 70 times a day. She moulded the first people from mud, taught them to have children, and became the goddess of marriage. On either side of her are cranes – symbols of longevity. Below them are heavenly dragons.

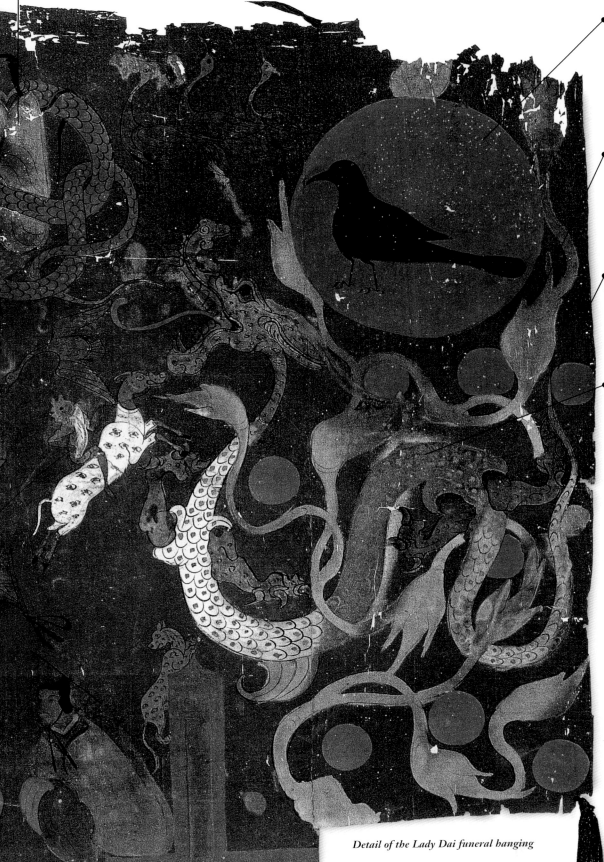

Detail of the Lady Dai funeral hanging

THE LEGEND OF HOU YI AND THE TEN SUNS

When the ten suns (see p.116) refused to go home, their father gave Hou Yi a new red bow and a quiver of ten white arrows and told him to "threaten my sons with this bow". But Yi became so angry at the sight of the dead and dying burnt people on earth that he shot first one, then another eight suns from the sky. When they landed, the people saw golden, three-legged crows (shown here with two legs), pierced with an arrow. Hou Yi was so angry that he had to be reminded to leave one sun in the sky.

FUSANG TREE

The ten suns lived in the legendary Fusang Tree in Tang Gu, a place beyond the eastern Sea. It had nine branches up its trunk and a special branch at the top. Each day, one of the suns would set off from this branch in a chariot pulled by six dragons, accompanied for a short distance by his mother. The tree features in many ancient myths, often relating to the sunrise.

CHILDREN OF THE EMPEROR OF THE EASTERN HEAVENS

The Emperor of the Eastern Heavens had ten children, each one a golden sun. Every day they took turns to go out and shine on the earth, having first washed themselves in the boiling sea. Every night their mother collected them and brought them home.

DRAGONS

Dragons are synonymous with serpents in Chinese mythology and represent wisdom, benevolent heavenly power, and the fertilizing earth currents. There are four dragon kings who live in the clouds and give out rain when needed. Local dragon-kings preside over streams, rivers, and wells. The dragons shown here are those that draw the moon and the sun across the sky.

CREATION MYTHS OF NÜ WA

Human beings were created by the goddess Nü Wa, either out of mud and water, or with her brother Fu Xi. Wanting the gods' approval, she and Fu Xi lit two bonfires and said, "If Heaven wants us to marry, may the smoke of the two fires mingle; if not, may it drift in separate ways". It mingled, so they married; but Nü Wa was shy and covered her face with a fan – as brides still do today. Nü Wa felt protective towards humanity. When Gong Gong, the Water God, made holes in the sky during a battle with Zhu Rong, the Fire God, and the whole world was unbalanced and ravaged by fire and flood, Nü Wa melted stones to plug the gap and make the sky as good as new. And, to make it extra safe, she killed a giant turtle and used its four legs as pillars to support the four corners of heaven.

THE EIGHT IMMORTALS

THE TAOISTS VENERATE EIGHT IMMORTALS who, through piety and virtue, have achieved eternal life. They have nothing in common apart from their immortality, and lived at different times in history, but they are usually depicted in a group, although myths and folktales attach to each of them individually. They live with the gods in the Kun Lun Mountains at the centre of the earth. Here, they feast and amuse themselves in the gardens of the Jade Emperor, the supreme ruler of heaven, where the magical peach-tree of immortality grows. Every 1,000 years, they are invited, together with the gods, to eat the peaches at a great feast given by the Jade emperor's wife, the Empress Wang.

HSIEN IS THE Chinese word for "immortal". The Chinese character for Hsien juxtaposes the characters for "man" and "mountain", signifying a man who lives on a mountain. The eight immortals are the most famous of the *Hsien.* Immortality is not just long life on earth, but eternal life in heaven.

AUSPICIOUS DEER
The deer is a symbol of longevity and good fortune.

MOUNTAIN PARADISE
The gods and immortals live on the Kun Lun mountains, the Taoist paradise sometimes called Shou Shan ("the hills of longevity").

THE STORY OF THE KITCHEN GOD

Once there was a mason called Tsao-wang who, no matter what he did, was always poor. Finally, he was so poor that he had to let his wife marry someone else. One day, without realizing it, he worked for the new husband. His ex-wife, who still cared for him, baked him some cakes, secretly putting a coin into each one. But because it was his destiny to be poor, the mason gave them away. When he discovered what he had done, he despaired and killed himself. But the ruler of heaven, on account of Tsao-wang's sad life, took pity and made him the god of the kitchen. Now, his picture hangs in every kitchen, and once a year he reports on each family's behaviour to heaven. Many people smear his mouth with honey or sugar so that he can say only sweet things.

TS'AO KUO-CHIU
Ts'ao Kuo-chiu left his home in shame after his brother was executed for murder. He devoted himself to following the Tao, "the Way". When he met the immortals Chung Li Chu'an and Lu Tung-pin, they asked him where the way was, and he pointed to the sky. They asked him where the sky was, and he pointed to his heart. They asked him where the secrets of perfection were, and he became an immortal. He is holding a court writing tablet.

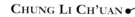

CHUNG LI CH'UAN
Chung Li Chu'an was a portly and rather flippant character.

Shou Hsing, God of Longevity
Shou Hsing (or Shou Lao) is the god of longevity, one of the three Star Gods or Gods of Happiness. He is depicted as an old man with a stick, and a bulbous bald head. He decides the date of everyone's death, and writes it down on a tablet at the moment of birth. Occasionally he has been persuaded to change his mind – one young man so pleased him with the offering of a jar of wine that Shou Hsing reversed the numbers 1 and 9, giving him 91 years of life rather than 19.

Walking stick

HO HSIANG-KU
Ho Hsiang-ku is the only female among the eight immortals. She was a Taoist ascetic in the reign of the Empress Wu. Sworn to virginity, she lived alone in the mountains, where the secrets of immortality were revealed to her in a dream. She is shown holding a lotus, and looks after unmarried girls.

CHANG KUO-LAO
Chang Kuo-lao was a famous hermit who resisted all attempts to lure him to the capital city. At last he made the journey, at the request of the Empress Wu, but when he reached a temple he fell down dead. His body decayed and was eaten by worms, yet he recovered. He travelled on a donkey which he could magically fold up into a piece of paper – this is what he is holding.

SOUL
Li T'ieh-kuai's soul is shown in the vapour rising from his gourd of life-preserving medicine, hovering above the beggar's body it inhabits.

LI HAI AND THE TOAD
Li Hai was a minister of state who one day received a visit from the immortal Chung Li Ch'uan (see below). The immortal proceeded to perform a trick, balancing ten eggs on top of each other with a gold coin between each egg. "Isn't that rather precarious?" asked Li Hai. "Not as precarious as your position," answered the immortal. Li Hai took the hint, resigned his post, and set off in search of perfection. On his journey he met the immortal Lu Tung-pin, who taught him how to turn gold into immortality pills; so Li Hai also became an immortal. He travelled the world accompanied by a three-legged toad. But the toad often slipped away from him and jumped into a nearby well, so Li Hai had to lure it out using a string of gold coins as bait. Li Hai is invoked as a god of prosperity, and is also the patron deity of needlemakers.

Chinese money

Li Hai stands on his three-legged toad with money in his hand.

LI T'IEH-KUAI
Li T'ieh-kuai, meaning "Li with the iron crutch", looks after the sick and is shown as an old lame beggar. Called to heaven to be instructed by the spirit Lao Tzu, the founder of Taoism, Li told one of his students to burn his body if he did not return in seven days. But the student, called to his mother's death-bed, burnt it after six. When Li returned he had to enter the body of a beggar who had just died of starvation.

THERE ARE THREE Chinese gods of happiness, Shou Hsing, the god of longevity, Lu Shen, the god of good fortune, and Fu Shen, the god of happiness. Lu Shen is sometimes replaced by Tsai Shen, the god of wealth. In Chinese art, they are often shown standing together.

LU TUNG-PIN
Lu Tung-pin was a moral philosopher. One day he met Chung Li Ch'uan, the first of the Immortals. While Chung Li was heating rice wine, Lu fell asleep and dreamed his future life, in which he was successful and happy, but ultimately lost everything. He awoke convinced of the vanity of worldly ambition and became Chung Li's disciple. He travelled the world fighting evil and helping people, and is shown carrying a magic sword given to him by a Fire Dragon.

Peach of immortality

LAN TS'AI-HO
Lan Ts'ai-ho was a wandering minstrel, and is often depicted with a lute. He was an effeminate cross-dresser – a kind of holy fool, who wore warm clothes in the summer, and slept in the snow in winter. One day, after he had passed out drunk outside an inn, he rose to heaven in a cloud. He looks after the poor.

HAN HSIANG-TZU
Han Hsiang-tzu was a student of Lu Tung-pin. A master flute-player, he can make flowers blossom at his command. He climbed the tree bearing the peaches of immortality, but fell off the top, attaining immortality just before he hit the ground. He is the patron of culture.

THE EIGHT IMMORTALS VISIT SHOU HSING
This plate shows the eight immortals visiting Shou Hsing, the god of longevity, who also lives in the Kun Lun Mountains. Clouds swirl around them all. The souls of good people, who are no longer reincarnated, may also dwell in the Kun Lun mountains although usually, they are sent to the land of Extreme Felicity in the west.

Chung Li Ch'uan
Chung Li Chu'an lived in the period of the Han dynasty. He discovered how to make silver from copper, but instead of keeping the money for himself gave it to the poor. He is shown holding a peach of immortality.

THE SACRED MOUNTAIN

THE SHINTO RELIGION, "THE WAY OF THE GODS", recognizes divine spirits, *kami*, in all natural phenomena. Sengen-Sama, the goddess of Mount Fuji, is the most sacred. Mount Fuji is so important to the Japanese that it has given rise to many myths. It is even believed to be the abode of Kunitokotachi, the Eternal Land Ruler, the invisible, all-pervading creator deity who arose as a reed from the primeval ocean of chaos. The legend illustrated below relates how the great 12th-century warrior Tadatsune went to Mount Fuji to confront the monsters who were terrorizing the local inhabitants. With two of his most trusted henchmen, he entered the great cavern at the base of the mountain and followed an underground river. Suddenly, Sengen-Sama appeared on the far bank with a dragon by her side. Tadatsune's companions tried to cross to reach her but she dispatched them within seconds. The goddess congratulated Tadatsune for his bravery but warned him not to try and cross over the river himself, as he would surely meet the same fate. Tadatsune bowed to her and retraced his steps.

Mountain Goddess
Sengen-Sama is the beneficent goddess of Mount Fuji. Pilgrims come from all over Japan to worship her. They climb to the top of the mountain to revere her in the rays of the rising sun.

SACRED TREE
Sengen-Sama holds a branch of the sacred sakaki tree in one hand, and a magical jewel in the other. The sakaki tree (*Cleyera japonica*) is one of the wonderful objects used to lure the sun goddess Amaterasu out of her cave (see pp.122–23).

JEWEL
Sengen-Sama holds a magical jewel in her right hand.

MYTHS OF THE AINU

In the beginning, the earth was a lifeless swamp, with six heavens above and six worlds below. One day, the creator, Kamui, sent a wagtail to make land. When the bird arrived, it had no idea what to do. Panicking, it beat the water with its tail (as it does today) and slowly, dry land began to appear. Seeing how lovely the world now was, the animals (who lived in the heavens) begged Kamui to let them live there. Kamui agreed and created the Ainu people, who had earth bodies, chickweed hair, and willow-stick spines (which bend in old age). Then he sent Aioina, the divine man, to teach the Ainu how to hunt and cook. When Aioina returned to heaven, the other gods complained that he stank of human beings, so he threw away his clothes. His discarded slippers turned into the first squirrels.

Dragon
Dragons are a symbol of the fertilizing power of rain. Taka-okami, the dragon god of the mountains, and Kura-okami, the dragon god of the valleys, were created from the blood spilled when Izanagi killed the fire god (see p.121). They control rain and snow.

MOUNT FUJI AND HER NEIGHBOUR, the male Mount Haku, once argued over which of them was the highest. To settle the matter, the Buddha of Infinite Light ran a pipe from the top of Mount Haku to the top of Mount Fuji. When the water spilled over Fuji's peak, the goddess was so cross that she beat Haku over the head and cracked his skull in eight places (now the eight peaks of Mount Haku). As a result, Mount Fuji is now taller.

Long ago, an old man found a baby girl on the slopes of Mount Fuji and called her Kaguya-hime. She grew up to be beautiful and married the Emperor. After seven years, she told her husband that she was not a mortal, and must return to heaven. To comfort him, she gave him a mirror in which he would always be able to see her. Vowing to go to heaven with her, he used the mirror to follow her to the top of Mount Fuji. But then he could go no further. His disappointed love set the mirror ablaze, and from that day smoke has always risen from the top of the mountain. Mount Fuji's last major eruption was in 1707.

DIVINE VISION
The gaze of the goddess as it falls upon intruders may bring either blessing or death.

IZANAMI AND IZANAGI

Izanami and Izanagi were commanded by the deities of heaven to shape the earth. Standing on the rainbow, the Floating Bridge of Heaven, they stirred the ocean with a jewelled spear and created Onogoro, the first island. Then they put up a pillar, walked around it in opposite directions, met, and coupled. Izanami then gave birth to the islands of Japan and various gods and goddesses. However, she was badly burnt at the birth of the fire god, Kagutsuchi, and died. Bereft, Izanagi killed Kagutsuchi and rushed to the underworld to beg Izanami to return. She agreed, but warned her husband not to look at her. But he broke a tooth from his hair-comb and lit it as a torch. In doing so, he saw that Izanami was rotting and covered in maggots, and he fled. Pursued by his demon-wife, Izanagi managed to escape just in time, blocking the exit with a huge rock. Trapped, Izanami angrily vowed to kill 1,000 people every day; Izanagi countered by promising 1,500 births for every 1,000 deaths.

Izanami and Izanagi
Izanami and Izanagi were the last of seven generations of gods. Here, they stir the ocean with a jewelled magical spear to create the islands of Japan.

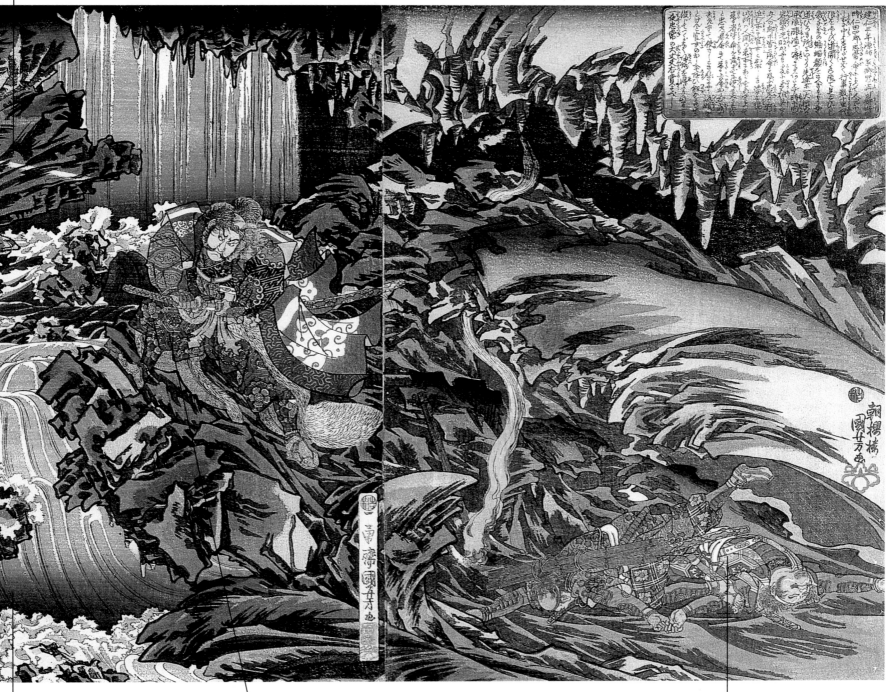

RIVER HOME
Every river has its own god, but is also home to evil dwarf vampires known as *kappa*, who drown their victims and then suck out their blood. The only way to outwit a *kappa* is to cause it to bow, thus spilling the water from its skull and dispersing its power.

TADATSUNE
Tadatsune was a vassal of the emperor Minamoto no Yoritomo, who became the first *shogun* (emperor) after his victory at the battle of Dannourra in 1185. His brother Yoshitsune was a legendary hero who appears in many Noh plays.

TADATSUNE AND THE GODDESS OF MOUNT FUJI
by Kuniyoshi *c.*1844
This Japanese tryptych shows the hero Tadatsune transfixed by the goddess of Mount Fuji after she has just killed his companions.

FALLEN WARRIORS
Tadatsune's companions – like him, samurai warriors – lie dead on the ground, victims of the goddess' displeasure after they attempted to trespass on her holy ground.

AMATERASU HIDES AWAY

AMATERASU, THE JAPANESE SUN GODDESS, Tsuki-yomi, the moon god, and Susano, the storm god, were born to Izanagi, the primal male, after he escaped from the underworld (see p.124). When they were old enough, Izanagi gave Amaterasu the rule of heaven, Tsuki-Yomi the rule of the night, and Susano the rule of the ocean. But Susano felt cheated, and threw a tantrum – he would rather go to the dark land of his mother, Izanami, than rule the waters. So he challenged Amaterasu to a contest – the one who gave birth to the most powerful deities would cede power to the other. But Amaterasu won, and Susano was so furious that he attacked the sacred weaving hall where Amaterasu and her maidens wove the fabric of the universe. He frightened and offended her so much that she withdrew to the seclusion of a cave, plunging both heaven and earth into darkness. The other gods were very concerned and determined to lure Amaterasu back into the world. They thought long and hard and finally decided to work on her curiosity by causing a commotion outside the cave, and tricking her into believing that they were welcoming a deity even greater than herself. This superior deity was, in fact, Amaterasu's own reflection in a mirror.

Cockerel
The first plan to arouse Amaterasu's curiosity was to simulate a false dawn by provoking cockerels – "long-crying birds" – to crow.

OMOHI-KANE
This is probably Omohi-kane, the wise "thought-combining" deity. He was the deep-thinking son of Takamimusubi, one of the five original gods. It was he who thought up the ingenious plans to arouse Amaterasu's interest and bring her out of her cave.

MUSIC OF THE GODS
The gods keep time for the provocative dance of Ama-no-Uzume by beating on a great drum, thus founding a tradition of music and dance in Shinto ritual known as *Iwata kagura*, music of the gods.

WITHOUT THE LIFE-GIVING warmth of Amaterasu, the sun, the world fell into chaos, nothing grew, and evil spirits ran riot. Amaterasu's reappearance ensured the future of the earth and thereafter, she only disappeared at night.

AMATERASU EMERGES
This tryptych shows the moment when Amaterasu emerges from her cave, amazed at the noise that is going on outside in the darkness. As she appears, the world is flooded with light and Ta-jikawa-wo, hauling back the stone at the entrance, is ready to grasp her hand and draw her outside completely.

❝*As you have blessed the ruler's reign, making it long and enduring, so I bow my neck as a cormorant in search of fish to worship you and give you praise.*❞
HARVEST PRAYER TO AMATERASU AT ISE

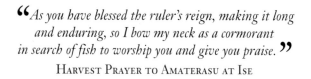

HAND-STRENGTH-MALE-DEITY
Ta-jikawa-wo, whose name means Hand-strength-male-deity, pulls aside the rock door behind which Amaterasu has hidden herself. He then takes her by the hand and leads her out, while another deity fastens a magic rope across the opening to prevent her return.

SAKE TUB
The goddess Ama-no-Uzume dances on an upturned sake tub. Sake appears in several myths, including the one about how Susano won his wife (see above). Here, the dancing floor reflects the licentious nature of the dance itself.

SUSANO, THE STORM GOD

Once Amaterasu had returned to the world, the gods punished Susano by cutting off his beard and his finger- and toenails and banishing him to the human world. Here, he saw a pair of chopsticks floating down the river and set off to find who owned them. He soon found the owners – an elderly couple devastated at losing seven daughters to the appetite of an eight-headed dragon, who was about to eat their last child, Kusa-nada-hime, the Rice Paddy Princess. Susano decided to rescue her, so he changed the girl into a comb, put her in his hair, and filled eight tubs of sake for the dragon. The dragon drank all the sake and fell asleep. Susano then cut off the dragon's heads with a magic sword, *aine no murakomo*, meaning "Clouds of Heaven", which he had found in its tail. Then he sent the sword to Amaterasu as a token of submission. Together with Amaterasu's mirror and jewels, it formed the Japanese imperial regalia. Susano then returned the Rice Paddy Princess to human form and made her his wife.

Susano no Mikoto preparing to kill the eight-headed dragon, 1832, by Keisei.

ALTHOUGH SUSANO is not evil, he has a tempestuous nature. For example, when the food goddess, Ogetsu-no-hime, gave him food that she had produced from within her own body, he killed her in anger. But from her corpse grew the staple foods of Japan: rice, millet, wheat, red beans, and soy beans. A version of this story is also told about Susano's brother Tsuki-yomi, the moon god, but it accords better with Susano's violent nature.

- **AMATERASU**
  Intrigued by the noise and laughter outside, Amaterasu emerges from the cave to see what all the fuss is about, bringing back light into the world.

IZANAGI, Amaterasu's father, gave a mirror to each of his children, instructing them to kneel before it every morning and evening and examine themselves. If they had evil thoughts, the mirror would be cloudy. A Japanese proverb says, "When the mirror is dim, the soul is unclean".

- **MIRROR**
  A sacred mirror, made especially by the Heavenly Smith, hangs from the sacred sakaki tree. As she emerges, Amaterasu is blinded by the reflection of her own light and is tricked into believing that the gods are celebrating the arrival of a new goddess, even greater and brighter than she is herself.

Sun Goddess
Chief goddess of the Japanese Shinto religion, Amaterasu is considered to be the ancestor of the Japanese imperial family. She has been worshipped at Ise since early times.

- **AMA-NO-UZUME**
  Ama-no-Uzume performs a kind of striptease outside the cave, provoking great hilarity among the gods, and curiosity on the part of Amaterasu who has no idea of what is happening. Because of her role in this myth, she is often described as a dawn goddess, but her name means "Terrible Female of Heaven".

- **VOCAL AUDIENCE**
  The gods gather, "eight-hundred myriad" strong, and create a cheerful racket. When Amaterasu asks why they are laughing, since the world is now in darkness, they reply that they are welcoming a goddess who shines more brightly than herself.

- **SAKAKI TREE**
  This tree is the 500-branched sacred sakaki tree that the gods dug up from Heavenly Mount Kagu. They set it up outside the cave and hung it with white cloth streamers as offerings to the goddess.

THE GREEK GODS

THIS FAMILY TREE, starting with the union of the sky and earth, Uranus and Gaia, shows the relationships between the Greek gods and goddesses mentioned in this book. The fourth generation became the deities of Mount Olympus and were the first to have children with mortals, thus mixing the divine and human bloodlines. The Olympians were led by Zeus, who was essentially a sky god. His brothers Hades and Poseidon ruled the underworld and the sea – the earth was held in common. Zeus is also called "father of gods and men", and his love affairs – too many to list here – resulted in the birth of numerous gods and heroes.

GAIA •x• URANUS

Cyclops   Giants   Other

TITANS

Cronus •x• Rhea
Saturn

Coeus •x• Phoebe   Oceanus •x• Tethys   Themis   Crius   Iapetus   Thea •x• Hyperion

Mnemosyne

Sea Nymphs

Menoetius   Epimetheus   Prometheus   Atlas •x•   Eos   Helios   Selene
    m Pandora   Hesperus   *Luna*

Asia

Hesperides

Dione *(Goddess)*

Mnemosyne *(Titan)*

The Nine Muses

Metis *(Sea Nymph)*

ATHENA *Minerva*

Themis *(Titan)*

Fates

Semele *(Mortal)*

DIONYSUS *Bacchus*

Leda *(Mortal)*

Castor   Polydeuces *Pollux*

Clytemnestra *m* Agamemnon   Helen *m* Menelaus   •x• Paris

Alcmene *(Mortal)*

Heracles *Hercules m* Hebe

APHRODITE •x• Anchises *(Mortal)*
Aeneas

ARES x

EROS *Cupid*

Europa *(Mortal)*

King Minos *m* Pasiphaë •x• Bull of Poseidon

Ariadne   Phaedra

Minotaur *(Half-bull, half-man)*

Maia *(Nymph)*

HERMES *Mercury m* Daughter of Dryops

PAN *Faunus*

Callisto *(Nymph)*

Arco

Leto *(Titan)*

APOLLO •x• Coronis *(Nymph)*

ARTEMIS *Diana*

Asclepius

Danaë *(Mortal)*

Perseus *m* Andromeda

ZEUS *Jupiter*

Leto ....

Hebe *m* Heracles *Hercules*

Eileithya

ARES *Mars*

HERA *Juno*

HEPHAESTUS *Vulcan m* **APHRODITE** *Venus*

Cadmus *m* Harmonia *(Goddess)*

Aristaeus *m* Autonoë

Actaeon

DEMETER *Ceres*

Persephone *Proserpine*

HADES *Pluto*

m Persephone *Proserpine*

HESTIA *Vesta*

POSEIDON *Neptune* •x• Aethra *(Mortal)*

Theseus *m* Ariadne
       m Phaedra

Key

Olympian gods	**HERA**	**HERA**	Roman name	*Mars*
Union	•x•		Descriptive	*(Nymph)*
Married	--*m*--			

ACKNOWLEDGEMENTS

Dorling Kindersley would like to thank Natasha Millen and Guo Zhiping;
Dr Anne Millard; Dr Will Rea, SOAS, London; Mr and Mrs CJ Rea; Jessica
Harrison Hall at the British Museum, London; Ken Mantel at the Narwhal
Inuit Gallery, London; Lori Cutler, Jill Barber, Joanne Logan at the Canadian
Inuit Art Information Centre; the Injalak Arts and Crafts Association of
Gunbalanya, Australia, Merlin Dailey at the Merlin Dailey Gallery, New York;
Henrietta Wilkinson for proofreading, and Hilary Bird for the index.

PICTURE CREDITS

Afrique en Créations /Dirk Bakker; 5 above, 90–91 centre, 90 above left, 91 below left
Akademische Druck-u. verlagsanstalt; 98–99 centre, 98 above left, 99 below right
AKG LONDON; back cover centre right, back cover centre right bottom, 78–79 centre, 78 above left, 79 below right /Alte Pinakothek, Munich; 24–25 centre, 24 left, 25 top right /Bibliothèque Nationale, Paris; 81 above right /Erich Lessing/Musée du Louvre, Paris; 38–39 centre, 38 top left, 38 top right, 58–59 centre, 58 below, 59 above /Gallerie Naz. di Capodimonte, Naples; 57 above /Moscow, Sammlung Familie Serow; 45 below left /Musée du Louvre, Paris; 20 above left, 48–49 centre, 48 above, 49 below right /Museo Capitolino/Erich Lessing; 67 below right /Museo del Prado, Madrid/Erich Lessing; 23 above right /National Gallery of Scotland, Edinburgh; 36–37 centre, 36 top left, 37 top right /Staatl. Antikenslg. & Glyptothek, Munich; 3, 59 below right
ANCIENT ART & ARCHITECTURE COLLECTION; 13 above right, 41 right
Stofnun Arna Magnussinar a Islandi; 70–71 centre, 71 left, 71 right
Artothek /Alte Pinakothek, Munich; 26–27 centre, 27 below, 27 top right, 32–33 centre, 32 left, 33 top right /Bayer & Mitko/Private Collection; 66 - 67 centre, 66 left, 67 above right
Birmingham Museums and Art Gallery; 80–81 centre, 80 below left, 80 above left, 81 above left
BRIDGEMAN ART LIBRARY, LONDON/NEW YORK/Agnew and Sons, London; 36 below left /Bibliothèque Nationale, Paris; 85 above right /Bradford Art Galleries and Museums, West Yorkshire, UK; 52 above left, 52–53 centre, 53 above right, 82 above left, 82 centre left, 82 centre right, 83 below left, 83 above left, 83 above right /Corbally Stourton Contemporary Art, London/ Aboriginal Arts Agency Ltd; 105 above, 102 above right /Faringdon Collection, Buscot, Oxon, UK; 25 top left /Ferens Art Gallery, Hull, UK; 65 below right, 64–65 centre, 65 above right /Fitzwilliam Museum, Cambridge, UK; 28–29 centre, 28 left, 29 top, 34–35 centre, 34 top, 35 below, 56 below right /Galleria degli Uffizi, Florence; 60–61 centre, 60 above right, 61 below /Guildhall Art Gallery, Corporation of London; 60 above right /Manchester City Art Galleries, UK; 84–85 centre, 84 left, 85 below right /Musée du Louvre, Paris; back cover top centre, 39 below /Musée du Louvre, Paris/ Lauros-Giraudon; 42 left /Musée du Louvre, Paris/Giraudon; 30 below, 31 below right /Musée du Louvre, Paris/Peter Willi; back cover top left, 46–47 centre, 46 above, 47 below right /Musée du Louvre, Paris/Giraudon; 30–31 centre /Musée du Petit Palais, Avignon/Peter Willi; 56–57 centre, 56 below, 57 below right /Museum of Fine Arts, Budapest; 29 right /National Gallery, London; 42–43 centre, 43 below

right, 43 top right /National Gallery, London; 62–63 centre, 63 below right, 63 above /National Museum of Iceland, Reykjavik; back cover bottom right, 69 below right /Nationalmuséet, Copenhagen; 62 left /Palazzo Sandi Porto (Cipollato) Venice; 4 left, 47 above /Private Collection; 7 below, 113 above right /Roy Miles Gallery, London; front cover top centre, 35 top /Royal Library, Copenhagen; 11 right /Simon Carter Gallery, Woodbridge, Suffolk, UK; 49 below left /Victoria and Albert Museum, London; 78 above right, 110–111 centre, 111 below right, 111 below left, 114–115 centre, 114 above right, 115 below left
BRITISH LIBRARY; 83 below right
BRITISH MUSEUM; back cover top right, back cover bottom centre, back cover centre left b, 4 above, 16 above, 17 below, 18–19 centre, 117 above, 118–119 centre, 118 below left, 119 above, 119 below /Peter Hayman; 15 right
Central Art Archives /The Finnish National Gallery/Ateneum, Helsinki; 75 above /The Finnish National Gallery/Ateneum, Helsinki/ The Antell Collection; 74–75 centre, 74 above right, 75 right
Jean-Loup CHARMET; 52 below left
Reproduced by kind permission of the Trustees of the Chester Beatty Library, Dublin; 123 above right
Cincinnati Art Museum /Museum Purchase, 1957.29; 20 centre left, 20–21 centre
C M Dixon; 8, 10 left, 71 below right, 110 above
Christies Images; front cover bottom/Cypress Book Company; 116–117, 116 below left, 116 above
Duncan Baird Publishers; 121 above right /The Japanese Gallery; 2, 122–123 centre, 122 above left, 123 below right
DK (special photography); 10–11 centre, 96 –97 centre /British Museum; 50 below /Glasgow Museums, St Mungo; 108 left, 115 below right /Jerry Young; 87 below right /Lynton Gardiner; 93 above /Manchester Museums; 4 right, 26 left /Michael Zabe; 6–7 centre /Mr & Mrs CJ Rea; 86–87 /Musée du Louvre, Paris; 33 below right /Universitets Oldsaksamling; 5 centre left, 72–73 centre, 72 above left, 73 below centre /University Museum of Archaeology and Anthropology, Cambridge; 9 left, 77 above right
Gemaldegalerie Alte Meister Dresden; 40 top, 40 below left, 40–41 centre
E.T. ARCHIVE /Tate Gallery; 31 top
MARY EVANS PICTURE LIBRARY /Arthur Rackham Collection; 68 below left
EXPLORER/C Regnault; 90 above right
WERNER FORMAN ARCHIVE; 70 above centre, 70 above right /British Museum, London; 99 below right /Field Museum of Natural History, Chicago; 95 below right /Statens Historiska Museum, Stockholm; 68 to 69 centre, 68 above left /Strouhal; 9 right
FOTOMAS INDEX; back cover centre left, 72 above right

PHOTOGRAPHIE GIRAUDON/Bridgeman; 12–13 centre, 12 left, 13 below right /Art Resource; 94–95 centre, 94 above left, 94 below left /Mantoue, Palazzo del Te; 22–23 centre, 22 below, 23 below right /Musée Guimet, Paris; 112–113 centre, 112 left, 113 below right
ROBERT HARDING PICTURE LIBRARY/Geoff Renner; front cover top right, 107 right Hamburgisches Museum für Volkerkünde; 106–107 centre
Michael HOLFORD Photographs; back cover centre right, 92–93 centre, 92 left, 93 below, 108–109 centre, 109 below right, 109 above /British Museum; 6 left, 14–15 centre, 14 above centre, 14 above, 15 below left, 21 above, 54–55 centre, 54 below, 55 above right, 87 above right, 88–89 centre, 106 right /Museum für Volkerkünde, Munich; 1, 101 above Musée de l'Homme, Paris /Cl. D. Ponsard; 89 below /Cl. D. Ponsard; 88 right
Arts Induvik Canada Inc.; 96 below
Barbara and Justin Kerr; 100–101 centre, 100 above, 101 below
Collection of Merlin Dailey, Victor, New York; 5 centre right, 120–121 centre, 120 top left, 120 below left
Board of the Trustees of the National Museums & Galleries on Merseyside /Lady Lever Art Gallery; 50–51 centre, 50 above, 51 above right
Manchester Museums; back cover bottom right National Gallery of Victoria /Injalak Arts and Crafts Association Inc.; 5 below 104–105 centre, 105 below right /Injalak Arts and Crafts Association Inc.; 104 above left /Warlukulangu Artists Aboriginal Association Inc. of Yuendumu; 102–103 centre, 103 below left, 103 below right
National Museum Copenhagen; back cover centre left a, 76–77 centre, 76 below left, 76 above left
REUNION DES MUSEES NATIONAUX /H Lewandowski/Musée du Louvre, Paris; inside front flap, 16–17 centre, 18 above left /Musée du Louvre, Paris; 19 right /Musée du Louvre, Paris; 44– 45 centre, 44 top, 45 below right
SCALA /Palazzo Poggi, Bologna; front cover top left; 64 below left

Every effort has been made to trace the copyright holders and we apologize in advance for any unintentional omissions. We would be pleased to insert the appropriate acknowledgement in any subsequent edition of this publication.